# International Marketing

## Fundamentals for Small and Medium-sized Enterprises

# International Marketing

## Fundamentals for Small and Medium-sized Enterprises

Bruno Roque Cignacco

**ATLANTIC**

PUBLISHERS & DISTRIBUTORS (P) LTD

Published by
**ATLANTIC**
**PUBLISHERS & DISTRIBUTORS (P) LTD**

7/22, Ansari Road, Darya Ganj,
New Delhi-110002
Phones : +91-11-40775252, 23273880, 23275880, 23280451
Fax : +91-11-23285873
Web : www.atlanticbooks.com
E-mail : orders@atlanticbooks.com

Branch Office
5, Nallathambi Street, Wallajah Road,
Chennai-600002
Phones : +91-44-64611085, 32413319
E-mail : chennai@atlanticbooks.com


Printed in Spanish by Ediciones Macchi (Buenos Aires, Argentina) in 2004
Translated from Spanish into English by Norma Capriolo

ISBN 978-81-269-1363-3



Printed in India at Glorious Printers, A-13, D.S.I.D.C.,
Jhilmil Industrial Area, Delhi-110095

# Acknowledgements

First and foremost, I would like to thank all the people who showed warm affection during the process of writing this book—very sweet and special people, like Lorena Sánchez, Hugo Francesconi and Elizabeth Razzari, who have been so understanding all throughout this writing period. I also thank Fernanda Castro and staff members of the accounting studio. It would be unfair not to mention my parents, who taught me values of self-discipline and improvement, both in professional and academic activities, and to Andrea, who watches my career development from the far distance.

I would also like to thank my former professors at the International Marketing postgraduate course in the *Facultad de Ciencias Económicas* of the *Universidad Nacional de Rosario*, especially Mr. Jorge Hollidge, and each one of those who showed me a way in the subject of international marketing, and continue to do so. I especially thank Dr. Eugenio Helman for his wholehearted support to my projects. I am also thankful to the students in courses and subjects in the different universities and business institutions, who taught me as much or more than they learned from me.

Finally, I extend my gratitude to Cignacco and Associates' clients, who constantly offer professional challenges and invite me to creative thinking.

**Bruno Roque Cignacco**

# Preface

I carefully thought about the idea that gave origin to this book some years ago. When working as a trainer in training courses, lecturing for students and professionals, and giving advice to business people on the various international marketing issues, I realized that, in some cases, a great majority of authors on the subject of international marketing approached the subject from a big enterprise-oriented point of view. Small and medium enterprises, which make up a relevant productive and commercial force in any country, have been relegated to a position of less importance in most of the excellent books on international marketing.

Besides, it can be noted that certain legal issues of international marketing (standards, regulations, resolutions and provisions) vary from country to country and are constantly being amended and updated, which makes it practically impossible to have an updated work that compiles all the regulations in force in a current time.

So, I have decided to focus on specific issues that make this work very peculiar, like:

— Including aspects relative only to international marketing, that is, the important range of marketing international strategies, policies and variables that appear as indispensable tools to gain access to external markets.

— Giving this work an orientation to exporting activities and other ways of penetration in world markets, like licencing, franchising and co-investment, leaving aside commercial aspects relative to goods import, which would take another book.

— Orienting the work towards theoretical-practical issues useful for small and medium-sized enterprises by considering the concerns that affect the international adventure.

— Giving fundamentals about international strategy, its design, implementation and control. This knowledge is always useful for long-term entrepreneurial activities. Moreover, these pieces of knowledge do not run the risk of becoming out of date, as it may happen with some topics such as international marketing customs regulations. This book also includes the most important ways that small and medium-sized enterprises may use to enter international markets, highlighting the importance of a global approach.

— Developing the topics from a deductive point of view, which allows to reach progressively from *macro issues* (such as globalization, regionalism) to *micro issues* (such as marketing variables) related to entrepreneurial activities.

— Explaining with clear and precise words international marketing terminology, using simple but specific words.

International marketing knowledge, unlike other areas, consists in academic systematizations of commercial practices applied by enterprises with levels of excellence in world performance, which allows to establish principles or guidelines that can be transferred to other organizations interested in internationalization.

Internationalization is a concept that will be treated many times along the text from different points of view, i.e. the importance of commercial alliances, problems within the company, state activities that favour international commercial actions, just to mention a few of them. Internationalization implies enterprise's stable and lasting commitments with external operators, which is why this aspect will be a conducting thread that guides the development of the different sections of the book.

The book is organized in seven chapters, conclusion and five supplements. Following this order, the subjects dealt with are the following:

The first chapter consists of a detailed explanation of the evolution of globalization and its impact upon companies. The main institutions and regional markets that compose the world scenario are also analyzed, ending the chapter with a brief analysis of the significance of cultural, political and economic differential environments for the design of efficient international strategies.

The second chapter describes the different barriers to internationalization for the small company, with an emphasis on the generation of creative alternatives to overcome them. The various advantages that the company gets in the penetration of external markets and the importance of state protection for the development of external activities are also analyzed.

The third chapter points out the significance of information for international actions, including what is the necessary information and which are the main sources where the entrepreneur can get access to it, with a thrust on economic sources. The main parameters that influence the selection of markets to penetrate are also considered.

The fourth chapter deals with the internationalization decision process as well as its main objectives and policies and the different strategic approaches of external activities relating to this process. The different stages that a company goes through in its internationalization, and the balance between diversification and concentration of actions in the different country markets are also evaluated.

The fifth chapter develops the main basic variables of international marketing. Their main components or subvariables are also explained with reference to the main strategies that can be efficiently applied to small and medium-sized companies.

Other topics analyzed are: standardization and adaptation, and the influence of country-image upon entrepreneurial activities.

The sixth chapter develops the diversity of marketing channels that a small and medium-sized enterprise may use for its international activities—from basic channels such as sellers—to more complex company structures such as export consortia. External market policies of penetration that exceed the concept of exportation, like franchising, production in destination, licences, among others, are also analyzed.

The seventh chapter develops the variables that I call "advanced controllable variables of the commercial mix". As relevant as those developed in chapter 5, these are called the four Cs of the marketing international mix [quality (this word begins with 'C' in Spanish: "calidad"), competitiveness, creativity and connectivity]. International certifications of quality, creative decision-making, the importance of the generation of alternatives for international access, external competitive attitude and e-commerce transcendence are among the principal topics discussed.

Supplements develop briefly some subjects related to international marketing strategy, for example, export documents, international means of collection, international carriage, negotiating principles and fundamentals of international classification.

With the strong conviction of having produced an integral work that links the topics in a didactic and entertaining approach, this book is presented to students, professionals, entrepreneurs, advisors and members of public and private bodies interested in the main factors that constitute the environment and strategy of the internationalizing organization.

**Bruno Roque Cignacco**

# Contents

# 1

# Globalization, Regionalism and International Environments

## 1. GLOBALIZATION

### 1.1. Background and Evolution of the Phenomenon

Authors like Fitoussi and Rosanvallon point out that there are three historical stages through which globalization developed: the first one, which they call *customs globalization*, in which a progressive tariff reduction aimed at increasing commerce among the countries involved, has been negotiated throughout different GATT (General Agreement on Tariffs and Trade) rounds of business; a second stage, which involves the great advances in telecommunication and information technology, and which produces the so-called financial globalization, which implies the existence of a foreign exchange market and other financial globalized products; and finally, there is a third stage, related to the fall of centrally planned economies of the communist system and their incorporation in the world market, as well as some countries liberalization towards the international market. The term "globalization", at present, appears as a word familiar to everyone, and not only reserved to the academic environment. However, it is a very controversial issue which causes heated debates and controversial opinions about its causes and effects.

### 1.2. Distinctive Features

Some trends consider globalization as either a myth or a continuation of tendencies. It is regarded as a phenomenon or group of real phenomena where there exists "a world without frontiers". In this global scenario, the Nation-State is turned into a fiction and the political variable has a reduced effective power.

There is an important association of factors that encourages and supports this trend. The 20th century is regarded as the starting point for this development. Other opinions, on the other hand, favour a more remote origin, after the Industrial Revolution. An easily recognizable concern is that globalization multiplies uncertainties. It presents the following features:

— **Shared scenario:** the globalization context appears as a scenario shared by all countries, but it does not internalize (does not impact) in every country in the same way.

— **Multifaceted phenomenon**: it embraces cultural, commercial, technological, information technology and financial aspects, making it a complex development with multiple interconnections.

— **Interconnection**: financial market globalization, information technology improvements, increase in travels, rise in commerce flow; all create a stronger interdependence and interconnection of the various national economies, which partially lose their autonomy.

— **Transitional**: the fact that this is an ongoing process makes it difficult to perform a complete analysis of this trend. It is impossible either to make a clear observation of its main features from due distance or to predict with certainty its evolution. Nevertheless, it may be observed that every feature becomes more established as time goes by. It can also be noticed that its multiple effects surpass the short-term, spreading as a trend with continuous wide projection in the long term.

## 1.3. Main Factors in the Global Trend

### *1.3.1. Existence of a Global World*

The world is regarded as an environment without frontiers. It is the global village, called like this by some specialists. This phenomenon implies a shortening of distances and a modification of time and space. Any world event affects directly or indirectly the whole planet. Besides, accelerated technological innovations that interconnect every culture in the world are produced.

### *1.3.2. Scientific Development Impact*

There is a strong connection between science and society, which is the result of company investments in the development of Research and Development (R + D) projects or in the introduction of new products, innovations in the materials used by particular industries, and new services for the consumer. These facts give rise to a stronger competitive field, because a great number of companies constantly launch innovative products to the market, and permanently transform these products lifecycle. These big R + D investments are so substantial that it becomes quite difficult to recover the money spent in an individual market. As a consequence, companies widen market portfolios at an international level to place their new products, establishing operations on the global scale.

These big enterprises deploy marketing on a global level because they want to distribute their fixed costs (R + D, marketing, etc.) in the greatest possible number of markets, in order to get lower unitary costs (what is known as economy of scale). Thus, a more competitive final price for the product is achieved.

Another important point is information technology and telecommunication innovations, as well as the Internet. Economic, social and digital areas are created, developed and consolidated. An evidence of the aforesaid is the increasingly generalized use of the electronic or virtual commerce (also known as e-commerce), the proliferation of sites, the circulation of the electronic mail (e-mail) and the chat (virtual conversation). These new means gradually superimpose on traditional means of communication and trade. This communicational revolution gives rise to the so-called digital economy (according to TAPSCOTT), which coexists with real economy. Technological development stretches towards other areas like biotechnology, robotics, the development of new forms of energy, etc. Also, a considerable and progressive interference of Science and Technology in many areas of society is observed, which produces a strong ambiguity and uncertainty about the consequences of such intervention. This fact is reinforced when scientific research evidence on issues of doubtful beneficial effects on humanity, or contradictory issues come to light.

### *1.3.3. Rise of Global Marketing Strategies*

There exists in the triad markets, made up by Europe, the United States and Japan, which concentrate almost three quarters of the international trade, a certain income levelling in consumers' lifestandards, which allows international operators to direct the commercial strategy of certain products (especially those that can satisfy varied similar needs in those countries), to intermarket or transnational segments, that comprise more than one country-market. A typical example of this can be seen in popular franchise brands that keep the idea of their product or extended service throughout the world market, but with adaptations to local features (cultural, legal, economic, etc.), as required by each specific country. Thus, the strategy is globally conceived, and then implemented with particular national environment peculiarities in mind, which implies product adequation.

Another aspect to be considered is global brands proliferation (the use of the same brand in different markets). This policy allows a better product positioning, and a reinforcement of the world perception of its attributes. Other relevant issue is internationalizing companies use of global communication elements (global advertising, international trade shows, global promotional material, etc.).

### *1.3.4. Development of Regionalism*

The constitution and development of different commercial blocks is one of the most important factors in the global trend. The integration of different national economies at a regional level permits the generation of two market spaces that affect the world environment. A first commercial space is developed within the integration zone, where main obstacles to commerce are reduced or eliminated for the block members. But, besides, another market space, which is affected by different tariff and paratariff barriers, is generated among the members of the regional agreements and external countries.

During the second half of the 20th century, within the ex-GATT (General Agreement on Tariff and Trade) frame of multilateral negotiation and in the present context of the WTO (World Trade Organization), the different signatory countries reached an agreement and produced a considerable lowering of tariff barriers (taxes on imports). However, a replacement in the use of tariff trade obstacles by the imposition of non-tariff or paratariff barriers is observed. This fact shows a paratariff trend that affects international trade flows. This fact can also be observed in the operations performed by countries of the main regional markets.

### *1.3.5. Determination of Competitive Spaces at International Level*

A totally relevant fact during the last century was the generalized fall of the socialist systems. These countries have progressively been entering the market economy. Some countries, in which the State used to control specific sectors of the national economy, have implemented progressive privatization policies of their state companies. As a consequence of these activities, a more complex competitive game to enter those private sector areas has been started.

At international level, particular companies develop a series of strategic operations. Partnerships among competitors in a sector are concerted, technology transference contracts between companies are signed, mergers and takeovers are produced. Other important issue is the structuration of global distribution chains and the creation of associative projects (exports consortia, coinvestment, etc.), based in different international markets.

A strong participation in this new competitive field of the New Industrialized Countries (NIC) is also produced. These are the so-called Tiger or Dragons of the Asian Southeast, with great technological development (high productivity) and plenty labour force (this last fact implies low income in this area, from a relative point of view, compared to the other countries). These NICs, in some cases, make world sales of their products in social dumping conditions (this means that the country internationally trades products whose most important compositive element is labour force, which is more abundant and economical in those countries). Labour force used in social dumping also has a much lower cost due to poor social security conditions, which generates, in some cases, labour situations of semislavery. The marketing of products in social dumping conditions pushes an international price fall of particular products.

### *1.3.6. Increase in the Number of Trips*

Technological improvement also affects transportation systems which are faster and more economical. These improvements affect goods cargo systems as well as passenger cargo systems. As regards, commodities international transportation low cost allows companies to offer more competitive final exportation prices and to offer their marketing strategy to farther markets.

From the passengers' point of view, transportation improvement brings about an increase in personal trips. This is why, as regards trade, consumers no longer stay in one market, but move through different country-markets. This fact impels the company to implement and reinforce a global strategy which takes this constant displacement and relocation of international consumption into consideration. These consumers also make contact with other cultures, and other tastes, and this contributes to the development of their global profile.

### *1.3.7. Reconsideration of Nation-State Functions*

The situation in which the national State is too small for the global world challenge, but too big for local issues is also possible. Each country policy affects the others and independence and autonomy are—to a great extent—lost, due to the interconnectivity developed among the different national economies.

It is held that, in particular performance fields, the "law of the States" is replaced by the "law of the markets". The State does not disappear, but many of its traditional functions (justice, education, etc.) superimpose to the activity of other national and world stage actors that form part of the so-called "subpolicy" (they are the Non-Governmental Organizations

—NGOs—and other social movements with global activities, such as, for example, Greenpeace). The lack of real cooperation international mechanisms among the different countries implies the creation of new game rules. Strategy rules should be win-win at the international level, in order to solve specific problems like unemployment, poverty, criminality and idle capacity not fully used by some industries, among others.

ROSENAU (cited by BECK) remarks that there has been a change from the national to the postnational predominance and hegemony. From a monocentric approach, in which decision taking is centred in the national States, there is a move to a polycentric approach, where there are also new actors (transnational companies, NGOs, and international financial bodies, among others) in decision taking at world scale. With these new protagonists, the national States share the power and must address their objectives cooperatively in order to correct problems that affect the different communities in the international field. In total agreement with this, HELD (cited by BECK) states that globalization limits national States sovereignty. This sovereignty is affected by decisions and activities coming from multiple bodies and actors in the international scenario.

### *1.3.8. Global Financial Movements Relevance*

Another substantial aspect is financial markets globalization. This includes bonds, papers, foreign exchange and money negotiation that different institutions manage at world level. International financing integration is the result of the development of satellites and information technology, which permits information transmission about operations, twenty-four hours a day in real time.

This global financial market is estimated to move money volumes worth 50 times the value negotiated in real commerce (that is, goods purchase and sale). It is held that the "vote of the citizen" is, in this global context, replaced by the "vote of the market". It has also been observed that this instantly transmitted information technology (in real time) links the different regions of our world (poor as well as rich), which causes, in turn, a total reorganization of the social institutions vital guidelines of the different regions, which goes beyond the merely financial aspects.

The need for financial help (which can be channelled through multilateral credit bodies) to the southern and eastern countries has to be considered within the frame of globalization, so that they could have foreign exchange to import machinery from Western countries. This measure would improve the productive structure and foster the development of economy and quality of life of the inhabitants of the poorest countries. This strategy, would improve the situation not only in the developing countries, but also in the Western countries, which would be able to sell their products to the poor nations. The approach win-lose, in which one country gains and the other loses would be left aside, and poor countries would not have to implement artificial measures of competitivity (i.e., competitive devaluation) that threaten world economic stability.

### *1.3.9. Development of a Global Society*

It is held that globalization produces a world redistribution of wealth and poverty, rights and absence of rights, successes and failures. As a result, this polarization produces two classes: the rich and the poor. Besides, hyperindividualism is generalized (the individual has to be autonomous), which causes great harm on the social structures of solidarity developed in other times.

Present-day society is considered a global risk society, since it puts itself at risk as a consequence of the different human actions of different origin like: industrial progress, exhaustion of natural resources (i.e. deforestation), uncontrolled world development of weaponry, among other factors. These risks go beyond the national frontiers and become global, seriously affecting the cornerstones of countries security. These situations create a global awareness and become intermixed with different ethnic and domestic conflicts, which happen inside and between the countries. These threatening situations ought to be faced by joint national governments, companies, middle bodies, and representatives of scientific world decisions. Shared guidelines about the main aspects (like "sustainable development" and "ecological modernization") related to these variables of uncertainty have to be established.

Another social aspect of the global phenomenon is discussed by BECK. This author says that, as a consequence of the capitalist system inserted in the global frame, there is a progressive destruction of sources of employment. Besides, there is unemployment expansion and redistribution. Only some companies, whose owners can improve their lifestyle, win in the process because they are financed by those affected: the national treasury and the salaries of those who are still employees.

### *1.3.10. Relationship between Globalization and National Comparative Advantages*

The concept of comparative advantage is very simple: each country has to specialize in the production of those products in which it shows more efficiency (or less inefficiency). The surplus of these goods has to be exchanged by goods produced by the rest of the countries. This concept of international economy, which expresses benefits in the long term, can give rise to unfavourable circumstances for some countries involved, in the short term. This situation takes for granted the issue of free trade among countries. However, this idea can be improved if each country applies a selective and temporary protectionism in those emerging sectors in which, even though they might not have a real comparative advantage at the beginning, this could virtually exist. Non-protection of particular sectors could completely eliminate the generation of a know-how, which could be used by other sectors of a country economy. It is objected that the country that looks for specialization only in the comparative advantage issues reduces the diversity of its offer and the capacity of adaptation to the conditions of modernity.

According to this, there is always going to be some degree of protectionism in certain areas of the national economies. This happens with the purpose of generating production structures that externalize their benefits to other areas. This means that free trade within the globalization market is not absolute, but appears as free trade degrees.

### *1.3.11. Generation of Transnational Chains of Value*

The expression chain of value refers to every activity deployed by a company or group of companies. The chain consists in a series of stages to which a component of value (adequate relationship between the benefits gained and the prices incurred) is added. This chain comprises the production and marketing of a product that looks for an efficient differentiation in competitive conditions as regards the products offered by the competitors.

This concept, extensively developed by some authors of the stature of MICHAEL PORTER, includes every activity from product design to those activities that go beyond the purchasing process (services, warranty, etc.). In the international field, some companies strategically locate and relocate in different countries important links in their chain of value, so as to be more efficient.

Given free capital flow, investments that correspond to some links in the chain of value are generally located in regions with low labour force cost and poor protective labour conditions (what is directly related to the "social dumping" problem). This happens because those capitals try to maximize their investment. Besides, international specialization and distribution is present at production level. In this work division, each country produces, above all, those goods in which it has a comparative advantage (that is, the most abundant factor in that country is extensively used).

Nations like those of Central Europe, or the United States produce goods or services which are intensive in qualified work, and countries with cheap labour force produce goods intensive in non-qualified work. This redistribution of industrial activities between regions creates, in some cases, a deindustrialization of some countries due to their companies relocation.

Products that are the result of a chain of value whose links are transnationally located all throughout the countries, are obtained. Thus, each stage produces only a part of the product, which is going to be assembled or improved later in other countries that complement the productive process. So, the proliferation of transnational value chains can be distinguished as a crucial feature of globalization.

### *1.3.12. Link between Globalization and Culture: Intersection of the Global and Local Variables*

According to the theory of the State as society containment element, every society presupposes a state control; that is, it is conceived from the national state point of view. So, this is about state societies, where the State exercises its power and sets an order in a territorial field, where collective identities are built with particular game rules.

Each State gives its society internal homogeneity allowing it to differentiate from the rest of the state societies. Nevertheless, the creation and development of transcultural social spaces, which have been studied by ALLEY-DETMERS (cited by BECK) is a very typical feature of globalization. This author presents Africa as an example of those spaces: it is not a spacial location or a geographical field; it is an idea, a conception, an aesthetics that goes beyond time and space frontiers and that refers to the features of non-identity, non-progress, and ancestral rites, among other symbolic elements.

ROBINS (cited by BECK) holds that globalization has strong cultural incidence, because there is a constant cultural transformation with a sustained convergence towards a global culture. There are some agents that try to universalize symbols at world level and such universalized convergence is reflected in society lifestyle and behaviour. However, the existence of a unique world commercial space is considered utopic, because it would threaten the entrepreneurial spirit of benefit maximization.

The great development that the media have had in the last decades and their expansion all over the planet, interconnecting different regions, is of great importance for globalization. This fact is intensified due to the entry of new competitors in the telecommunications field, as well as because of a policy of partnerships, mergers and acquisitions, which have pioneered in the line by multiplying their settlements in the global field, in order to develop and consolidate their technical knowledge.

Roland Robertson (cited by Beck) conceptualizes glocalization by emphasizing the deep transnational interdependencies that exist and go beyond time and space. Real globalization and the one showed by the means of information appear as one and the same thing. The coexistence of attributions, responsibilities and images that are particular of people and individuals, and foreign to them is very important. These issues are reflected in the coexistence of global (that what is external, suffocating) and local features (what is small and specific), which may, in turn, be seen as an aspect of globalization.

*Glocalization* may be analyzed mainly from a cultural kaleidoscope, bearing in mind related issues, such as ethnicity and cultural heritage, among others. Ties that transnationally link societies generating new communities are produced. In some cases, they appear in a context of conflict in which institutionalized and standardized symbols coexist with local cultures.

The global issue is very important, but this does not mean that the local field has to be discarded. From the marketing point of view, companies cannot trade totally standardized products to all the country-markets because the products need some kind of adaptation to the legal, economic and cultural requirements of each one of the destination markets. Czinkota and Ronkainen remark that some transnational companies design their global marketing strategy, but once this strategy is implemented, bearing in mind the local features of the target countries (which is called marketing strategy glocalization). In practice, there are no companies that produce an absolutely standardized unique product for every destination market; hence the importance of localism (related to the part of culture that is alive) within the globalization frame.

### *1.3.13. Other Global Issues*

More international weight and more relevance is given to services: a progressive participation in the tertiary sector (telecommunications, transport, financial services, professional services, etc.), in world trade. This is the result of four factors exposed by Lobejón Herrero: the appearance of new services, the deregulation of many tertiary activities, the development of new technologies related to services and the tendency towards product differentiation. This last aspect implies marketing processes with a greater proportion of services to satisfy consumers' needs.

It is now estimated that foreign trade associated to the tertiary sector accounts for the fourth part of the world negotiated merchandise volumes. Within the Uruguay Round, which gave rise to the World Trade Organization, the GATS—General Agreement on the Trade of Services—, that establishes common multilateral regulations for that sector, has been established.

Other aspect to highlight is the importance of ecological and environmental concerns. Some buyers from developed countries markets request products that do not damage the environment in order to close commercial deals. Also, there are the 14,000 ISO standards that certify quality standards taking into account the environmental impact that the entrepreneurial chain of value causes. The problem of environmental protection is shown in a conception that analyzes the impact of economic development on the natural environment, especially when considering sustainable development, which implies a long term vision that comprises the world's future generations. This trend encourages some countries (especially those with great relative economic development) to adopt strict rules about the environment. Even though there have appeared economic "green" fields, many operators produce and trade many products in ecological dumping conditions (that is, they get products at a low cost as a consequence of the non-fulfilment of ecological standards). These companies threaten the companies that strictly observe natural environmental aspects to conditions of inequality.

Another important aspect which features this complex phenomenon is intraindustry commerce increase (commercial flow increase among different companies of the same industry).

## 2. THE WORLD TRADE ORGANIZATION AND OTHER INTERNATIONAL BODIES

### 2.1. Main Bodies of International Relevance

After the Second World War, important international bodies that approached different topics were created:

### *2.1.1. International Monetary Fund*

The IMF, originally, was created to help in the disequilibrium in the different national trade balances. Another fundamental function is the granting of credit to the different national States. This financial help has conditionality features, because the body requires some state conditions to free those funds. The State takes the commitment to make specific structural reforms in different aspects of its national economic policy (of taxation, social security, and monetary character, among others). The Fund representatives apply direct supervision measures over the countries that receive help, in order to be sure about the compliance with the commitment taken.

### *2.1.2. World Bank*

WB gives financial assistance with different objectives: development plans, social assistance, infrastructure works, development of capital markets, etc. These funds are granted directly to the State or state bodies. This body has different facilities that consider loan refund with grace periods and more favourable conditions as regards refund money rate. These conditions favour, above all, those loans granted to developing countries.

Other relevant international body is the United Nations Organization. Among its multiple activities, its contribution to world peace stands high.

## 2.2. Origin and Development of Multilateral Commercial Agreements: From the GATT to the WTO

### *2.2.1. World Trade Organization Origin*

After Second World War, from the commercial point of view, there was the idea to create an International Trade Organization (ITO) but, for different reasons, it was not consolidated as an international body. Instead, agreements were made from 1947, known as the GATT (General Agreements on Tariffs and Trade), with the primary objective of promoting a series of measures for the progressive liberation of commerce. On several occasions, the countries held different meetings so as to reach consensus to progressively diminish international trade barriers (tariff and paratariff barriers). These agreements were reached through different rounds (name given to the meetings among the national representatives of the countries), in order to reach a consensus about the progressive deregulation of commercial flow. The Uruguay Round gave origin to the World Trade Organization (WTO), which is, at present, a solid organ for discussion and solution of controversial issues that may arise between the countries as a consequence of the international operations that relate them. This international body has incorporated all the agreements timely reached within the GATT frame.

### *2.2.2. Principles that Rule the Functioning of the World Trade Organization*

The WTO has rules that also governed the GATT agreements. Non-discrimination, which includes the clause of the Most Favoured Nation and which establishes that concessions (or benefits) granted by one country to another (for example, reduction of trade barriers to imports), should be extended to other countries that were not the original beneficiaries (they have to be multilateralized) is one of those principles. If a country reduces its tariff barriers in order to import products from another country, this benefit has to be made extensive to the rest of the countries. However, there are some important exceptions: the existence of regional markets like free trade areas and customs unions (where countries can grant benefits to the member countries without extending them to those that are not members), preferential trade among countries and their colonies, and the Generalized System of Preferences (GSP). The GSP is a system in which particular countries (many of them developed countries) grant concessions (like reduction on imports tariffs) to specific native products from certain developing countries. Those advantages are granted without the need to multilateralize the benefits and without reciprocity obligation from the countries benefited.

National treatment, which expresses that imports cannot be subject to less beneficial conditions than the ones that affect local production, is another important clause. A typical example is the rule that says that imports cannot be reached by value-added tax (VAT) higher than those applied to sales in the internal market.

A very important principle is transparency in external market access, which means that the countries have to anticipate the use of tariff barriers and avoid imposing paratariff barriers. These barriers are monetary and so, easier to detect than paratariff barriers.

There is also a principle that stimulates friendly discussion. It is called "consultation principle". It refers to the search for consensus in the event of commercial differences or controversies among the nations. Countries are expected not to take unilateral measures that may affect other countries. This principle also rules negotiating issues discussed in rounds, so as to reach consensus in the different agreements.

### *2.2.3. Importance of the Uruguay Round*

The Uruguay Round was a meeting of national representatives that extended over a period of years. The World Trade Organization emerged from there. The WTO is an international body, on the same level as the IMF or the World Bank. After nearly fifty years the unconcluded project of the creation of a body to deal with the liberalization of foreign trade operations (originally the ITO) turned real. This body incorporates the ex-GATT principles and agreements negotiated until that time in the different rounds. It also includes the following features, among the negotiation issues of its members: international marketing of services (and their application, with principles similar to those that rule the marketing of products) and intellectual property rights (with fundamentals for the adequate protection of these intangible assets).

Agricultural products were included in this round, as negotiable products for barrier reduction. Those sectors had not been included in the ex-GATT agreements. Another important issue dealt with was the reduction of international tariff barriers and the conversion of paratariff barriers in force into tariff barriers, process called barrier tariffication.

Another remarkable aspect of the Uruguay Round is the attempt to progressively dismantle the Multi Fibre Agreement

(MFA) that affects most of the international marketing of textiles. Another measure refers to the greater precision required in the parameters of determination and investigation of unfair trade practices (certain subsidies and dumping). Another important issue is the determination of some parameters in common to reach consensus about phytosanitary control of internationally marketed products.

## 3. REGIONALISM

### 3.1. Constitution of Regional Blocks in the Global Scenario

Regionalism is a trend within the global phenomenon of constitution of regional markets. The terms "regional markets", "commercial blocks" and "integration systems" will be used in this section with the same meaning, even though some authors make a difference between them.

Regional markets are fields made up by two or more countries in which differential aspects as regards third countries are present. Differentiated fields which benefit the intrazone (for the members of the commercial block) issue as regards extrazone (that refers to the situation of the block members towards the countries that do not belong to the block) are present. These issues may comprise from a simple tariff reduction to a more complex integration (which may imply a tariff structure for common extrazone and harmonization of economic policies, among others).

Dr. BALASSA presents economic integration "as a process that comprises measures oriented to eliminate discrimination among economic unities that belong to different nation States". This author makes a differentiation between cooperation (that includes activities oriented to reduce discrimination among countries) and integration (which implies elimination of discriminatory systems among the different countries).

These markets are supported by agreements among the countries involved called treaties or protocols. Integration systems can be open or close (depending on the possibility of inclusion of additional members different from the ones of the original commercial block).

### 3.2. Different Forms of Integration

There are different integration models based on the degree of bond development and the magnitude of the objectives among the member countries. Next, the different theoretical models of integration will be exposed, from the least (the simplest, with limited objectives) to the most complex form of integration (with more ambitious goals). In practice, international existing commercial blocks coincide with some of the models that are going to be explained.

Regional markets that in practice are in an integration state inferior to the one presented in their objectives are shown. At present, there is only one market: the European Union, whose objectives have been totally fulfilled and so, its theoretical integration goals have been achieved.

#### *3.2.1. Tariff Preferential Area or Zone*

In this integration fashion the member countries look for a tariff barrier reduction and other obstacles for intrazone trade (that is, within the regional market). But the same individual tariff structures of each country in regards to commerce with other countries is maintained (that is, for the extrazone).

For example, in a situation prior to integration, country A has tariffs which are 10 per cent for certain product and country B has a 20 per cent tariff for the same product. Once the tariff preferential zone is constituted between A and B, a reduction of 50 per cent of the tariffs is agreed. This implies that if A imports a product from country B, it pays a 5 per cent tariff (that is, 10 per cent minus 50 per cent tariff preference); but if A imports the product from a third country that is not a member of the integration (for example, C) the product will pay 10 per cent (that is, the tariff without the reduction). If B imports the product from A, it will pay a 10 per cent tariff, and from C, a 20 per cent.

#### *3.2.2. Free Trade Area*

Similar to the previously mentioned integration state. The difference is the will to look for barrier elimination for the intrazone. But just as the tariff preferential zone, individual tariff structures for extrazone are maintained by each one of the members of the block.

### 3.2.3. Customs Union

Its objective is the free circulation of goods intrazone (that is, elimination of trade barriers for commercial operations among the member countries). Other important objective is the determination of a common tariff structure for extrazone (common external tariff). In the example above, both countries (A and B) will agree on the same tariff for imports coming from C. Besides, it is possible that this stage of integration required the creation of a common Customs House for the regional market (which would imply the elimination of the national customs). This body would be in charge of foreign trade taxes collection and control, redistributing revenue among the member countries.

### 3.2.4. Common Market

It adds to the customs union objectives free movement of factors (work, capital, technology) that may move without barriers throughout the regional market. It also seeks policy macro-economic harmonization among the countries. This market pursues the accomplishment of common regional features and greater connection and contact in the implementation of those policies.

### 3.2.5. Economic Union

Apart from the common market objectives, this adds the adoption of a common currency among its member countries (which implies the existence of a common monetary system). Thus, national currency disappears. Besides, it demands the determination of certain policies in common (agricultural, environmental, etc.).

### 3.2.6. Confederation or Total Integration

In this integration model, countries behave and function as a unique country. This is due to the unification of positive rights in force among the members of the integration.

There are different reasons why countries try to develop regional markets like: the accomplishment of better political relationships with the other members, normalization in migratory issues among the different countries and obtention of marketing benefits. Other causes are: an increase of negotiating capacity for each member of the integration block, the implementation of structural reforms at regional level, and the possibility to remain in the regional trend.

## 3.3. Main Regional Agreements at World Level

Some of the main international markets will be mentioned. The reader is referred to more specific literature for some detailed aspects of these markets.

At present, the main commercial blocks are:

### *3.3.1. North American Free Trade Agreement (NAFTA)*

Composed by the United States, Canada and Mexico; its objective is the creation of a free trade area. This agreement also covers issues like: intellectual property right protection, development of intrazone investment and environmental care, among other topics.

### *3.3.2. Asociación Latinoamericana de Integración (ALADI)*

This market is formed mostly by the main countries of the South American sub-continent. Its objective is the creation of a Latin American common market.

As with the NAFTA, it is in an initial state of integration, that is, a tariff preferential zone. Many rules and regulations link the member countries. There are bilateral, plurilateral and regional agreements of partial or regional scope where members of the block grant concessions for intrazone operations.

### *3.3.3. Mercado Común del Sur (MERCOSUR)*

Composed of Argentina, Brazil, Uruguay and Paraguay. Its objective is the creation of a common market, but in practice it is considered an imperfect customs union, because intrazone trade is free and there is an External Common Tariff (ECT). That free market and the ECT extend to most tariff products, not to all of them. Besides, there is an exemption system for some products. In addition, treaties to form free trade areas between the Mercosur and Chile, and the Mercosur and Bolivia have been signed. In the year 2006, Venezuela was incorporated to the MERCOSUR. This country is now in the transition towards customs union integration.

### *3.3.4. European Economic Union*

It is composed by most of the countries of Western Europe. The incorporation of new European nations to this regional market is constantly being negotiated. It is the only commercial block that has reached its objectives. It is a monetary union with one monetary system (with a unique currency, the euro, and the European Central Bank). It functions as a protectionist market. This block applies the greatest variety of tariff and paratariff barriers known by products coming from the extrazone.

It develops regional policies, like European agricultural policy and fishing European policy. These sectors develop with the help of the national States and the communities. It comprises supranational bodies (European Council, Commission, Court of Justice and Parliament) that give rise to rules of community law and apply them. There are certain less integrated countries of the area and they constitute the European Free Trade Area.

### *3.3.5. Free Trade Area of the Americas (FTAA)*

Nowadays it is not a regional market, but a continental integration project, whose commercial agreement covers from Alaska to Tierra del Fuego. Its objective is the creation of a free trade American zone.

### *3.3.6. Other Markets*

There are ASEAN (Association of South East Asian Nations: Brunei, Indonesia, Malaysia, Myanmar, Philippines, Singapore, and Vietnam), CARICOM, Cooperation Council for the Arab States of the Gulf, Economic Community of West African States, Andean Integration System, among the most relevant.

## 3.4. Regionalism Related Effects

These effects vary considerably according to the integration level reached by a regional market. Nevertheless, in general terms and due to market extension, the following features are present:

### *3.4.1. Intrazone Trade Increase*

Also known as the creation of trade within the integration area. The countries involved in the regional block increase their imports and exports volume as regards the members of the area. This is due to the reduction or elimination of tariff barriers and other trade barriers, which encourages the generation of big volume operations.

This increase in trade brings about an intrazone production increase. This production, when extended, permits the development of economies of scale (better distribution of fixed costs). It also implies an extension of the competitive field that stops being a national field to become a regional competitive environment. These factors encourage the companies to get a higher level of efficiency.

In some cases, there is some trade diversion. This diversion happens in customs unions when a country that is member of a block imports a product which was less efficiently produced within the frame of a trade agreement than the product produced extrazone. This happens because that product is protected by an external tariff in common, which rises the price of similar products of countries that are not members of the integration block.

### *3.4.2. Increase in External Investment and Technological Updating*

The integration area is a very attractive target market for the location of productive investment coming, not only from the extrazone, but also from companies that are based in one of the member countries. Investing companies design a strategy to start production in one of the block countries, to be marketed later in the extended market.

Direct investment, as well as the increase in intrazone trade flow, are propellers for the renovation of the intrazone technological system. This renovation is produced with the signing of know-how transference contracts, and the incorporation of capital goods, among others.

### 3.4.3. Improvement in Intrazone Consumption

Consumers are highly benefited by integration, because prices of products imported by a country from another member of the agreement are reduced. This decrease is the result of the elimination of intrazone trade barriers that made them costly. With the increase of intrazone imports and exports, block consumers widen the variety of selection of products they can choose from.

### 3.4.4. Improvement of Political Relationships between the Countries Involved

There is an important link between trade and international politics. More fluid diplomatic relations between the States is the result of an increase in trade. This friendly link favours the signing of new agreements among the countries.

### 3.4.5. Determination of Regional Rules and Standards

In some cases, the constitution of commercial blocks allows to reach consensus among its members, which permits to determine some points in common. There can be rules in common that deal with different subject areas like: customs issues, packaging, transportation, quality standards and obligatory certifications, among others.

### 3.4.6. Negotiation of Other Agreements at Block Level

A synergic attitude in the negotiating capacity of the members is produced. The block may negotiate new commercial agreements (by increasing its power and negotiating ability) with other countries or with other integration systems.

### 3.4.7. Proliferation of Panregional Entrepreneurial Strategies

Some intrazone or extrazone located companies devise and implement panregional marketing strategies, considering every country in the integration system as a unique target market. The aim of these strategic activities is to have access to a commercial block, trying to position products aimed at panregional segments (for consumers with similar tastes or needs in the different member countries). In this way, it is possible to get the standardization of certain variables of the marketing mix at regional level (for example, using the same brand, or the same packaging to have access to different market-countries intraregionally).

### *3.4.8. Relocation of Some Industries*

Intrazone changes may be produced because industries want to obtain the benefits of the existing comparative advantages enjoyed by other member countries. This dynamics produces a total or partial restructuration of the national productive structures. As a consequence, there may be a national reconsideration, about the specialization of their productive structures, as regards the regional field.

### *3.4.9. Organization of Intraregional Strategic Alliances*

Trade agreements can become a propitious field for companies of different member countries, due to market expansion and increasing regional competitiveness. Joint projects, in which different companies from the commercial block integrate and complement in issues like marketing, production, supplying and/or financing in order to develop a regional strategy may be beneficial.

### *3.4.10. Other Effects*

Another important effect is the substitution of commercial relationships with extrazone countries in favour of exchanges with economies that form part of a regional agreement. A drop in transaction prices and a greater transparency in intrazone prices is also relevant. This last effect is produced, above all, in the regional markets that reach a common currency, as is the case with the European Union.

## 4. INTERNATIONAL ENVIRONMENTS

### 4.1. Impact of Differential Environments on International Marketing

There are a lot of features in common between a marketing strategy design for the internal market, and a world market marketing strategy. However, one of the main distinctive issues between domestic and international marketing is that between local and world markets there exists a series of differential factors.

These differences can be of different character. They configure in each external market (or country-market) certain international environments that differentiate them from the national environment.

These environments differ from country-market to country-market, even though similarities between the environments may appear. This fact creates psychological proximity between the markets, which generates a more propitious field to market the products.

## 4.2. Main International Environments

The differences presented in these environments and their variation from country to country (and, in some cases, the existence of different internal subenvironments in a country), are what precisely makes international marketing activity complex. The entrepreneur must know and handle these differential features efficiently in order to adapt the most appropriate strategy for each market. Later, some strategies like standardization, which minimizes the impact of the differences will be developed (by offering the product attributes without modification to the different markets).

The most important environments are:

— Economic, financial and technological.

— Cultural.

— Political and legal.

### *4.2.1. Economic, Financial and Technological Environments*

The economic, financial and technological environment consists of different factors that vary remarkably from one country to another. It is very relevant to adequately consider this environment when establishing marketing strategies. Every one of these factors interpenetrates the competition and consumption activities in the destination market. Some of the components of this environment are part of a structure of resources (in a wide sense) of a country like the climate, natural resources, etc., and other factors that are determined by the interaction between companies, consumers and state activity (GDP, per capita income, unemployment rate, etc.).

The economic, financial and technological environment comprises the following items:

— Domestic gross product and gross national product.
— Number of inhabitants and demographic growth rate.
— Population composition by age groups and its distribution in the national territory.
— Per capita income and income distribution structure.
— Productive structure and national strategic sectors.
— Productive and commercial structure concentration levels.
— Number of national small and medium enterprises and their features.
— Economic development level.
— Composition of average family.
— Indebtedness level.
— Money and inflation rates.
— Indebtedness level and public sector financing options.
— Technological development level in the different sectors of economy.
— Level of state intervention in economic and commercial activity.
— Entrepreneurial financing options.
— Foreign trade and international operation incentive supporting programmes.
— Country risk (this is a political and economic factor).
— Imports volume and discrimination by sector and product.
— Exports volume and discrimination by sector and product.
— Balance of payments.
— Infrastructure (communication, road system, transport, distribution, etc.).

— Features of the national financial system (capital market, money market and foreign exchange).
— Development of technological segments.
— Private and State investment level in R + D (research and development).
— Exchange system and exchange rate risk.
— Degree of economy liberalization (existence of tariff and paratariff barriers).
— Policies of external investment promotion.
— Economic growth rate.
— Country participation in a regional market and its relative importance.
— Existing natural resources.
— Human resources (or human capital) and environmental care policy.
— Geographical features (climatic, topographic, etc.).
— Life quality and unemployment level.
— Tax burden and structure.

#### *4.2.2. Cultural Environment*

The cultural environment is composed by multiple factors, it is multidimensional. Culture is made up by a series of behaviours, beliefs and values that constitute every social activity. Cultural tradition is transmitted from generation to generation. There is a great resistance to change in the cultural aspects and these factors persist almost invariably through time.

Cultural sensitivity or culturization is the adaptation capacity of a company to a specific cultural environment. Cultural incompetence refers to the entrepreneur's incapacity to detect and interpret the cultural differences between the national and the external markets. Cultural imperialism implies the determination of an entrepreneurial strategy that does not consider cultural differences between the countries of origin and destination. This attitude promotes the imposition of cultural values of one country upon another.

Some international cultural environments give great relevance to the context in which operations develop. These are cultures of high context, like, for example, the Arab countries and Japan. Words have a less explicit meaning in these cultures, but there is a greater consideration of the person as a guarantee of commitment and responsibility in the compliance of his or her obligations. These environments require less legal formalities to make commercial deals.

There are some other cultural scenarios in which context is not so important. In these fields, words transmit the whole message in an explicit way (i.e. the United States). In this type of cultural environment, the safety of a commitment comes from the fixing of some formalities and legal precautions that relate the parties in the compliance of their responsibilities. The important thing is not the person, but the agreements and documents that he or she signs (low context cultures).

The sharp existing differences in the cultural and international environments involve a responsible analysis of the environments mentioned. A strategy of access that takes into account foreign values, features, uses and customs has to be defined. The entrepreneur is required to have an emphatic attitude (as if he or she were from the foreign market) considering the cultural particularities of every external market. A simplified analysis based on the local cultural features of the market of origin has to be avoided.

Some of the main variables about the different cultural international environments that the company has to consider are:

- — Language and shades of meaning (language is relevant to communicate the product attributes and to get information about the destination market).
- — Religious factors and popular beliefs.
- — Consumers' lifestyles.
- — Consumers' attitudes to everything foreign.
- — Usage and consumption of a specific product.
- — Social values (solidarity, cooperation, etc.).

— Main social institutions recognized by society.
— Aesthetic issues (this has to do with the use of specific colours, design preferences, shapes or materials, etc.).
— Factors that encourage the purchase, and different social behaviour patterns.
— Non-verbal language (useful to negotiate commercial agreements with external market representatives, or when devising advertising strategies).
— Education levels of the population (possibility of gain access to basic education, illiteracy rate, percentage of the population with superior studies).
— Social stratification features.
— Society access to new techological forms.
— Customs and uses.
— Other features (individualism, importance of woman in society, average family size, ecological care, attitude towards elderly people, importance of ethics).

#### *4.2.3. Political and Legal Environment*

Autodetermination as regards legislation and the establishment of a political system that protects the activities performed by the institutions and inhabitants of a country is a feature of sovereignty. As it is already known, regulations change sensibly from one market to the other, according to particular economic cycles that belong to each nation. The entrepreneur has to analyze numerous political and legal variables, which may directly or indirectly affect the marketing of the product in a particular external market. Among them, the most important are:

— Present political system.
— State intervention degree in economic activity (regulation of some operations, creation of bureaucratic bodies of control).
— Existence of pressing groups (lobby).
— Different commercial barriers (tariff and paratariff barriers), that hinder the access of products from other countries.

— Existing level of political risk in the country that may affect security in the development of commercial activities (existence of war conflicts, *coups d'etat*, revolutions, strikes, terrorism).
— Governmental activities that may affect the constitutional real property and others (confiscation, expropriation, etc.).
— Relationship between state and religion.
— Force of laws against disloyal commerce practices (dumping, subsidies).
— Imposition of commercial penalties to particular countries.
— Features of national regulations protective of copyrights (patents, trademarks, designs, etc.).
— Enforcement of environmental protection laws.
— Character of the prevailing legal system (based on written laws or customary law).
— Existence of economic policies that affect the international flow of commerce (fixation of maximum prices, controlled foreign exchange system, etc.).
— Legal system that tolerates corrupting activities in the private and public environments.
— Bilateral or multilateral political or international agreements that might achieve more beneficial marketing conditions.
— Validity of regulations that promote the organization of international marketing associative activities.
— Existing customs regulations.
— Legislation about foreign direct investment introduction (IDE).
— Other type of important regulations are those that deal with the following topics: commercial contracts and documents, functioning and regulation of normal and multimodal transport, promotion of capital goods

or critical supply imports, consumer protection, and competition.

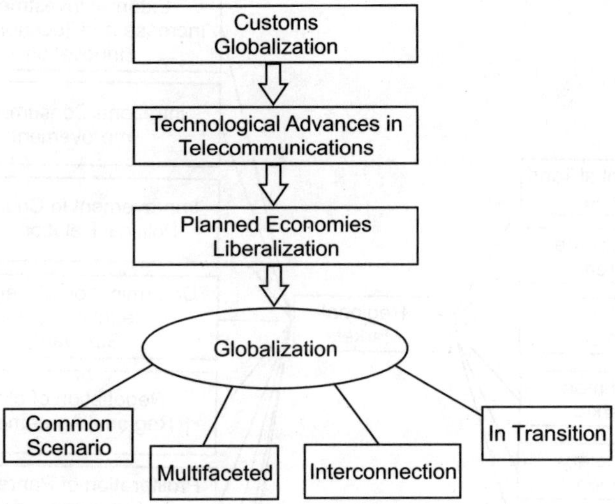


**Figure 1.1.** Globalization Stages and Features

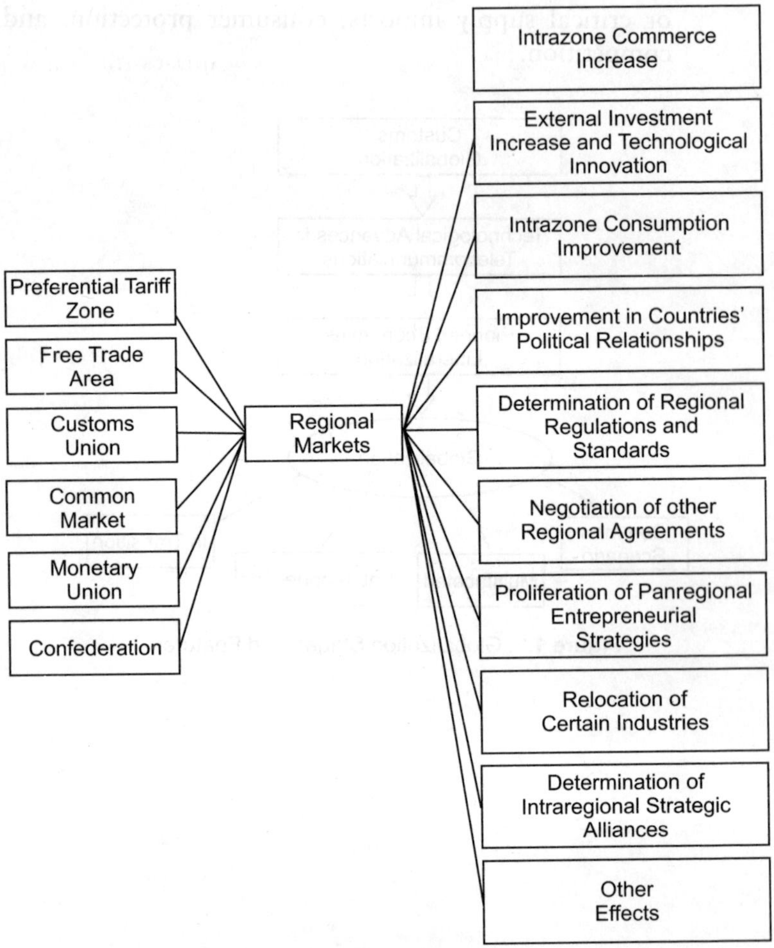


**Figure 1.2.** Regional Market Types and their Effects

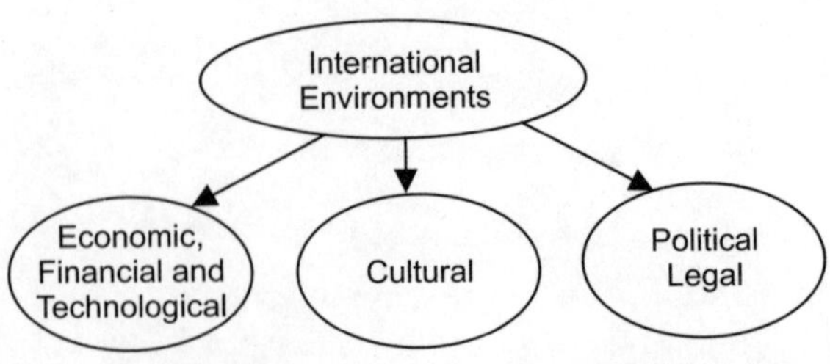


**Figure 1.3.** International Environments

# 2

# The Enterprise and the International Markets

## 1. SMALL AND MEDIUM-SIZED ENTERPRISE CONCERNS

Within the small and medium-sized company vast concerns there is an important series of issues that affect internationalization.

The first obstacle entrepreneurs, especially those unexperienced in external markets, have to face is the lack of exporting conscience.

### 1.1. Exporting Conscience

#### *1.1.1. Main Features*

The exporting conscience is a positive entrepreneur's attitude, which allows him or her to develop a progressive link at international level, through the assumption of medium and long term obligations with the external markets.

Thus, an exporting conscience can be qualified as:

— *Mental:* It is an attitude closely linked to entrepreneurial thought and executive strategy. That conscience is in the entrepreneur's mind, impelling and encouraging him or her to penetrate and develop commercial activity in the world markets. This positive conception as regards international marketing must not be isolated in the hierarchical levels of the company; it also has to expand to basic or operative levels. Every member of the company, from an employee with the lowest salary to the most hierarchical executive, has to be imbued with this exporting conscience. It is very common, however, for this attitude to appear first at the top levels and then to spread to the rest of the members of the organization.

— *Reasonable:* This reasonability based attitude gives the entrepreneur who has exporting conscience the ability to understand the complexity of global markets and develop a rational and progressive marketing strategy in order to internationalize the article.

— *Positive:* It is aware of the difficulties that world market penetration implies, but a motivated entrepreneur remarks the potential benefits that the development of international activities (greater earnings, better distribution of costs, use of idle capacity, risk diversification, etc.) can bring to the company.

— *Gradual:* This attitude favours a decision-taking process that allows the company to familiarize progressively with the different international marketing activities. Besides, as different situations are experienced in the external markets, a process of feedback is produced within the company. This attitude generates a learning capacity and decisions based on that capacity permit the exporting conscience to self-generate through time. This step-by-step procedure implies that, with the acquisition of international experience, the entrepreneur will diversify the markets that the company will progressively penetrate. Also, as time goes by, the degree of difficulty of the markets accessed (from the simplest to the most complex) will progressively increase. This means that the company will have to develop an increasing allocation of monetary, financial, productive and human resources towards international markets as well, as it consolidates in those markets.

— *Stable:* This exporting approach is presented as a strategic attitude. External markets access can be thought of as a company mission. International access can be one of the main objectives which will guide the other secondary objectives. This is not just a behaviour with short term effects. It is an entrepreneurial vision with objectives in the long term, far beyond the present situation.

### *1.1.2. Factors that Affect its Formation*

Some factors that may threaten the development of an entrepreneur exporting conscience or undermine the development of this positive attitude are:

— ***Fear to the unknown and resistance to change:*** In some companies, international markets complexity and heterogeneity appears as an unsurmountable difficulty at the beginning. The company watches external markets with a great load of uncertainty. The entrepreneur clings to the known context which he or she better manages, the internal market.

— ***Unsuccessful experiences:*** If the company was unsuccessful in previous international operations, doubts about the feasibility of external marketing and company competence for this activity might appear. The entrepreneur must evaluate if those experiences have been carried out without planning. It is also important for the organization to consider the implications of some failed attempts, such as the need of adequate technical counselling and a requirement of minimum necessary information to gain access to international activity.

— ***Ignorance about the positive aspects of international marketing:*** The entrepreneur must not only emphasize the challenge that international marketing poses, but also know about the different incentives that international marketing activity may have for the company. Some very relevant are: rise in earnings and credit, or tax incentives.

— ***National market security:*** The security the company has in national market operations is a factor that may threaten the creation of the exporting conscience. When the entrepreneur develops certain level of operations in the domestic environment, operation diversification towards other markets may be considered unnecessary.

This factor can also be supported by increasing national sales and the high purchasing power level of the segment to which product is oriented in the local environment.

— ***Knowledge about global reality:*** The entrepreneur may have some degree of naivety and not be aware of some present global context principles. Some globalization factors, such as the progressive and irreversible interconnection of national economies by means of commercial, financial, and communicational flows, constitute keys to the entrepreneurial activity. Unawareness about this increasingly globalizing trend that interpenetrates constantly the national context where the company develops its activities, can bring about serious consequences for the organization. Ignorance about these issues can make the small and medium-sized entrepreneur think that his or her product is marketed at a local level of competition, totally disconnected from the international environment. These distorted perceptions can also make executives believe that their product can only be accepted by the domestic market and is not fit for the global market.

### *1.1.3. Solutions to the Problem of its Absence*

Among the solutions, the so-called company internationalization promoters are really important. These factors may be very different and they act direct or indirectly upon the entrepreneur. These promoters support, motivate, and accompany the organization in its change in attitude. Among them, the following can be pointed out:

— ***Different situations that may cause the entrepreneur or some of the employees to get some level of openmindedness towards international markets:*** The main enhancers are the execution of international marketing training courses, international subject conference attendance and knowledge updating through informative bulletins or programmes about international marketing issues. Attendance to trade shows and commercial missions as well as acquisition of knowledge on international activities performed by the local competitor may also help.

— ***Different people that may influence in the company change of view:*** Generally, this is about operators or intermediaries that perform activities directly or indirectly linked with internationalization as, for example, personnel with knowledge of international marketing that has been incorporated to the company staff, consulters in international marketing, international carriers, brokers and marketing companies. Customs agents, development governmental bodies advisors, external sector financial institutions, among others, are also important.

— ***Certain economic or structural junctures of the local market:*** Some aspects of local market economic depression or recession that cause a drop in sales and a decrease in domestic consumption, or the existence of a wild competitive national market environment that impedes participation in the market, may be exporting conscience generating factors. These issues can open a new horizon of entrepreneurial change, determined in some cases by a strong reason of survival or by a search for alternative commercial ways. The important thing to remember is that if some of the reasons mentioned are junctures, the entrepreneur must not leave aside exporting attitudes due to national improvement. It is important that once the exporting commitment has been assumed, international activity must not be neglected, no matter what favourable subsequent changes may appear in the domestic environment. The company attitude must be to support and strengthen the international strategies that it may have been deployed in national market unfavourable times, even though the local environment juncture could have improved later.

## 1.2. Exportable Volume and Quality Problems Consistent with the External Market

### *1.2.1. Differences between Exportable Balance and Offer*

Another problem that entrepreneurs may have to face at the beginning of their internationalization activities is the lack of exportable volume and an adequate quality to satisfy the minimum requirements of international demand. Generally, foreign buyers' orders have the following features:

— They are very significant, which means that certain cases exceed the total production of the small and medium-sized company in the market of origin.

— They require quality level that may be sustained throughout time.

As regards exportable volume or amount devoted to international markets, a difference has to be made between exportable balance and supply.

Exportable Balance

It is the difference between a company's total production, national market sales deduced. The balance is fluctuating, because it decreases when national sales increase and *vice versa*. There are variations in this balance due to internally marketed volume fluctuations.

These balances do not allow to assume continuous and serious commitments as regards foreign operators. The exportable balance does not allow the entrepreneur to determine a medium or long term export strategy, due to its fluctuating and discontinuous character. When speaking about exportable balances, the domestic market has the priority in production assignation. International market is the adjustment variable; only production surplus without local consumption is used.

Exportable Supply

It is a continuous and stable volume assigned for international markets, which allows to make commercial agreements that exceed the short term. This volume is assigned preferentially to the international market in relation to local consumption.

It positions the exporter as responsible and reliable before world operators. It allows compliance with a certain quantity for the external buyer and thus complies with international commitments.

Supply represents a great responsibility in the assumption of external commitments that are going to be totally satisfied. So, no matter what happened with local market sales and consumption, the foreign buyer will have, for sure, a part of the exporter production in accordance with the contractual agreements signed. In this case, the adjustment variable is the internal market, which means that production that is not part of the exportable supply is assigned to the national market.

It is noticeable that a small entrepreneur exportable supply is insufficient compared to the minimum amounts required for the world market. These specific concerns may be traditionally or creatively approached.

### *1.2.2. Solutions to Exportable Supply Concerns*

Traditional Solutions:

— Acquisition of new equipment, enlargement of productive facilities, increase in working hours and number of workers in order to produce. Any other rise in company productive resources that allows to manufacture more products for world insertion is also appropriate.

Creative Solutions:

— ***Associativity:*** It is a joint project to gain access to external markets. Associativity may be an effective solution for small producers with insufficient exportable supply. By associating different exportable supplies of the same article produced by small-sized companies, an *exportable offer package* to efficiently satisfy international demand may be created.

— ***Manufacturing contract:*** It is very useful for the producer that cannot totally satisfy external orders with its own production. In this case, it subcontracts the necessary amount of goods to reach the exportable offer to one or more companies, then, buys this production (that the companies manufactured by order) and integrates it to the exportable volume. The subcontracted company produced the goods, which were then bought, to send them to the world market, according to the specifications and regulations of the ordering company.

### *1.2.3. Importance of Product Quality in International Operations*

As regards homogeneous quality concerns of the product offered to international markets, the company must accomplish the same product features and attributes in each lot produced. Those goods must satisfy the foreign buyer's or user's needs without ups and downs. Besides, a quality relation among all the pieces or parts that make up the product has to be achieved. They have to have the same performing level for use or consumption. An adequate relation between product quality degree and an economic life has to be looked for.

Total quality has to be an objective, which implies the application of parameters not only in product manufacture and finish, but in the whole of the entrepreneurial process. The local entrepreneur will have to face these problems related to quality when he does not comply with certain quality standards stipulated by legal regulations in the destination country (like the use of specific materials, the avoidance of certain artificial preservatives, etc.). These parameters may be considered, in some cases, paratariff barriers. In other cases, the barriers are not legal (also-called "*de facto* barriers"), when they are established by external buyers who wish their supplier in origin to incorporate to their system of quality.

### *1.2.4. Solutions to the Problem of Quality of Volumes Offered*

One of the solutions for quality concerns is that a total quality management system should be included in the company in order to get some kind of national or international certification following quality standards. For example, at international level, there are the so-called ISO Series 9000 and 14000 standards, relevant in the world market. This type of international quality management implies the hiring of a quality advisor for the entrepreneur. A company quality plan has to be followed according to the Standard Order Procedures Manual, in order to get certification from the lawfully authorized body, which will ratify that all or part of the industrial process is included within the standardized parameters.

Generally, getting these certifications may be quite costly for the small company, which makes it impossible for the company to start formalities. Nevertheless, if the company participates in any associative structure (for example, an export cooperative), it may get better positioned to obtain quality certification. A qualitative control system cost of implementation for internationally marketed products, by means of a joint structure, can be shared by all the members of the associative project.

A second solution to comply with certain quality aspects is for the company to make periodical revisions and analyses of the production shipped. Verifications are performed by independent laboratories or specialized consultory agencies that issue documents called "quality certificates", and control certain aspects of the manufacturing process or product attributes. Quality issues to be analyzed vary according to the product (i.e. control of resistance, radioactivity, level of humidity, etc.). So, the external buyer may be offered the inclusion—among international commodity shipment commercial papers—of quality certificates, which constitute the documentary support to the verification of exported products specific attributes, performed by independent bodies in order to demonstrate a uniform level of quality.

Highly economically developed countries generally have higher quality requirements. This is why the entrepreneur may also consider a change in penetrated markets objectives, at least in a first stage, as another alternative solution to the subject of quality. Marketing of goods in less developed or developing country markets may be considered with less quality stipulations.

## 1.3. Financial Problems that Affect Internationalization

### *1.3.1. Importance of These Concerns*

Lack of funds to internationalize is another small and medium-sized entrepreneur concern. Financial resources are among those resources necessary to gain access to world markets (human, productive, etc.). These financial entrepreneurial problems prevent the company from carrying out operations that could directly or indirectly link it to the external markets. Financial difficulties may be the result of company inaccessibility to credit facilities from financial institutions or of lack of capital of its own.

Depending on each particular case, financial lack of capacity prevents certain expenses which are important for external market penetration from being assumed.

Operational Expenditures:

— In international marketing, collection cycles are longer than in the internal market. Generally, export operations have an average collection cycle of 90 to 180 days, which is highly superior to internal market commercial practices collection cycle. This is why it is very difficult for the entrepreneur to maintain that cycle (that goes from production and shipment to the effective collection of goods), without income to cover operative accounts.

— Offering of quotation abroad with certain price clauses that imply carriage payment and other price components by the seller (an example is the incoterm CIF clause —cost, insurance and freight—, by which the seller is responsible for the payment and inclusion of the cost of the product, as well as international carriage and insurance in the price offered).

Production Costs:

— Raw material purchase, inputs and other components necessary to produce a product for marketing in other countries.

— Enlargement or modification of the productive structure to make it adequate for product manufacturing.
— Productive process controls, through quality audits, national and international quality certifications.

Marketing Costs:

— Development of research studies of external markets.
— Preparation of multilingual leaflets, brochures and catalogues (with high costs of design and translation).
— New container design and testing, according to the legal requirements of the destination market.
— Participation in international expositions and trade shows.
— Participation in commercial missions and business trips.
— Web page design and maintenance.
— Promotional material delivery (samples).
— International brand design and registration.

### *1.3.2. Solutions to International Marketing Funding Concerns*

This kind of problem may have different solutions:

#### Traditional

It consists in the procurement of credit lines at more beneficial interest rates. They are the so-called "exports prefinancing credits", which allow to financially settle the production of goods for the international market. Financing credits are those that support financially the cycle that goes from exported product shipment to operation collection. Postfinancing credit lines to the seller aim at regenerating the company operative cycle after operation cashing. In some cases, there are also credit lines to extend the productive structure through the incorporation, in advantageous conditions, of national and/or imported capital goods for exportable articles.

In the case of government actual assistance, governmental bodies can help, especially the entrepreneur, in certain marketing aspects: management of programmes for small entrepreneurs' participation in official stands (generally shared by several companies) in international trade shows and expositions, with lower cost of access to these events. Also, some state bodies consider the organization of business trips whose costs may be shared among several entrepreneurs. Some state agencies give free or low cost consulting services to the entrepreneur, as regards quality management, package design, etc. In some cases, there may be governmental programmes that grant subsidies to carry out some internationalization activities or to create associative company structures for international marketing (exportation consortia, groups of exporters, etc.) and support their activities. In other cases, the State may take part in the organization of commercial events (trade shows, international entrepreneurial events, etc.), which allows to generate contacts between the local and the international business force.

### Creative

Associativity allows the small and medium-sized entrepreneur to face up to certain expenses that relate him or her to the external market (such as investigation markets, international leaflets, trade shows attendance). The expenses are shared among all the members of the joint project, with unitary much lower costs for each entrepreneur than if he or she had to pay those sums individually. These associative structures may get, through a system of joint or centralized purchases, more economical costs for input purchase, machinery and raw material and longer purchasing terms for their partners. In some cases, company structures may get more beneficial credit conditions for their components, or act as guarantors to get individual financing. As associative structures have a greater negotiating capacity when buying from abroad than the capacity when acting individually, sometimes they may get shorter financing operations terms (shipment-collection cycle is reduced) in direct proportion to the importance of the business concerted.

Other possible solution in case of financing problems is through the constitution of a joint venture or coinvestment. This is an international association (contractual or through the creation of a new partnership), that allows intervening companies to assign different resources (capital, labour force, technology, etc.) for world markets access. A joint venture may be composed by a medium-sized national company and an international company. In this example the national company would contribute productive structure and human resources, among other resources. On the other hand, the international company would contribute *capital for the operative process*, technology, information about potential business opportunities, or international contacts for the exporting project. In the world environment, there are official programmes that promote this type of ventures, of which Al-Invest is one of the best known. This programme is promoted by the European Union and favours partnerships among companies of that regional market, and those of other countries.

## 1.4. Problem of Knowledge about International Marketing Dynamics

### *1.4.1. Importance of These Concerns*

An obstacle the small and medium-sized enterprise has to face is the lack of knowledge (or know-how) about how to gain access to international markets. It is a very complex problem that shows great entrepreneurial ignorance about important issues on:

***Operational management and exportation:*** International freight contractual aspects, advantages in the selection of a particular means of transport, calculation of a container capacity and its logistic management, and analysis of the different components that make up an export price. Other aspects must also be considered, like merchandise insurance and the convenience of the use of different international insurance clauses, issuance of different commercial papers (bid, quotation, proforma invoice, packing list, etc.) and the management of other documents (certificate of origin, phytosanitary certificates, among others).

***Customs aspects of exportation:*** Main ways to declare an export before customs service, use of tax free areas, documents required by customs control, customs body functions and control sectors. Other significant factors are: the use of fiscal deposits, sampling, knowledge about the main promotional benefits for international marketing (refunds, drawbacks, temporary admissions, etc.), tax collected by the customs body, and violations and penalties for those illegal acts, among other topics.

***Banking and financial international marketing aspects:*** Knowledge of the forms of payment used (documentary collection, draft, documentary letter of credit, etc.) and the advantages of each one, presentation of documents to the correspondent bank of the letter of credit, international collection management initial stage, and issuance of a bill of exchange. Other issues to be considered are: prefinancing procurement, financing and postfinancing credit lines.

***International commercialization aspects:*** Collection of information about business opportunities in the external markets, detection of the main existing trade barriers for international market access (tariff and paratariff barriers), product brand and package adaptation to legal, economic, and cultural requirements of the countries of destination, international distribution channel detection and/or design, different international means of promotion (trade shows and expositions, catalogues and leaflets, web pages, etc.), implementation of the most adequate international price policy and marketing channel selection for each market, considering different factors (market size, existing marketing barriers, similarity with the market of origin, etc.). The company may also ignore how to emphasize certain product attributes in order to achieve differentiation with its competitors in the external markets. Some of the company strengths for differentiation are: low costs, attractive and safe packaging, popular brandname, good postmarketing services, adequate discount and bonus policy, technological innovation and quality, qualified salespersonnel, etc.

All these concerns are mainly based on the lack of appropriate information about how to carry out, efficiently, activities in the external markets. The company does not possess the technical knowledge to perform some aspects of international operations. The entrepreneur does not have the operative or executive qualified personnel necessary to carry out the internationalization basic activities of a company. In conclusion, expert and detailed knowledge about international marketing main aspects is something companies lack.

### *1.4.2. Solution to the Concerns about International Operation Knowledge*

There are three specific solutions to these concerns:

— *Tertiarization:* Also-called "outsourcing" or "externalization". It implies leaving unknown operations and undertakings, related to world markets penetration, in the hands of external intermediaries (consortia, trading companies, brokers, consultants, etc.) that will perform the actions unknown to the company.

— *Training or development of internal structures:* It refers to personnel training at the company at different levels. The objective is to prepare employees on the main aspects of international marketing, by means of courses and seminars so that they can have a good performance in the company's international marketing activities. In other cases, employees with knowledge on these topics can be incorporated, in order to create an international marketing department within the company.

— *Mix strategy:* It consists in a mixture of the previously mentioned, that is, the development of certain company's internal level skills on international marketing, and also tertiarizing some internationalization functions.

In certain cases, and for some specific activities, the use of service tertiarization may be important. This could be due to the fact that training is a process that requires learning internalization time before practical application. Before certain actual business opportunities or situations, or in the case of the first internationalization stages, the company needs to respond with certain speed and efficacy. In these cases it would be more convenient to ask a specialized and experienced agent to assist the entrepreneur in the international adventure. As the organization operates and consolidates in the external markets, the use of internal structures and resources of its own may be considered.

Externalizing functions also has to do with the company business volume in the external markets. Tertiarizing may be an important choice; more than developing internal resources in the case of a small volume and a low number of operations or few exploited markets. The company executive will have to assess whether it is antieconomical or not to implement and support an internal administrative structure to handle and supervise operations. In some cases it may be useful to outsource part of the functions; in others or all of them.

These variables must be observed in order to evaluate whether to outsource or internalize all or some of the functions of international marketing:

- External structure cost versus internal structure cost.
- Number of penetrated markets.
- Volume of monetary business generated by exports.
- Internationalization stage in which the company is occasional, experimental or consolidated export.
- Market importance and complexity to gain access to it.
- Geographic (distance) and psychographic (similarity in trade practices, languages, cultures, official language, legislation, etc.) of the selected international markets compared to the market of origin.

## 1.5. Problem of Determination of International Competitive Prices

### *1.5.1. Importance of a Correct Determination of Export Prices*

Sometimes, the company cannot develop attractive exportation prices in order to close international commercial agreements. It is a problem of costs; these are very high and leave the organization out of the competition world. The problem is that prices offered by the company to external markets, being so high, do not position it as competitive in comparison with the other offering international environment.

Prices may be very high due to two definite reasons:

**Internal company reasons** (susceptible of variation):

— Incorrect imputation of the components that make up the exporting product. The company wrongly includes some components within the international price. It may include items that do not correspond to the exported product price or, just the opposite, essential costs may be disregarded.

— Certain components carry a high cost or incidence upon the product final price (packing, containers, inputs, etc.).

**External company reasons,** that is, causes related to its environment and upon which the company has little control:

— Existence of strong taxation, social security and energy loads that negatively influence competitive price fixation. A country generally is asymmetric compared with others. An entrepreneur is going to be affected by his or her country's asymmetry compared with others at the international level. Asymmetries are competition differences among the different countries, due to existing legal differences among them. It is a relative concept, and competition difference among different countries may be based on specific legislations in force in them (exchange, taxation, energy, work, industry). Due to the fact that the production and enforcement of different legislations (laws, decrees, resolutions, etc.) is in each of the different national bodies power, (parliaments, ministries, etc.), the legal environment that differentiates a country from other may negatively affect entrepreneurs' costs. An example may be a country with a legal policy of workers' social security which is taxed to entrepreneurs with higher retirement and health insurance contributions as compared to other countries. Supposing that these high "taxes to work" existing in this first country were higher than the ones in force in a second country which possessed a more permissive legislation and lower labour cost; this situation might contribute the first country to be less competitive as regards prices as compared to the second, especially on exports that take intensive labour force. A more obvious aspect as regards asymmetries comes with exchange rate policies within an economic plan. Certain countries affect exchange rate through national currency devaluation (with the objective of empoverishing the neighbouring country) to make exports more competitive in price issues relative to the international market.

In some cases, a conjunction of several regulations issued by different national governmental environments is produced. These norms may affect a series of operations and steps that the exporter has to perform obligatorily. This intricate net of legal requisites and steps (authorizations, controls, presentation of papers) constitutes a highly bureaucratic national environment with an antiexporting bias.

— Inexistence of an adequate national infrastructure, that may have a positive effect on price calculation. International marketing infrastructure comprises every kind of systems that facilitate exports, directly or indirectly (as, for example, bridges, airports, ports, warehouses and warrants, free trade areas, waterways, bioceanic corridors, etc.). If the infrastructure existing in a country or region were efficient, it would allow cost and time savings in international operations development. The development of this infrastructure ought to be within the main functions of the State, as part of a national support policy and country's international marketing promotion. However, States usually go to the private sector in order to get contributions in the development of certain infrastructural systems.

### *1.5.2. Solutions to International Prices Concerns*

Several solutions are offered:

— **Associativity**: Through association with other companies, the small entrepreneur can share expenses necessary for international access. These costs, within the joint project, are paid among all the entrepreneurs (especially, fixed expenses). In this way, a lesser incidence of those amounts is accomplished upon the exported price at individual level, which allows the generation of competitive offers abroad.

— *Price revision:* The entrepreneur must carefully study everyone of the components that make up price, and only charge those items that really correspond to the exported product. This implies that the entrepreneur has to make a detailed analysis of internal as well as international market price fixation (cost audit). There will be expenditure in which the imputation will only correspond to the internal market price (example: advertising in the country of origin), and others that will belong only to the exported product price (example: international literature). Surely, there will be expenses whose assignation will correspond not only to internal market price but also to export prices. Besides, price assessment also has to consider how to account for more efficient costs of everyone of the items (inputs, raw material, package, etc.). In some cases, the possibility of importing product components that the company buys or manufactures, will have to be evaluated. In other, customs strategies like, for example, temporary admission of components to incorporate to a product that will be exported after manufacturing may be developed.

— *Outsourcing:* In some cases, the company may tertiarize part or, in others, the whole of the product that manufactures, by diverting activities to foreign companies with a more efficient manufacturing process. Thus, costs that make up exported products are diminished.

— *Reduction of state duties:* This solution is out of entrepreneurs' direct reach even though they may participate actively in the formation of lobbies. Through these pressure activity groups, States can be petitioned to implement the reduction of duties that affect exports directly and to generate entrepreneurial cost reduction economic policies, both in the internal as well as in the international market.

— *State and private investment in infrastructure:* State as well as private sector participation will be encouraged. This joint activity goal will be the development of channels and structures that speed times and allow the reduction of internationalization costs.

## 2. ADVANTAGES OF EXTERNAL MARKETS ACCESS

The starting up of international activities is not only problems for the small and medium-sized enterprise. World market penetration has a series of actual benefits of different kinds (related to tax burden, customs, credits, etc.), which, in some cases, local entrepreneurs ignore.

### 2.1. Customs Benefits

As regards customs advantages, most exports are benefited by a series of state stimula. The best known national incentives are tax refunds and drawbacks. They provide the reimbursement of internal taxes paid at each productive stage (in the case of tax refunds) and taxation corresponding to products imported by the company (in the case of drawbacks) that may affect exported product price. Besides, each country has customs regulations that benefit international operations like: import and export temporary system, delivery in consignment, export on behalf of third parties, and use of free trade areas, among others.

### 2.2. Credit Benefits

As regards the credit issue, there are special lines for exporters, granted by the main official and private banks. These credits are called prefinancing or financing export credits, and have more beneficial terms and rates than those assigned for domestic activity credits.

### 2.3. Tax Benefits

From the taxation point of view, unlike sales made in the internal market, exports do not have to pay most of the main taxes like: Value Added Tax (VAT), Stamp Taxes,

Internal taxation, etc. Besides, as regards VAT, generally, exporting companies may—as regards tax paid in purchases and expenses—credit it, compensate with sales in the internal market, ask for a refund or transference.

The purpose of most States is to exempt international operations from domestic market operations taxes. Thus, the producer may form more competitive exportation prices without "exporting taxes". There is a generally accepted principle in international marketing: "taxation in the country of destination". The aim is to exempt exports from most taxes in the country of origin, so that the countries of destination could be the ones to tax the goods, through import operations.

## 2.4. Image Benefits

The start up and consolidation of the small and medium enterprise international operations allow to generate a better company image. This affects the firm positioning in the external market. The internationalized enterprise assumes commitments in the different world markets and may supply the different requirements they make. This attitude gives the entrepreneur a higher status among the organizations in that sector and gives the company a position of prestige. Besides, continuous contact with international operators, improves company's image and symbol communication to the consumers, the competitors, and society in general. The internationalized company's activities are positively perceived, especially world markets obstacle overcoming and responsibility and reliability in its management to assume commitments of great international importance and comply with them.

## 2.5. Market Diversification Benefits

Another important incentive achieved by the exporting company comes from operation risk diversification between national and external markets. This issue may be more important when, due to national market crisis or economic recession, international scenarios are penetrated. A national market with recession or economic depression makes entrepreneurs who have not gained access to world markets constantly affected by a decrease in sales and generates a productive capacity surplus. A similar situation appears in those national markets in which there is a strong competitive environment which prevents the company from getting more participation in the domestic market. The same happens in saturated markets, in which the product is in its maturity or declination stage. Every aspect described reinforces the importance that exportation has for small and medium-sized enterprises. The entrepreneur will be able to evaluate the possibility of penetrating other markets more interesting from the purchasing power point of view, with a greater number of consumers, or less saturated. The organization will have to look for those environments with a lesser number of competitors than the domestic markets, or those country markets with different lifecycles for their product. When external operations are developed, all the efforts and resources are not concentrated on the national market, and, in this way, the effects of internal market instability that may affect the business are diminished.

## 2.6. Benefits of Increase in Commercialized Volumes

Certain price and quality competitiveness advantages can be obtained when products are internationally marketed. Besides, by getting an increase in earnings, exporting companies get other benefits. One of them is a better distribution of some fixed costs as a consequence of an increase in total sales that generates a greater production volume. In this way more reduced fixed unitary costs and more competitive prices are accomplished (through economies of scale, economies of marketing and economies of R + D).

Besides, internationalization may solve problems of company idle capacity. The implementation of an international strategy allows to reach a greater production quality, because of the constant contact with other stricter cultures and with world environment competitors. Processes and product design are improved as international exposure is increased.

## 2.7. Benefits of Differentiation

It is possible to discover that a particular product, in certain external markets, appears as a totally differentiated product from the rest. This situation may turn it into "unique", be it for its technological advantages, design or provisions included. It may happen that a product is not very well-known in some markets or little used and consumed, as a result of being in the first stages of its lifecycle (for example, product introduction stage). This issue may incentive penetration in that country-market with the company products. It should be verified that differential issues perceived upon certain attributes (quality, design, technology, costs, etc.) of a particular market product are about real differences and not erroneous perceptions.

## 2.8. Benefits of Exclusive Information

An important factor that boosts exportation is the access to exclusive information about business opportunities in the world markets. These data may come from trade shows attendance, market informal studies, business trips or other means. They may be about specific orders from a particular country, about a specific product, or data concerning potential buyers. These elements represent an important advantage for the entrepreneur who possesses them, until they reach competitors' hands.

## 2.9. Benefits of Associativity

When an export company strategy is used through different joint structures (like consortia, cooperatives, etc.), the enterprise may hire technical personnel specially qualified in different international activities (market studies, international quality certifications, trade shows attendance, etc.). Without taking part in those associations it would be very difficult to pay for those expenses individually. Besides, synergy (consistent union of forces) among the different exporting partners of the project is produced, which allows to get better negotiating conditions with the international marketing different operators and auxiliaries (clients, suppliers, carriers, customs agents, etc.). Each member is contained by a company structure of cooperation in the international access stages.

In some cases, some enterprises opt to export by imitating their competitors' attitude because they have already internationalized. Thus, they try not to be left aside from the relative advantages of the international marketing enjoyed by the competition. However, in some countries, especially in the developing countries, the presence of small-sized companies in the international environment continues being absolutely limited.

It is important to reflect on the relevance of international markets and the advantages of positioning, in order to adopt a positive attitude to internationalization. The assumption of external commitment has to be gradual and decisions must be adopted beyond the present state of affairs that may affect companies. Entrepreneurial attitude must not be based on the marketing of balances not sold in the internal market (exportable balance). There has to be a strategy to allow the exportation of stable and continuous volumes (exportable offer), to generate lasting commercial relationships with customers abroad.

## 3. STATE FUNCTION IN EXPORT PROMOTION

### 3.1. Importance of Government Planning in International Marketing

It is important for the central government as well as the governmental institutions at the different state levels to fix an exporting integrated policy. Is it the state function to help in the design of a country exporting profile? The State ought to be one of the main promoters for big companies to have an additional support in their international marketing. Governmental bodies must become supportive of small and medium-sized enterprises that do not have the capacity to design international marketing policies, establishing contacts or detecting business opportunities. Small organizations should be assisted to relieve their vast shortages: administrative, financial, economic, and productive, and the lack of exporting attitude.

External sector is an important variable for any country, so, an adequate, coordinated and balanced plan to enhance international markets has to be provided. It is necessary to design and implement a national master plan of exports promotion, which will allow the effective insertion of companies in the external markets. The setting of this plan constitutes an important official measure, which is a frame for an adequate decision taking process in the private sector.

This plan must comprise the following features:

— **Articulation:** Interconnection and coincidence with other plans of vital importance that should be simultaneously developed, such as:
  - Productive, quality and technological innovation national plan.
  - Internationalization adequate infrastructure development plan.
  - Other plans (those that contribute to the efficient use of the public budget, pursue an adequate exchange rate policy, that try to redesign the national taxation system so as to reduce tax burden for enterprises, etc.).

— **Complementation:** These government activities must accomplish a complementation with those developed by international marketing institutions. Among the main agents there are the international marketing and entrepreneurial chambers, banks that manage international payment instruments, carriage and insurance agents, international marketing consultants, different non-governmental organizations, etc. This joint activity allows to assist companies that do not have exporting tradition to beat apathy towards world markets.

— **Gradualism:** Its application has to be coordinated and in stages. There has to be an efficient implementation of the different basic policies, as well as the performance of the different operative programmes. Asynchronies that may appear during the operative start up have to be anticipated. There must not exist superimposition of functions in the different bodies involved.

— **Integration and coherence with economic policy main objectives:** The plan will be supposed to serve a specific and vast contribution to the different economic objectives of a country (efficient resource allocation, price stability, balanced balance of payment, full employment, sustainable growth and development).

These goals will be approached from different angles: economic, commercial, social, etc. Its design and implementation must have a long term strategy, beyond the national juncture. It has to be projected not only for the present society, but also for the development of the future society.

## 3.2. Main State Aspects of Internationalization Promotion

State activity ought to be oriented towards local producers with production and productivity, regionalism, infrastructure and logistics, financing, international marketing promotion policies, information about industrial process improvement, paratariff barriers and subsidies, exportation normative and operative aspects, country-image and other policies in mind.

### *3.2.1. Production and Productivity*

The government will have to guide companies as regards productivity goals to achieve economic prosperity. Authentic regimes of production and exportation promotion based on incentives to companies efforts and competition will have to be established.

Counterproductive governmental policies like protectionism and subventions which may affect internal production should have to be avoided. It is the state duty to support companies in their production, not only of final products, but also of parts or pieces. The government has to promote the complementation of the different productive structures of the companies and the creation of industrial strategic alliances. With these integrations income yield capacity is expected to improve in each of the companies involved. These strategies permit to obtain higher volumes of exportable supply and more competitive prices to supply the most attractive and rentable external markets.

A diagnosis of the present productive structure has to be made previously to objective design and policies implementation. The State can fix differentiated and sectorial state policies to promote product international marketing of certain subsectors that may have a greater multiplier effect on the national economy, to support the growth of those productive systems that have a greater level of externalities. These are connections between a main productive sector or subsector, and different secondary areas that take advantage of the benefits "granted" by the main area.

The existence of policies to promote one or a few competitive products specialization and to promote local producers association (horizontally or vertically) is important. Complementation actions that favour industrial and commercial efficacy will be given priority. They will also support those between local and foreign producers. Apart from this, productive reconversion policies for sectors affected by foreign competition will be implemented.

Foreign investment promotion, in its pure form or through the constitution of mixed investment of national and foreign capitals (coinvestment) will also have to be considered in this plan. These undertakings will have to be promoted in the main sectors of the national productive system. Thus, the local industrial structure may feed from technological development and know-how, from quality systems developed by the foreign companies.

### *3.2.2. Regionalism*

It is fundamental to consider the benefits relative to regional integration experiences. These commercial blocks create greater flows of commerce among the members, attract more external investment and improve competition environments and internal consumption.

The State, at every level, has to support those integration systems of which it forms part, to increase the volume of the commercialized products and the welfare of every country member of the integration. Sustained elimination of any intrazone marketing barrier that may exist inside the blocks has to be a firm objective.

Another primary goal will be to establish policies shared with the other member States of the block, so as to reach a progressive liberalization of production and service factors among the member countries. Besides, progressive correction of asymmetries, among them, in fiscal, laboral, and tax-related aspects will have to be coordinated. In some lesser ways of integration like free trade areas, the only objective will be the liberation of intrazone trade.

Every commercial effect which results from integration will have to be taken advantage of. New regional and multiregional agreements will have to be signed to use their advantages. Some key points to observe in the constitution of new regional blocks are: total compatibility with the World Trade Organization agreements, provision of adherence and origin regime clauses, establishing of ambitious integration objectives and limitation to antidumping actions, among others.

Non-economic benefits derived from integration systems must also be taken into account. For example: strengthening of bonds, control of migratory currents, increase in block negotiating capacity, or protection of incipient regional industries.

### *3.2.3. Infrastructure and Logistics*

National infrastructure deficiencies must be reduced in order to get better costs in carriage, communication, ports, airports and energy, among other areas. An inadequate infrastructural system limits the range of economies of scale and competitiveness achievements in cost and time issues. The implementation of governmental policies that promote storage structure increase (fiscal deposits, silos, warehouses, etc.) results in higher logistic efficiency. The development of storage platforms allows to perform the strategic storage of certain products for export (as, for example, agricultural products), and to market them in periods different from the production period. With the use of these strategies, the producer may obtain higher international prices. The development of specialized logistic systems and structures (terminals, ports, etc.) to facilitate export containerized load and the use of multimodal transportation are also necessary.

The State has to continue with this process of privatization and deregulation. Improvement in policies of physical integration like roads, highways and bioceanic corridors in order to penetrate other world markets has to be agreed upon. A total legislative consensus on carriage in the regional environment as regards frontiers crossing among the countries is very relevant. The creation of physical integration agreements and protocols among different countries is a subject that has to be insisted upon.

It is important to support waterways works to improve navigability considering dredging and buoying of international rivers. New systems of railways and roads have to be built and border crossings and third generation ports increased (with facilities for container traffic and greater capacity of TEUs—for twenty-foot equivalents—movement).

### 3.2.4. Financing

State support is very important to carry out an international marketing policy, due to the lack of sufficient financial resources that most small and medium-sized enterprises suffer. So, it is going to be vitally important to establish credit lines and special financing plans to exporting productive activity. Besides, the State will have to configure an adequate and solid national financing system, with clear rules for national and international operators.

Financial help to exporting companies must be a part of the main objectives of state banks to improve the weak financial reliability that affects most small-sized companies, which, in certain cases, results in a barrier to penetrate international markets. To do this, reduction of financial costs through a reduction in the interest rate will have to be considered. A crucial factor is to achieve a continuous development and modernization of national stock exchange.

The government has to promote other non-traditional or scarcely spread financiation sources among entrepreneurs. Among them, there are issuance of negotiable debentures, leasing (renting of a property with an option of purchasing) and factoring (bank discount of exports invoices).

### 3.2.5. Policies of International Marketing Promotion

Governmental initiatives have to give priority to external market promotion and provision of market studies of products manufactured by state agencies in the different levels. Assistance to the exporter has to be configured within a decentralized advisory policy relative to international marketing. This support policy is immersed in a national development policy, but it has to have operative structures of advising and answering questions on internationalization aspects with a local basis (that is, located in small cities or regions).

The objective of this decentralized system is that state support may help the entrepreneur who is not based in the main cities of the country. A greater connection between the official advisor and the entrepreneur that ignores international marketing aspects is a priority. Besides, this allows government agents to have more knowledge of productive sectors and of the economic local reality.

This locally based government help to the entrepreneur in international activities preludes a more precise and specialized advisory help. This decentralized help adequately estimates the different peculiarities relative to existing productions in each regional economy.

Other of the state activities consists in stimulating producers to participate in international exhibitions and trade shows, commercial missions, and business rounds. Some events may provide for entrepreneurs' training through courses, seminars, talks, and publications on international marketing. This type of meetings promotes favourable expectations among entrepreneurs as regards export operations.

Commercial attachès—who are representatives of a country's embassies and consulates abroad—must carry on a double flow of information with the state government. These officials have to provide the different governmental agencies with updated information about the external market (opportunities of business detected, lists of importers and international events), so that it can be sent to the interested companies. On the other hand, the government, at every level, has to provide certain information to the different commercial sections abroad. Data provided will consist of a list of national producers with interest in exporting to those markets. That information will have to be permanently updated. In this way, integration, perfectioning and interconnection of state informative systems and attachès at international level is obtained. This benefits the entrepreneur who requires information about world markets.

The objective is that government agencies, attachès and other brokers integrate and complement their databases. As a consequence of this, a national information system about the external markets will be able to be gradually built. These goals could be more efficiently reached by establishing **a greater number of commercial** regional offices or official points of contact in the main countries of the global market.

Most small and medium-sized organizations need some institutional support in external activities. The State may help by providing useful information about international environments. Agencies and government attachès may provide valuable product market studies. Collaboration and assistance could consist in a joint participation, between private and state sectors, in international events and salons. In some cases, it is important that information on internationalization be published in manuals, leaflets or instructive sheets, to allow the entrepreneur to train in the most relevant aspects.

### *3.2.6. Information about Industrial Process Improvement*

Information about the improvement of industrial processes, as well as about other aspects, has to be publicized through different bodies:

— ***Controls:*** through different certifications, of industrial process efficiency and safety aspects different stages of a product for export. The objective is to advise the entrepreneur about the different aspects of product adequation to the regulations of the countries of destination and the requirements of foreign buyers.

— ***Quality:*** information about international quality standards requisites (ISO 9000 and 14000). Data on national or regional regulations. Advising about costs and benefits of a quality certification. Lists of the main specialized national consultors in this subject.

— ***Tests:*** making of tests as regards different aspects of the product for export (physic-chemical features, resistance, etc.).

— ***Training:*** programmes of practical training and entrepreneurial awareness of the importance of quality control and new technologies for external markets.

— ***Package and packaging:*** aspects related to export package and packaging (design, materials used for their production, adequation to the means of transport and to the geographic distance, etc.).

A communication of this knowledge among the companies through publications, training programmes and a technical support system available to organizations with technological problems or obsolescence of productive processes, which may be a barrier for export, is an objective. Advice will also have to integrate the different private and state universities with different specialists in the area. To do this, universities and state bodies will make agreements, to perform interdisciplinary activities.

The State has to provide support and help in an integrated way together with the other international marketing institutions. To do this, the government has to perform a vast communication upon the various aspects of international marketing. The State must comply with the function of giving information about commercial opportunities on documentary, financial and operative external issues. Besides, technical innovations that directly affect exporting industrial activity, especially those facts that improve company competitiveness, will have to be communicated.

### *3.2.7. Paratariff Barriers and Subsidies*

As for imports made by local entrepreneurs, the central government has to abandon the creation of, with protectionist character, paratariff barriers that hinder the normal and habitual flow with a foreign country (like, for example, excessive regulations and bureaucratic customs steps, standards on technical or sanitary requirements that make the penetration of products difficult, demands for quality warranties, among others). Importation of those products that constitute critical inputs, as well as that of those that allow the reconversion of the national productive system (machinery, capital goods, turn-key plants, etc.) will have to be promoted.

As regards subsidies, the local government must avoid to grant those which are specifically forbidden by the World Trade Organization. Subventions not allowed by the WTO are those direct or indirect helps granted by the State to producers that affect the result of exports. This has to be considered to prevent exported products from being taxed by compensatory rights in the destination countries affected by those subsidies.

### *3.2.8. Legal and Operative Export Aspects*

Integration and simplification in normative relative to international marketing customs, operative, and financial aspects is yet something that has to be analyzed. Generally, there exists an important group of regulations that affect exports and which are issued by different governmental bodies. In certain cases, the different bodies involved may issue contradictory normative.

This normative inconsistency carries a great complexity for the company to interpret and analyze legislatively, which seriously affects the performance of international commercial activity. These legal dispositions are quite complicated, even for specialized advisors in the topic.

It is relevant for the norm to have stability and continuity all through time, regardless of governmental policies. The entrepreneur will produce a horizon of world market medium and long term operative planning, if there are clear and stable national game rules that regulate exports.

From the regulative point of view, the State ought to strengthen the implementation of the various legal scenarios that promote the performance of international operations such as: tax refunds collection, reimbursements and drawbacks, regimes of temporary admission, delivery on consignment, export in charge of third parties, free trade areas, among others.

### *3.2.9. Country Image*

The State ought to campaign through a specific body in order to position the image of the country well in the different world markets. This body will highlight particular attributes of some local or regional products (for example, natural, without preservatives, etc.), so as to contribute to the creation of an adequate country-brand abroad.

It is possible to promote the country by homogeneous regions nationally relevant and with distinctive features. These actions allow the development of company strategies for the marketing of products closely linked to the local environments of the promoted country.

### *3.2.10. Other Policies*

Finally, a progressive lowering in the cost energy inputs, labour costs, social security, and taxation, among others, must be achieved. These components may influence negatively the determination of international prices. All these activities will have to be framed within an economic policy of efficient use of the public budget in its different levels. Another transformimg aspect comprises a foreign exchange policy with an adequate exchange rate balance that could allow balance between a country imported and exported volumes.

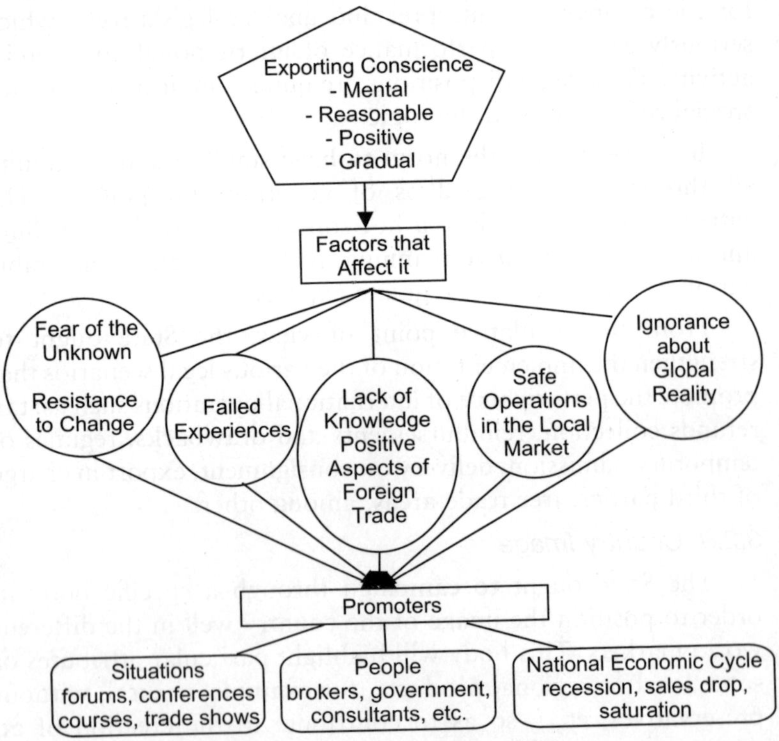


**Figure 2.1.** The Exporting Conscience

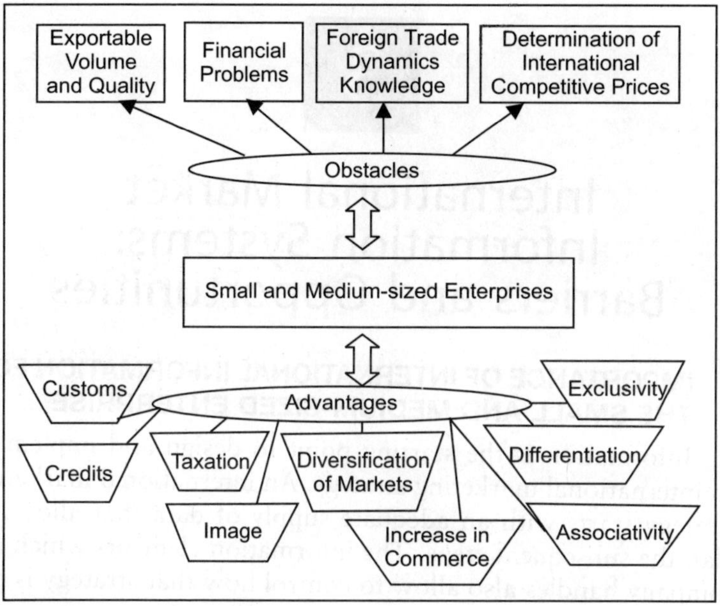


**Figure 2.2.** Problems and Advantages of Internationalization

# 3

# International Market Information Systems: Barriers and Opportunities

## 1. IMPORTANCE OF INTERNATIONAL INFORMATION FOR THE SMALL AND MEDIUM-SIZED ENTERPRISE

Information is the starting point to design and implement an international marketing strategy. An international marketing strategy starts with an adequate supply of data that allows to plan the subsequent steps. The information elements which the company handles also allow to control how that strategy is put into practice.

Even though information is vital to design an international business plan, data flow must feed the development at every single stage, and help in the execution of the necessary adjustments upon the results (which are also informative elements).

A fundamental concern for the small and medium-sized enterprise is the lack of knowledge about what information is useful to introduce its product in the international markets. Besides, there is also lack of knowledge about where to get external market data (the company does not know which are the most appropriate data sources).

Creating, in quite a structured fashion, an information system about the international market should be an entrepreneurial duty. This system would be of great importance in activities such as: collection, updating, analysis, refinement, registration and consultation upon the various legal, economic, cultural, commercial, technological and consumer aspects in the international environment. Information will be, in some cases, general and, in other, more specific. For this reason, complementary sources of multiple access are needed.

## 2. INFORMATION SYSTEMS ABOUT EXTERNAL MARKETS: FEATURES

Information systems have to meet the following requirements, both for a big as well as for a small-sized enterprise:

— **Multiple sources:** A valuable piece of information does not necessarily come from one source, it isn't corroborated by a unique source either. Information is obtained through a large number of sources. Thus, the searching and compilation information process does not exhaust after the first providing source.

— **Complementarity:** Some information may be completed, extended or restricted as a result of the use of that diversity of means for information access.

— **Provisional character:** This provisional character shows two features:

- Specific information (for example, a country's statistics on imports, numerical information about a specific market consumption, etc.) has to be periodically updated in order to remain valid for use in international entrepreneurial policies.
- Every piece of information collected has to be stored, though apparently some of it appears to be irrelevant for the aims pursued. The elimination and discarding of data that appears to be irrelevant to the objectives in a first analysis should be avoided, even though there might not exist direct connection with the market or product investigated. Collected information can be multifunctional; that is, it can have more than one specific use. It can be useful in a subsequent stage, as complementary or extended strategic information. Unintentionally obtained information can contribute to market development or to the marketing of goods not included in the original plan of the company. It is also possible to discover worthwhile market opportunities for the company. Thus, the information filtering and

discarding process will only be part of a subsequent period of evaluation.

— **Easy systematization for filing and consulting:** Collected data has to be filed in an accumulative database system defined as informative classification by sources (direct, indirect, etc.), product, market, company and date. This organization allows the enterprise to enjoy database information availability to implement specific decisions and policies.

Some other features of information systems are:

— **Complexity:** Sometimes, a great volume of information can be accessed. This amount of information needs to go through a permanent administrative system organizing process of processing and filing in order to keep it available.

— **Partiality**: Information in general, particularly that referred to specific external markets, is not complete. It does not provide every perspective of a market or a product. This information is perfectible, because some data on the variables will always be incomplete and so, it will not be completely true to all the changes in an external environment. The company gets partial information on the behaviour of some variables, which can only be true at the time of the investigation and a possible future behaviour. This feature shows a certain degree of uncertainty about some aspects of the information in a specific system.

## 3. TYPES OF INFORMATION: PRIMARY AND SECONDARY; FORMAL AND INFORMAL RESEARCH

### 3.1. Basic Classification of International Information

Information can be of different types. General information, known as secondary information, is the information obtained by the entrepreneur which uses sources which have compiled the data in different times and with different aims (as compared with the time and goals of the research carried out by the company). Examples of secondary information are:

macro-economic data of the destination country imports, population, per capita consumption, etc. (this information may have been surveyed by governmental organizations, before the time of the investigation).

Information "built" by the surveying company is known as primary. It is much more detailed and specific, and can make use of direct sources (that is, investigating in the destination market). Examples of primary information are: discount policies of competition markets in destination, packaging used by companies in a particular country, consumer's purchasing attitude and behaviour towards a particular brand, etc.

As regards secondary information, this gives us important introductory notions about a specific international environment. Sometimes, the reports are so complete (particularly those coming from formal investigations or market profiles) that it is not necessary to resort to complementary information (for example, primary information).

Secondary information is basic for the small-sized company. It can be applied as a starting point to identify and select specific markets. Its procurement implies a small effort (sometimes, almost null) for small and medium-sized enterprises. Some sources are provided for free (commercial attachés, governmental organizations related to international trade) and in some other cases at a low cost (chambers of commerce and entrepreneurial chambers).

In general, more resources (financial, human, etc.) are required by the company to get access to primary information. This has a higher level of precision than secondary data and a complementary character to secondary information, and completes aspects that cannot be obtained by other means.

In order to comply with the objectives proposed, it is possible that data searching should have to be formalized in a structured plan of international market investigation.

## 3.2. Other Ways to Classify External Market Information

Information can be classified in personal and direct. Personal information requires contact through different channels (personal interviews, business trips, telephone communications, etc.), which establish communication links with various foreign trade auxiliaries (agents, representatives, government officials, importers, destination country residents). On the other hand, direct information always implies the company's personnel or executives physical visit to the destination market with the aim of getting first-hand knowledge (with a wider perception) of external market specific conditions.

Besides, information can be accessed through a market formal study. This consists of a series of stages: data collection is structured and it usually resorts to primary information sources (surveys, interviews, etc.). This study is costly, which makes it, in most cases, inaccessible from the economical point of view for the small and medium-sized enterprise that is starting to internationalize. The first aspect in a formal investigation stage is the design of investigation objectives (to make it clear which are the aims of market prospection and what kind of information is required, as a result). Secondly, the design of the data collecting instruments and sample size are made (topics like the use of questionnaires, qualitative and quantitative surveys, and upon which representative part of the population those instruments will be applied, are defined). The next stage consists in putting into practice the investigation in itself (i.e. conduction of surveys, questionnaires), in the selected country market. As last but one stage, data interpretation, which implies interrelating and evaluating the variables subject to investigation. The final stage consists in getting results and incorporating them in the company international marketing information system. Here, a redesign or readjustment of some stages in the international marketing global strategy of the company such as, for example, a review of the internalization objectives, a redefinition of the introduction channels in the world markets and the modification of the commercial mix variables, is carried out. A small organization can get access to this kind of investigation when, as part of an associative project (consortium, exports cooperative, etc.) a consultant who performs the pertinent studies is hired jointly.

Informal investigation is the most widely type used in small and medium-sized enterprises. It has a low cost; it gets its material mainly from secondary information sources (reports, markets profiles, lists of importers, public listings of commercial opportunities published by official entities, among others). Generally, there is not a series of set stages, but it is always guided by some "intuitive" plan from the entrepreneur's point of view. It can be sufficient to reach certain markets, especially in the first internationalization stages.

## 3.3. Sources of Information

Every source is equally important, since in some cases they complement one another. It is possible that data provided by a source could not be accessed through another. When a company makes use of a larger number of sources, it can complete the different pieces that make up the international scenario. Among the main sources we can mention:

### *3.3.1. Commercial Expositions and Trade Shows*

These events can be accessed as an attendee or an exhibitor. In either of the mentioned roles information about product competition at a comparative international level may be obtained. Besides, it is possible to collect data about particular channels that operate internationally (agents, distributors, brokers, etc.). It is feasible to generate potential contacts with suppliers or international clients and, when a company exhibits in a trade show, it can become aware of issues related to the interests and motivations of potential product consumers, through questionnaires, surveys, etc.

### *3.3.2. Other Events*

Foreign trade training courses, entrepreneurial conferences and regional or international economic forums are other instances where the organization can get world market specific information.

### *3.3.3. Technical Reports and Specialized Literature*

There is local, regional, national and international literature that can give the entrepreneur precise information about the global market.

### *3.3.4. Formal Market Research made by the Company*

As it has already been mentioned, this way is too burdensome for the small and medium-sized enterprise.

### *3.3.5. Business Roundtable*

This foreign trade way of indirect contact demands the intervention of an event organizer. The company or governmental body that organizes this event previously enrolls the interested parties that will be part of the database, so as to make them take contact with one another. Afterwards, interviews among the potential buyers and sellers of the product are arranged, so that mutual proposals can be made.

### *3.3.6. Business Trips or Missions*

Organized by governmental agencies, chambers, or private institutions, they consist in producers' visits to their product potential buyers in a particular destination country. These trips are made in the time period set by the organizers and destination companies. The itinerary is short but the rhythm, intense. Every detail is coordinated by the organizer, and interviews with government officials of the destination country can be included. These events allows for entrepreneurs' more personal contact with the foreign market and a more direct relationship with their product potential importers.

### *3.3.7. Commercial Attachés in Consulates or Embassies of the Country of Origin Abroad*

This subject is going to be developed in full in 3.4.

### *3.3.8. Commercial Sectors of Foreign Countries Diplomatic Representatives in the Country of Origin*

Consulates and embassies are linked with the country they represent by big flows of information. It is possible to access very valuable data both to export to that country-market and import from it.

### *3.3.9. Government Agencies, Foundations and Associations Related to the Exporting Activity*

Every State has one or more bodies or specific sectors that stimulate entrepreneurial management of international businesses. The State, at every level, has a ministry, body, secretariat, subsecretariat, sector or department devoted to the promotion of foreign trade. These organizations give free advice on various international topics: requisites to reach a particular market, importers and commercial attachés' listings, studies and research on specific markets and particulars on merchandise classification, among other data. Those bodies constantly receive updated information about product orders that come from external markets (called "commercial business opportunities") by commercial attachés. Other sources of consultation could be: private, mixed and intermediate sectors. These usually organize training courses on the topic of foreign trade, forums or meetings on the topic of world operations.

### *3.3.10. National Statistics and Official Reports*

Every country has its statistical system centralized in a ruling body in charge of making compilations, analyses and official reports on import and export activities. These are macro-economic data, but also constitute important secondary information that describes, introductorily and generally, aspects of export markets (volume of operations, historical trends, relative percentage over total of exports). Apart from this, there is relevant information compiled in foundations reports, international advisors, and other private agents. Further, there are international statistics carried out by bodies like the World Bank or the UN, which can be very useful as complementary information on certain markets.

### *3.3.11. Meetings or Personal Interviews with Foreign Trade Operators in the Destination Market*

They allow a direct contact with importers, trading companies, distributors and other foreign brokers, thus facilitating the access to a particular type of information that, due to its extreme sensitivity, demands for a personal encounter. It is difficult to obtain the information by other ways, and it is almost always primary information. These interviews make up the itinerary of a business trip. Similarly, valuable information can be gathered through personal and sensory observation in the destination market. An example of this is the trip made by the entrepreneur in the different destination points of sale, to see how the competition product is presented and positioned in comparison with his or her own products. This personal observation can be part of a trip without marketing objectives, such as a trip abroad for pleasure.

### *3.3.12. Binational Chambers*

They are highly qualified and specific sources of information. Those that link the country of origin with the country-market selected are relevant. These chambers can be situated both in the market of origin as well as in the destination market. They have listings of both countries main importers and exporters and of the products marketed at a binational scale. They know in detail about the specific requisites to import and export the different products between those markets. This information can be provided for free or accessed at a very low cost.

### *3.3.13. Foreign Trade Advisors*

They generally offer wide advise from marketing research to business opportunities localization. They detect existing destination trade barriers for a certain product access and advise on obligatory governmental interventions for exportation. Besides they can negotiate freight and hire insurance; and help in the issuance of commercial and financial papers, among other functions.

### *3.3.14. Financial Institutions*

Most banks have a foreign trade sector which provides support in areas like: most popular forms of payment in certain markets, operative and legal requirements for the management of financial instruments, collection due dates, foreign currency trading among others.

### *3.3.15. International Carriers*

They give information about itineraries to get access to particular markets. They quote the different freight options (and other related services, such as commodity consolidation), offer help on packaging requirements and adequation to the means of transport, and give information about loading capacity and usage of unitary loads (pallets) and containerization systems (containers).

### *3.3.16. Insurance Companies*

They help about the most common risk coverage for a particular product, market and means of transport. They give advice on the different types of policies (floating, individual) used in the international market and about more specific forms of insurance (like surety insurance).

### *3.3.17. Customs Agents*

Their main activity is centred in document presentation and operative procedures required by customs control. They also estimate and settle taxes favourable to customs service due to external operations, and handle the collection of foreign trade promotional benefits (repayments, drawbacks). They are highly qualified in the valuation and classification of goods, sampling and management of temporary import and export operations.

### *3.3.18. Internet*

This topic is going to be specifically developed in the E-commerce Chapter. Search engines allow for the detection of potential importers and distributors for the exporting company.

### *3.3.19. Other Entrepreneurial Structures Associated to Foreign Trade*

Agents, distributors, brokers, general entrepreneurial chambers, sectorial entrepreneurial chambers and foreign trade chambers are some of the structures that make up foreign trade functioning mechanisms.

## 3.4. Commercial Attachés of the Country of Origin Located in Embassies and Consulates in the Selected External Markets

### *3.4.1. Their Importance as a Source of Information for Small and Medium-sized Enterprises*

Attachés or commercial advisors are specialized representatives that work in the embassies or consulates that a nation has in different country-markets.

They present the following features:

— They are located in a particular external market, so they are in permanent contact with it.

— They have knowledge about commercial practice, legal and cultural features, and destination market competitive aspects.

— They have an important database about the country-market where they are placed.

— They have updated information about those markets.

— They provide free information about the different features of the destination country.

Generally, commercial attachés' listings can be accessed through, for example:

— Foreign trade governmental bodies.

— Entrepreneurial, binational and foreign trade chambers.

— Foreign trade foundations, bodies and private associations.

— Via Internet, through search engines, using key words such as: "attachés", "advisors", "consulates" or "embassies".

In some commercially relevant and geographically large markets, there can be more than one commercial representative, and each commercial attaché in this market can have a different piece of information. In some small markets, commercial sections are divided in regions or areas of influence that extend over more than one country. In this case, there is only one attaché that compiles the information of the different neighbouring countries. This information varies, depending on the attaché and the country. Most attachés have an e-mail address, suitable, economical and practical tool to ask for information and get it.

*3.4.2. Data that Commercial Attachés can Provide*

The vast information that these foreign trade agents can provide to the company includes:

- — Listings of importers, distributors, brokers, supermarket chains (name, corporate name, domicile, telefax, e-mail address, commercialized products, imports—if there are—from country of origin, etc.).
- — Listings of entrepreneurial chambers, governmental bodies, foreign trade associations located in that country.
- — Schedule of the most important events in that country (trade shows, expositions, congresses, business roundtables, commercial and entrepreneurial meetings, among others).
- — Precise updated listing of that market business opportunities.
- — Macro-economic data relative to the destination country (imports volume, most required products, etc.).
- — Main tariff and paratariff barriers in the market.
- — Existing market studies and profiles about a particular product, and official reports on definite sectors of the country-market in destination.
- — Potential partners for joint projects at a binational level (coinvestment, strategic alliances), legislation for marketing and/or production branches in destination markets.
- — Main web pages with some of the information already mentioned.

Attachés can, in some cases, arrange entrepreneurial interviews with private and public organizations located abroad. This service is useful for the company that decides to make a trip, to arrange personal meetings with potentially interested parties.

Much of the aforementioned data can also be granted by most of the other sources cited in 3.3 (governmental bodies, associations, chambers). The comparative advantage that commercial attachés have upon these is that they possess an *in situ* connection with the market to be penetrated. This feature places them in a comparatively privileged situation, because they have wider and more updated information and, in some cases, become information sources to other sources.

### 3.4.3. Market Profile

Other necessary reports are market profiles, which comprise a great amount of information, such as:

— Product features and duty classification.

— General tariff regime of the product in the destination market: import duties and taxes.

— Existence of paratariff barriers which affect the company welfare (exemptions, licences, sanitary certificates, production standards, quality controls; all of them obligatory).

— Ranking of main countries which supply the product to that market.

— Importation values and volumes. This statistical information presents total and unitary quantities and prices, differentiated by origin, that is, by country, as well as the evolution and trend of that numerical information.

— Data about the product national manufacturing in the destination market.

— Validity of agreements signed with the country of origin and preferential tariffs granted through them. Requirement of certificates of origin.

— Main buyers (distributors, retailers, etc.) in the destination market and their requirements. Most usual distribution structure. Well-known consumer centres in this market and most convenient access to them.

— Existence of chambers, entrepreneurial associations and other institutions related to the product. Events in the destination market (trade shows and expositions), related to the product.

— Aspects concerned with the presentation and packing of the product. Labelling requirements. Packaging concerns (use of boxes, palletization, containers, or in bulk).

— Whether operations with the market of origin have already been performed.

### 3.4.4. *Model of Information Request to the Commercial Attaché*

The electronic letter (or fax) addressed to the commercial attaché must include at least:

— Commercial attaché name to which the consultation is made.

— Name of the company that requests the information.

— Name of the product, detailed commercial and technical description. The product tariff item has to be mentioned according to the Tariff Nomenclature (based on the Harmonized Commodity Description and Coding System), in order to facilitate the search task of the requested information.

— A clear identification of the specific and precise information requested. An example would be: "listing of the main distributors with indication of name, telefax, e-mail and address, based in city A that import product Y".

# 4. RELEVANT INFORMATION FOR THE SELECTION AND PENETRATION OF A PARTICULAR EXTERNAL MARKET

## 4.1. External Market Information: Different Aspects

Highly relevant information may consist of *current data* (for example, per capita GDP corresponding to the year previous to the investigation), or trend data (i.e. GDP variable per capita of the last five years). In this last case, the analysis of this series can determine an increase or a decrease of the variable for a particular period.

The data can be quantitative—susceptible of being expressed in numbers (statistical figures)—or qualitative—not able to be expressed in numbers or percentages (for example, particular purchasing behaviour and brand loyalty). There could also be quali-quantitative information (for example, the report on a survey that shows that a particular percentage of a market has a specific lifestyle or preference).

Data about the foreign market under consideration can cover the following items:

— general features;

— paratariff and tariff barriers;

— consumer market;

— competition and/or sector and commercialized product;

— market existing infrastructure.

### 4.1.1. Information about General Characteristics

This information shows, in a broad sense, macro aspects of the country upon which the country of origin company can be interested in developing business:

— Information about the principal economic and demographic variables (population, demographic growth rate, birth rate, GDP, GNP, import-export volume, level of indebtedness, country risk, unemployment, balance of trade and payments, etc.).

— General information about the country (religion, language, education, prevailing political system, etc.).

— Industrial, fiscal, monetary, exchange rate, labour policies.

— General economic policy of the destination country. Information about policies in force that could have an indirect or direct effect upon international trade and investment (economy liberalization coefficient, existence of foreign companies location laws, defense of competition and consumer laws, antimonopoly laws, etc.).

— Existence of regional agreements (free trade area, customs unions) or special cooperation and development treaties between the country of origin and that of destination that create trade preferential operations.

### 4.1.2. Information about Tariff and Paratariff Barriers

These are barriers established by most States with the objective of:

- — Protecting the national economy of the destination market.
- — Obstructing the access of foreign company products to a particular market. Generally, most of these companies make the natural dynamics of the imports flows in the destination market difficult.
- — In some cases, they generate fiscal revenue for the State of destination, as a very important source of collection.

#### 4.1.2.1. Tariff Barriers

Commercial barriers are divided into two groups: tariff and paratariff barriers. Tariff barriers consist in the imposition of tariffs or taxes to international marketing flow (in general, they affect most of the imports made by the destination country). They are transparent, which makes it easy to get information about them. They are monetary because their effect on imports can easily be quantified. In general, these barriers increase the imported product price and have a protective effect for the destination country producer. Besides, they rise the imported product price for the external market consumer. Apart from this, these barriers are the only ones that generate revenue for the importer country-market national treasury.

It is advisable to have a correct technical and commercial description and an adequate tariff classification (see supplement V) so as to obtain information about the barriers that could specifically affect a particular company product. Barrier application changes from product to product. Some goods can be subject to the imposition of greater commercial barriers than others, depending on the destination country commercial policy approach.

Among the great diversity of tariff barriers there have to be mentioned:

- — ***Import rights:*** These are duties that tax imports made by buyers abroad. It can be a percentage, called "*ad* *valorem* rights", or a fixed amount per unity imported (or specific tariff). Besides, there are compound taxes, which are a combinatory of *ad valorem* and specific tariffs, continuous tariffs, with an application all through the year and seasonal, when they are applied during particular periods of the year. Other classifications are: antidumping rights, that affect products that come from origin in dumping conditions, and compensatory rights which are taxed on products that come from origin with an incidence of subsidies.

— ***Official Values:*** They are prices that act as a legal basis for the application of taxes to the *ad valorem* import. Either official price or real value, the one that is higher, is taken as a base to estimate the tax. In this way, the State that puts them into force tries to determine a tax collection system ground and discourage under value invoicing illegal business (which is the declaration of product value inferior to real).

— ***Less taxation burden for more local added value:*** More than a tariff barrier it is a tariff trade system. The products with higher level of industrialization exported to a market will pay higher import taxes than the ones that have less added value. This is a clear example: the import of a finished car pays more taxes than the import of its parts without assembly. This system is generally adopted by most countries in the world. Its objective is to encourage the import of goods that necessarily incorporate some added value in the destination market and discourage the purchase of finished products.

— ***Variable tax:*** It is an import tax whose objective is to level the internal market price (especially in products that are not very competitive at the international level), with the international market price in force. It is used for commodities, which are internationally quoted products, that is, their price is determined by the world supply and demand. The product protected at a national level has a higher price than the international quotation. As the international price of the products varies constantly through time, also the tariff modifies to accompany the international price and get a uniform protection level.

Other tariff barriers may be:

— ***Other charges:*** They are retributions paid for particular services rendered in the destination country due to import. They can be payed by statistical compilations, complementary services of imported merchandise verification, verification service of the destination assigned to the nationalized product.

— ***National taxes:*** Goods imported by a country are subject to the same taxes as goods sold in that internal market (for example, value-added tax or its equivalent). Those duties have identical treatment for commercial operations carried out between members of a regional agreement. Internationally, the general criterion declares that the exported goods should not be taxed by the country of origin predominates. It is an international trade principle not to export taxes. The marketed goods are only going to tribute following the destination country criterion. Consequently, goods will be taxed when import is made.

— ***Export taxes or duties:*** These are taxes that some countries establish to export particular products. The taxes increase the price of the exported product and are estimated on the FOB price or similar. The main objective of their existence is to increase tax revenue of the exporting country. Another objective may be export taxation on products with low level of industrialization. In this way, the export of products with great national added value, which will not be taxed with those tributes, is officially encouraged.

#### 4.1.2.2. Paratariff Barriers

These barriers are called, "non-tariff" or "paratariff", and include a wide variety of commerce barriers. These barriers have been proliferating in international marketing throughout the last decades. As with the tariffs, they are imposed by the national States and they are obligatory.

They include all the ones that do not have a direct or indirect relationship with import or export tariffs. They can be quantitative (when one or more States establish limits in the amounts commercialized) and qualitative, and, among the most important, can be mentioned:

— ***Norms and legal requirements:*** They have different characteristics. Customs requirements force to comply with particular bureaucratic formalities at the customs control bodies of origin or destination, when dealing with commodities. The documentary rules established the legal delivery of certain documents to import or export. Quality rules set parameters for product manufacture according to control standards. Package requirements limit the use of certain materials in the packaging or its design. Sanitary monitoring deals with product healthfulness and consumers' health protection, and control is carried out through official institutions of origin and/or destination.

— ***Import or export quota:*** They are the maximum amount to import or export. As regards amounts that limit the volumes imported, these create product shortage in the destination market. An insufficiency in the imported products offer is produced, if they are limited by quotas and destination imports demand is high. These quantitative barriers create a higher level of protection to the national industry than tariffs.

There are different kinds of quotas: Global and assigned. In the first case, the first to complete the import quotas are benefited by this regime. In the case of the assigned quotas, parts of those are generally distributed among the potential interested importers through a system similar to bidding. Quotas can be simple or tariff. The last case is a quantitative limitation that, if exceeded, allows to import with the payment of costly tariffs.

— ***Subsidies:*** These are direct and indirect forms of help that a country grants to particular local producers.

When the company wants to enter a market, in which the State has granted subsidies to its national producers, that company is in unequal conditions. The local companies benefited by the subsidy will deduce from its sale price the benefit of the subsidy and, as a consequence, will develop more competitive prices. Due to the help granted, these organizations will be able to compete in the international markets and not only in the local one. The granting of certain subsidies is forbidden within the frame of the World Trade Organization. Those assigned to get better results in an export process are not admitted. Investigation about the existence of subsidies has an additional condition: that they damage the industry of the importer country in the products subsidized. The affected countries may start a process so that taxes and compensatory rights could be applied. Subsidies assigned for international marketing are regarded as unfair commerce policies and so is dumping.

— ***Government purchasing policy:*** This type of barrier appears when the purchasing terms and conditions of the state system in the destination market establish "customized" requirements for national companies. Those requirements can only be carried out by the local companies, leaving foreign competition out of the game.

— ***Exchange:*** Also known as bartering in its different modalities (compensated exchange, barter, etc.). It applies to the export of goods in exchange for products instead of foreign currency. This barrier limits the exporter's capacity of choice. The exchange is considered a barrier because the exporter receives some goods from abroad (for the payment of the exportation) which limits the export company's range of choice, as compared to an operation paid with currency.

— ***Commercial agreements:*** There are different kind of agreements. Some can consist of quotas, both for imports and exports. In this way, commerce between the agreement signatory countries is structured and hindered. An example of this type of barriers is the Multifiber Agreement (MFA), which regulates textiles commerce. With the agreed conclusions in the Uruguay Round, and within the WTO frame, the FMA was being progressively dismantled.

— ***Foreign exchange control:*** Foreign exchange is foreign currency deposited in an account abroad. With this barrier, entrepreneurs need the intervention of the financial system state control to buy and sell foreign money. It is possible that customs bodies could contribute, complementarily, with exchange rate management. This system can establish the following restrictions: maximum and minimum quantities to buy and sell foreign currency, international payment and collection due dates, deadlines to pay off exchange collected in exports. When the purchase and selling of negotiated foreign currency is limited, a direct control is exercised upon the volumes imported and exported, because these are closely related to the amount of existing foreign exchange in a country. The lack of knowledge about the existence of exchange control, either in origin or destination markets, can hinder export operations.

#### *4.1.3. Consumer Market Information*

Consumer market information is very vast and includes several aspects.

Among the main to be considered there are:

— ***Consumer's features:*** This area has to do with a market segmentation process. The total market for a particular product in the destination area is too vast, this is why it has to be divided into units with homogeneous features called "segments". Market segmentation allows the company to estimate for the market operations and concentrate the efforts on that segment more efficiently. With this policy it is possible to provide for consumers' needs and the actions of the competition.

There are different ways to segment a market, according to different authors (ACERENZA, KOTLER, STANTON). Ultimate consumer market can be divided according to socio-economic features (sex, age, work, economic status) or by consumers' psychographic features (interests, lifestyles, motivations and other personal features), and behaviour issues (reactions or responses to a product). Other markets may be segmented according to intermediaries' features (number of operations, specialization, coverage, etc.). In the case of industries, some valid criteria are: product final use, volume and frequency of operations, company geographic location, among others. Generally, the company uses more than one segmentation variable, always following consumers' or users' distinctive features in the destination market.

As regards segmentation and in order to define the qualities of the consumer market, it is important to consider:

- General features of the product demand. If the product in the destination market has a rigid demand, the consumer will not change the amounts bought despite product price fluctuations. If the demand is flexible, volumes of purchase will be modified with price fluctuations.
- Purchasing process. It is necessary to identify who starts the process of purchase and why, reasons for repurchase, etc. It is also important to detect if purchases are the result of rational or compulsive behaviours.
- Principal channels used in the purchasing process. It is necessary to observe whether it is about general stores, small grocery stores, specialized points of sale, etc. And to detect what are the services provided by those marketing systems beyond the product process of sale.
- Consumption or use of substitute or ancillary products. Substitute products are products that can satisfy, in a similar way, the need covered by a particular product of the company. Complementary products are those consumed in connection with other product.
- Consumer's demand for specific presentations, product quality and packaging.

- Consumer's requirements of particular services such as warranty, installation and repair, that can vary depending on the product considered.
- Existence of cultural variables such as religion, fashion, particular habits and customs, which condition a process of purchase. In particular markets intercultural differences are so strong that the product is pushed to be adapted to them.
- Some nationalistic aspects that may encourage rejection towards foreign products and promotion of local ones.

### *4.1.4. Information about Competition, the Industrial Sector and the Product*

In general, the collection and analysis of information about the competition can have different approaches. It can be seen from a macro-economic or general point of view with a present and historical evaluation of the product production sector in the destination market or of its imports. Pertinent data includes total sales volume, total imports, interannual trends, origin of imports, among others. A micro-economic analysis implies the identification of each competitor, its name and personal data, and market participations; it is information specific to the producers and importers located in the destination market. Besides, the marketing policies performed by the operators of that market have to be identified.

- Features of the local industry in the destination market to be taken into account:
  - — If it is a sector concentrated in a few companies or whose competition is divided among numerous firms.
  - — The presence or absence of state or monopoly activities, and the participation of multinational companies in the operations of that sector.
  - — Global or local features of the industrial structure in the destination market and future strategy of the exporting company.

- — Present situation, its evolution and adequation to the different economic policies in the destination country.
- — Relationship between local production in that market and imported product volume.
- — Existence of legal rules that benefit imports or the settlement of investments in the foreign country.

- Marketing strategies used by the producing or importing companies in that country-market:
  - — Communication strategies implemented: Information about means used to promote the product, types of messages issued, product positioning strategies, organization of communicational events, etc.
  - — Distribution strategies used by those companies: Data about short or long distribution channels use, functions and services supplied by each intermediary, contractual links that connect every level of the distributive system, distribution policy used (selective, exclusive or massive), aspects of communication within the channel, channel coverage, among others.
  - — Price strategies used: Existence of price leaders and followers, and discount and rebate policies, different components that make up the cost of the imported product in destination, incidence of financial and taxation aspects upon final price, etc.
  - — Product strategies used: Quantity and types of trademarks existing in the market, containers policies implemented by companies and different presentations by which the product is marketed. Materials used, technical features, product quality, technological development of the marketed product. Other issues are governmental requirements that affect the manufacturing and marketing in the destination market, packaging rules, components, preservatives, etc. It will also be analyzed in which

stage (introduction, development or growth, maturity or declination) of the product lifecycle that market is.

The small and medium-sized organization has to compile and evaluate the information referring to the competition (and the sector), and the products offered in the selected country with the purpose of designing a differentiation strategy that could highlight the main attributes of the product for the market objectives.

### *4.1.5. Information about Market Infrastructure*

In a wide sense and from a commercial point of view, infrastructure consists in those facilitating systems which help in a direct or an indirect way with marketing the product in the destination market. Infrastructure existing in a particular country-market presents different aspects:

— ***Financial.*** It includes existence of a solid financial system; great number and variety of national and foreign banks, both public and private; consolidation in the destination market of a safe and fluid platform for international operations payment and collection; developed capital market; alternative financial mechanisms validity (factoring, leasing, etc.).

— ***Logistics.*** It comprises development of roads, highways, railways, bridges that facilitate market access. Also, ports efficient operation, airports, container depots, fiscal deposits, tax free areas that contribute to better commercial performance in destination. Besides, carriage companies location, storage and insurance companies in that market.

— ***Commercial.*** It refers to distributors, importers, trading companies, agents, wholesalers, as solid and reliable distribution channels in destination. Further, advertising agencies, media, marketing studios, professional studios and consultors as part of the chain of value in the external market.

## 5. CRITERIA FOR MARKET SELECTION

Criteria for the selection of a market among several potential markets are varied. These processes that consist in determining the most adequate relationship company-product/country-market is called "macrosegmentation" (according to GARCÍA CRUZ), and some of its most relevant features are:

### 5.1. Market Size

A study of the macro-economic variables of a country has to be made: number of inhabitants, Gross Domestic Product, rate of demographic growth, and volume and trend of total imports and of product. With this information, the company has to anticipate and estimate data towards the desired segment.

### 5.2. Psychographic Closeness

Also-called "psychological closeness", consist in the similitude existing between the market of origin and that of destination in the marketing practices, commercial legislation in force, consumers' habits, language and certain cultural features. It allows the entrepreneur to observe the external market with a vision more familiar with the national market. So, a mental state towards a more reliable and certain vision of internationalization is generated.

### 5.3. Purchasing Power

It is important to evaluate the purchasing power of potential consumers. Some hints can be perceived by the per capita GDP.

### 5.4. Geographic Vicinity

A very relevant factor is the ease of access and the vicinity of the selected country. This factor affects everything related to the cost of international transportation of the merchandise and logistics complexity. It is convenient for a company in its first internationalization stages to start by concentrating its exports in the closest markets, reaching to neighbouring countries.

### 5.5. Degree of Economy Liberalization in the Country of Destination

It can be measured by the relationship between the total imports and the Gross Domestic Product. Another indicator is the level of duties and the paratariff barriers imposed to the company product.

### 5.6. Country-market Risk

This has to be measured from a wide point of view that takes into account not only economic but also financial, legal and political aspects.

### 5.7. Relevant Economic Indicators

Some interesting indicators could be: illiteracy rate, average salary, minimum salary and energy consumption, among others. These indicators provide for consumers' general characteristics.

### 5.8. Product Modification

The number of adaptations to a product due to cultural, economic or legal aspects has to be taken into account. Some changes could consist in the obligatory use of particular components or packaging, labelling rules, technical requirements and quality standards.

### 5.9. Simplicity and Speed to Operate

The agility, simplification and celerity of the product introduction procedures in the country of destination have to be analyzed. These include all the bureaucratic activities, documentation procedures, granting of permits and licences, registration in control bodies, among others.

### 5.10. Existence of Government Incentives

It has to be known that some foreign countries grant financing lines to local producers to use them in certain imports. Other issue to analyze is the validity of advantageous and ample foreign investment laws for the companies of origin. These regulations can motivate the entrepreneur to manufacture the product in the destination market, through production branches that benefit him or her in taxation and finance.

## 5.11. Product Lifecycle

Those markets in which the company product is in an initial stage have to be clearly distinguished from those in which it is in the development stage of its vital cycle. These cycles vary from market to market, because of cultural, economic and technological reasons.

## 5.12. Existence of Regional Homogeneous Markets

A very differentiated feature appears in those country-markets that are members of a commercial block. The company may consider a direct or indirect subsequent access to the rest of the regional market.

## 5.13. Company Resource Level Applied to Internationalization

The selection of the international market to penetrate has a close relationship with the amount of monetary, financial, productive and human resources that the company is going to make use of in its international strategy. It is important to examine the company internationalization stage. The organization can be in an initial stage, as, for example an experimental or sporadical export, or consolidated in the external markets through continuous export.

## 5.14. Other Relevant Features

Among others, the amount of potential business opportunities detected and the structure and infrastructure of the competitive environment in a particular external market are of great importance.

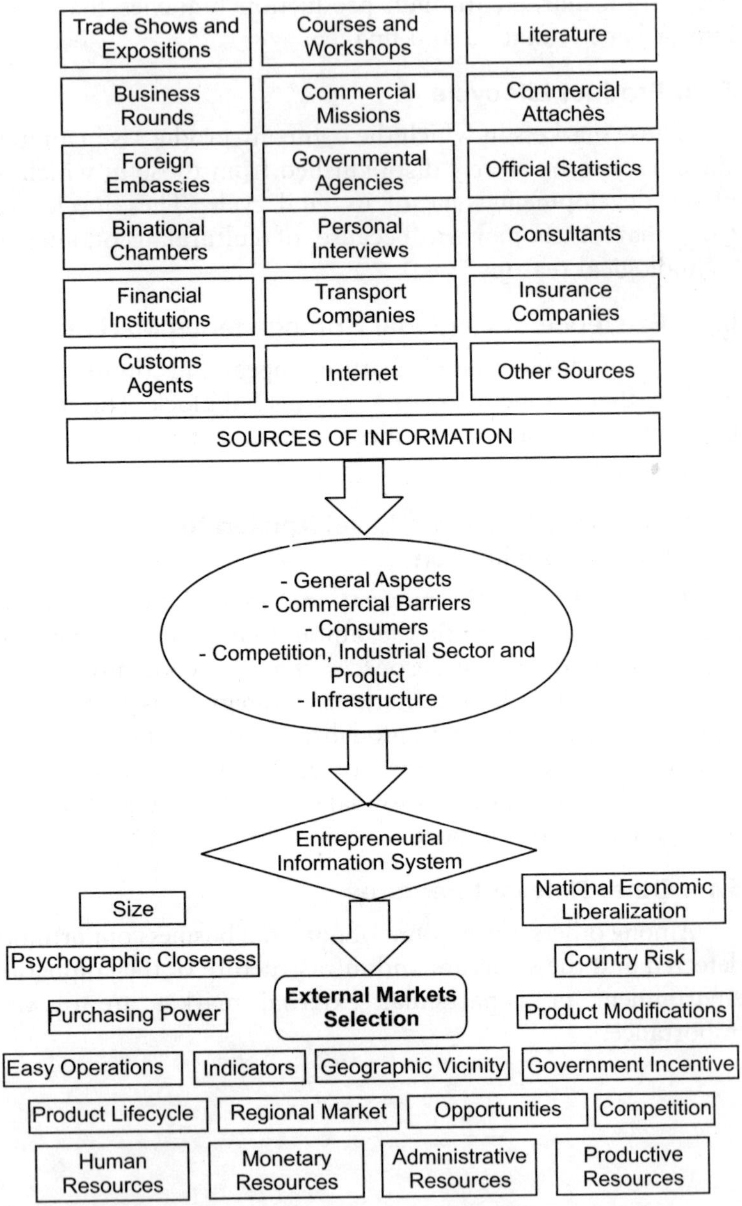


**Figure 3.1.** Importance of Information for Internationalization

# 4

# International Marketing Strategy

## 1. THE DECISION TO INTERNATIONALIZE

### 1.1. Influential Factors on Decision Taking

Firstly, the small and medium-sized entrepreneur who decides to internationalize establishes the objectives related to that issue. Different alternative courses of action to the international operations (increasing internal market coverage, approaching new segments or widening the product line in the national market) are taken into account. Subsequently, the probable results of the steps taken, due to those decisions, are analyzed. And finally, an adequate evaluation of those results is carried out.

During the decision taking process of access to the external market, the company has to deal with conditions of some uncertainty. Entrepreneurs are never totally sure about the result of their actions as a consequence of these uncertainties upon several variables that are out of reach (competitors' reaction or demand behaviour). Nevertheless, the company has to plan its activity within a strategic plan frame, taking into account available resources and time, and different courses of action, among other significant factors. Also, restrictions at the company internal level have to be considered (restrictions in its production capacity or in its internal operative financing procedures to export) as well as those at the international level (existence of tariff or paratariff barriers in the destination market).

The concept of opportunity cost is very significant when we speak of a business selection among alternatives (among which the access to a specific external market could be included). This cost refers to what the entrepreneur forecasts he or she does not gain (or loses) because of a choice of a certain course of action over others. When considering the possibility of international access, the organization has to anticipate whether exporting has a lower opportunity cost than concentrating the activities in the internal market.

It must be highlighted that entrepreneurs always take decisions upon the results they perceive as likely to happen, which implies some degree of uncertainty, ambiguity and undetermination upon the future events. The company makes a "bet" on a future issue, which carries some risk due to the choices made.

### 1.2. Features of Internationalization Decisions

When an organization analyzes the convenience of international marketing, it always has a partial outlook of the variables involved in the company's choice, among others. These decisions are not taken in conditions of certainty, but constitute approaches to the desired results. In every decision, the entrepreneur attempts to organize reality, limit its complexity and reduce its uncertainty.

This decision-making process has a mental character. Entrepreneurs, rooted in the present, try to modify some current conditions of the company dynamics with which they are not content (idle capacity, drop in sales, high indebtedness). Besides, particular results are also desired for a future time (higher profitability, higher status for exports made, unitary fixed costs decrease for higher sales).

A decision taking process to operate in the world market implies a process which presents the following features:

— Rationality and coherence. However, there exist decisions that could include intuitive or emotional components.

— Planning and anticipation of the results of external market access.

— Responsibility and commitment.

— Creativity (evaluation of non-traditional alternatives).

A decision to internationalize comprises a series of additional decisions which branch off the main objective, like: obtention of information, product adequation to market requirement and choice of the most adequate penetration policy, among others.

Decisions taken for external market access can be strategic (also called political). This decision is linked to global, long term decisions, that consider all the factors globally involved, in an environment of great uncertainty. There are tactical or directive decisions, when some strategic planning aspects are considered, for the short term. Lastly, there are the operative decisions which put tactical decisions, through specific actions, into practice.

An example of a strategic decision relative to the external markets would be: exporting to the city of Miami, United States of America. A tactic decision referred to this issue is: choice of a distributor based in Miami to sell the product in that area. An operative decision in agreement is: reaching consensus and signing the international distribution contract, with geographical exclusivity clauses, minimum volumes of sales, stocks levels, etc.

### 1.3. Evaluation of Internal Resources for International Insertion

The organization must determine, among other things, whether it has export potential or not, that is, capability to internationalize. To do this, firstly, a macro-economic evaluation of the country of origin (such as the competitiveness of the country due to its currency exchange, export support system, the country's comparative advantages in certain sectors, etc.) has to be made. Secondly, data referring to the selected countries of destination (trade barriers, economic indicators, regional commercial agreements, existence of business opportunities). But, above all, in internationalization decision-making, the existence of enough resources within the company appropriate for an exporting project will be checked:

— Managerial.
— Technological.
— Human operative.

— Commercial.
— Financial.
— Productive and intellectual property related.
— Administrative and organizational.
— Logistical.
— Creative.

## 2. STEPS TO AN INTERNATIONAL STRATEGY

A strategy is a plan with predetermined objectives that starts from the present situation, forecasting a future situation. Different courses of action are included so that a different state can be reached in the short run. There is an implicit idea of change, transformation, reconversion or renovation of the current state of affairs and of generation of improvement actions and new realities.

The strategic attitude is proactive, has a long term vision and contains a provision for future scenarios. There has to be a strong company commitment in order to design and implement a strategy, and flexibility and creativity should serve those goals. The entrepreneur must concentrate efforts and efficiently assign resources, among them timing, to achieve the goals established in the design stage of the strategy.

The strategy must always be oriented towards company value creation for the enterprise as well as for the consumer and must follow a clear differentiation of the organization as regards its competitors. It will have to be in accordance with the company's mission. In order to do this, it will have to answer this question: what does business consist in for the organization?

The international marketing strategy follows a series of steps:

1. Design.
2. Implementation.
3. Control and adjustment.

Many small and medium entrepreneurs wrongly think that an international marketing plan has to be carried out only by big-sized companies. This conclusion is based on wrong and simplistic ideas that relegate the small-sized company plan. Every enterprise that would like to internationalize must have its own plan of external business.

To design an adequate strategy, a number of steps relevant to any company will have to be followed, no matter its size. Among them, there are:

— Search for information to take decisions.

— Ordering of a series of stages (assignation of priorities and deadlines) to follow, in order to get access to external markets.

— Company internal resources (human, monetary, etc.) assessment for international penetration.

— Quantification of objectives and supervision of their observance.

— Putting into practice of the different policies so as to accomplish the set goals.

— Strategy different steps adjustment throughout the implementation of the plan.

## 2.1. Strategy Design

Strategy design stage includes a series of substages:

### *2.1.1. Acquisition of Information about International Markets*

This issue has already been developed in detail in Chapter 3. However, some aspects on the topic are going to duly discuss the subject in full. This stage comprises a series of steps to follow:

— fixing of objectives about what the international market information wanted is;

— information inquiry instruments design and definition of the research acting field;

— determination of the different traditional and alternative sources of information (especially for informal market research);

— acquisition of data elements (historical or current information and trends);

— analysis, comparison, register, accumulation and interrelation of the information obtained;
— drawing of conclusions of the information obtained and analyzed.

The initial investigation on international market is going to throw light upon certain issues like:

— Determination of the most attractive country-markets for a particular entrepreneur's product. If there is a great number of equally attractive markets, and the budget assigned to international markets is meagre, or the company wants to concentrate on a few markets, different factors will have to be considered to select them: similarity between external and national markets, number of legal regulations or cultural issues that imply product adaptation, and competition features, among other factors.
— Particular commercial mix policies (product, price, promotion, market) or penetration strategy to be used (agents, distributors, etc.).

International market acquisition of information has a value for the company, which is reflected in some features: exclusivity, reliability, precision, specificity, uncertainty reduction, etc. Information acquisition has a cost (in money or time). The entrepreneur must always make an adequate analysis of the value-cost ratio, when compiling international information.

This primary goal of this stage is the selection of the most adequate markets for the company products. Afterwards, the next stage will proceed.

#### *2.1.2. Fixing of Objectives for Market Access*

##### 2.1.2.1. Objectives as International Activity Conducting Structures

These international strategy objectives are always determined in relation to a specific product and a particular market (or submarket). In order to design them, the following aspects have to be taken into account:

— ***Company internal resources:*** Funds bound for international operation development, personnel affected to the international undertaking (human talent development), productive structure capacity to satisfy international demand (process technological updating) and existence of company product differential elements (quality, costs, material and packaging innovation, popular brand name, patents and services offered).

— ***Selected market features:*** Existing commercial barriers, regulations that affect the marketing of the product, local competition structure and behaviour in destination, dynamics in import, motivations and other features of demand in destination, market segments and niches detected, unsatisfied needs, among other issues to be considered.

### 2.1.2.2. Objectives Features

Objectives in general have the following features:

— There is a time limit to their completion and evaluation.

— They fall into the frame of the company mission (coherence).

— They have to be quantified, that is, turned into goals, for the subsequent measurement of results. If the objective cannot be measured in numbers, there should be, at least, a valid parameter that could permit to easily verify its completion.

— They provide for an appropriate assessment of commercial and financial risks, which implies the development of activities for their completion.

— They evaluate the existing restrictions in the company as regards assigned resources quantity and quality.

— They consider the different alternatives for process activities development. In practice, there is always more than one alternative for the company's goals.

— When there is conflict among several objectives, priorities and considerations will have to be established, and they will have to be divided into main and secondary.
— When multiple objectives are established, it is important to analyze the degree of similarity, compatibility, as well as simultaneity or chronological arrangement.
— It is important to consider that some objectives can be autonomous and others are going to be conditioned by the previous completion of lesser objectives.

#### 2.1.2.3. Examples of Internationalization Objectives

Among objectives pursued by the company are:

— Achieving certain exports percentage (estimated upon company total sales) for each market.
— Reaching a specific fixed amount of sales or certain amount of unities per market selected.
— Covering a particular market share, in a particular country.
— Acquiring a certain profit level (gross or after taxation) in international operations.
— Achieving certain profitability from external market activities.
— Gaining access to particular cities or regions (submarkets).
— Fixing minimum or maximum amount of monthly exports.
— Carrying out a specific amount of shipments.
— Other objectives: performing a certain amount of promotional activities, making commercial and distribution agreements.

### *2.1.3. International Commercial Mix and Marketing Channel Design*

International marketing mix design comprises a series of different policies (product, price, distribution, communication policies) which are interrelated. Each one of these variables, known as the international marketing mix four Ps (product, price, promotion and *distribution*[1]) will be treated in full in Chapter 5.

### 2.1.3.1. International Product Policy

International product policy makes reference to all those attributes, functions and differentiated features that the product has, to satisfy international demand needs (consumers and users). This important policy includes the following aspects:

— Necessary materials and components for production.

— Design and international registration of one or more brands appropriate for the product line.

— Product colour, shape, style and aesthetic planning.

— Product forms of use or operating instructions.

— Aspects of product quality and economic life (durability).

— Functional and communicational aspects related to packaging.

— Technical, material and logistic aspects of export packing.

— Services associated to the product (installation, training, parts replacement, reparation, warranty, etc.).

— Product adaptation according to destination market different factors: consumer purchasing power, government regulations, consumption patterns, external client behaviour and economic aspects, among others.

### 2.1.3.2. International Price Policy

Price policy comprises all those components that influence the determination of export final prices: costs, demand behaviour and competitors' attitude in the external market. This policy includes the following aspects:

— Exported product production cost (with legal, cultural, economic or technological external market issues in mind).

1. N.T. In the original in Spanish, the word is plaza.

— Financing costs.
— Administrative costs.
— Marketing costs (includes distributors' margins and retributions of the other intermediaries that participate in product delivery).
— Export costs (documents, customs formalities, carriage, etc.).
— Costs of product-related services.
— Other commercial issues (discounts and bonuses, advance or partial payments, etc.).

#### 2.1.3.3. International Distribution Policy

The distribution policy comprises all the commercial, logistical and communicational issues among the different intermediaries that make up an international distribution channel.

— Distribution channel structure.
— Distribution channel coverage.
— Functions at each distribution channel.
— Number of intermediaries at each channel level (density).
— Communication styles within the channel.
— Contractual issues and retributions at each distribution channel level.
— Intervention of intermediaries who facilitate international distribution (carriers, warehouses owners, etc.).

#### 2.1.3.4. International Communication Policy

Communication policy (or promotion) refers to different transmission aspects to various recipients (consumers, suppliers, employees and society) of different messages about the product and the company features and attributes that allow the building of a differentiated image of them:

— Sales promotion.
— Advertising activities.
— Sales force.

— Public Relations.

— Packaging visual features.

Every product, price, promotion and distribution policies are intimately linked with one another. For example, a product oriented towards a high purchasing power segment will need high quality components, and container and product intangible attributes will be highlighted, such as the status that promotes consumption. In this case, the product price will fit a high level, and its distribution will not be massive, but exclusive of certain channels. Besides, advertising will be carried out in certain selected media, specialized magazines, and publications consumed by people with a high standard of life.

This commercial mix design for international market products is more complex than the one devised for the national market, because most variables (product, price, promotion and distribution) will be affected, in a greater or lesser extent, by economic, financial, political, legal and cultural environments differential features of each external market.

### *2.1.4. External Market Access Channel Selection*

International marketing channel design implies the selection of the most adequate company structure for external market access. When evaluating international market penetration policy, entrepreneurs will have to consider some factors that will affect their decision: size and knowledge of the market to be penetrated, tariff and paratariff barriers, consumer and competition features, type of product, segment orientation, among others. The main marketing channels are:

— Sellers.

— Agents and distributors.

— Brokers.

— International concession.

— Export licensing and franchising.

— Manufacturing contract.

— Administration contract.

— Associative strategies (exports consortia and cooperative, joint ventures).
— Marketing companies.
— Sale branches and subsidiaries.
— Foreign Direct Investment (FDI).
— Other channels (piggy backing, technology transfer administration contracts).

## 2.2. Implementation

In this stage, the designed strategy is put into practice and the operationalization of all the variables involved in the strategy (commercial mix and marketing channels) is pursued in order to comply with the objectives. This strategic implementation will be developed according to international market information collected throughout the design stage and will be applied to all the selected external markets.

It is an operative or active stage, in which the company assigns material, human, monetary and productive resources, for the actual completion development of the different goals set in the previous stage. The entrepreneur transforms what has been planned, stipulated and projected in the marketing strategy into real, tangible activities.

An example of the activities at this stage could be: if an internationally market accessed product has been designed with a particular packaging to be manufactured by the company; suppliers who may offer material of the desired quality for that packaging will be required; meetings between the visual designers and the manufacturers will be held, pursuant to the set design stage stipulations. Once manufactured, durability and functionality tests will be carried out.

## 2.3. Control and Adjustment

This is a fundamental stage in international activities, because feedback from the implementation stage actions is necessary. In this stage, information about the results of the international marketing strategy put into practice is analyzed and these features may be verified:

— degree of completion with objectives;
— correct international marketing channel functioning and structuration;
— consistency and adequation of each of the marketing mix variables.

From this analysis, it may turn out that all the objectives (fixed in the first stage of the strategy called design) may have been totally met, and this will allow the entrepreneur to establish higher objectives for the next period according to the experience gained through internationalization activities.

The fixed goals may not have been satisfied or they may have been met partially, which leads to two subsequent analyses:
— evaluating whether operative activities have been correctly carried out;
— considering whether the chosen objectives are too ambitious for this stage. In this case, the entrepreneur will have to consider the creation of more realistic and easier to achieve goals.

As to the marketing channel and the international commercial mix, necessary adjustments may be detected at this stage. This redesign may appear as a consequence of new information accessed during the implementation stage (for example, consumers' reaction to the product, competitors' reaction, etc.) which was not available to the company during the strategic design stage.

Usually, the enterprise gets information about its international activities constantly, in each stage, and this information provides various adjustments to the designed strategy. With this in mind, marketing strategy main quality must be flexibility, in order to produce the different modifications, according to the entrepreneur's results in the external market operations.

## 3. DIFFERENT INTERNATIONALIZATION STAGES OF A SMALL AND MEDIUM-SIZED ENTERPRISE

### 3.1. World Markets Gradual Connection

International markets access of a company involves stages characterized by:

— a gradual connection with external markets;

— a progressive resource assignation to internationalization activities;

— a cumulative learning of the international marketing different issues (which generates a greater company security and solvency in external performance).

Through the development of worldwide operations, the small and medium-sized enterprise gets familiar with the exporting "know-how", thus reducing the initially perceived uncertainty. Generally, a company is not exporting born, because at the beginning it possesses neither the experience nor the knowledge about international marketing. It becomes an exporting company through the empirical development of external activities. An organization vision on the world dynamics can only be acquired through a continuous exporting practice.

### 3.2. Main Stages in International Insertion

Following Dr. JARILLO, it is noted that a company can start getting access to international markets through occasional export, which implies a company passive marketing activity. The company that occasionally gains access to the global market does not generate any proactive strategy to internationalize. In this stage, small scope operations are carried out as a result of external companies' orders. The organization does not deploy an exporting strategy; it is the foreign buyer the one that approaches the company. There is a null or scarce company management of the international marketing mix variables, thus defined by the external buyer.

In a second stage, called "experimental export", pilot operations are carried out in a few markets, and exportable national balance (production surplus not commercialized in the national market) is assigned abroad. In this stage, the company controls very few components of the commercial mix, among them, product cost and internal design, and most marketing variables are stipulated by the external buyer.

Marketing companies or other intermediaries locally based in the country of origin may also be used at this stage, through indirect export structures.

In a subsequent stage, called continuous or consolidated export, the number of operations as well as of markets accessed increase. This greater volume of business may require the creation of an export department within the company. Different international marketing channels may be used (company sellers, agents and distributors, indirect export, licences, franchising, etc.). A greater control over marketing mix issues, such as product external design and fixing of active policies relative to price and communication to retailer buyers and distribution in destination is built up.

There are two subsequent stages which are: marketing branch establishing and indirect investment abroad (also called production branch). When setting a marketing branch, the company takes charge of the different functions previously in the hands of intermediaries (distributors, agents, etc.). This allows to develop the marketing strategy much more efficiently, due to direct contact with the selected market. A branch for commercial activities based in the destination market, makes it necessary to assign an important series of resources for the development of branch activities (salespersonnel, premises, warehouses and means of transport). The rise in the use of resources allows to hold an almost integral control of the main product items at external level and to assume promotional activities towards the different distribution intermediaries in destination.

In indirect investment, the company manufactures the product totally or partially in destination. When all the production is in destination, there is no export activity, but when it is partial in destination, the company may export parts, sketches or unfinished products, which are later finished in the production branch. There are different reasons that may motivate the entrepreneur to place productive structure abroad, like: fiscal benefits for foreign investment, more economical inputs in that market that justify production in destination, high international costs of loading transport, existence of high barriers in that country-market, among others. Thus, the organization has an almost global control of the international marketing strategy.

However, it is important to remark that the company does not necessarily have to get to the last stage, but, at least it should get to the continuous export or consolidated stage.

## 4. INTERNATIONAL MARKETING STRATEGY: DIFFERENT APPROACHES

According to different authors (KEEGAN, GARCÍA CRUZ, CATEORA), external market strategy approach may be different, that is:

— **National or domestic approach:** The company does not consider the possibility of exploring external markets, neither does it develop any contact with international operators; its marketing strategy only considers local contextual factors (competition, domestic commerce practices and national consumers). This strategic approach generally lacks exporting conscience, and does not take any world risk or commitment.

— **International or extension approach:** The company is already involved in the internationalization process, but gives more importance to the national market and a secondary place to external markets. There develops an ethnocentric approach, which deploys the same national strategy in the different external markets, without any kind of adaptation to the different international environments (economic, legal and politico-legal). The entrepreneur believes that national strategies successfully implemented in the internal market must also function well at world scale. So, the marketing strategy implemented in the local market is extended to the different country-markets, presupposing their homogeneity and similarity. This strategy is generally applied in the first stages of the company internationalization, when the aim is to penetrate markets similar to the national market (psychographic closeness).

— **Adaptation or multinational approach:** The company gains access to international markets taking into account the particulars of each country. A specific marketing strategy is designed for each country, considering adequations to each market local needs. It is a multicentric approach, in which each country-market is individually considered for international strategy design and implementation. The existing legislative, cultural, economic, legal, technological development and political issues differences among the different markets make it necessary to individualize access approaches. This approach is generally adopted after an extension approach, when particular markets needs are recognized to satisfy them. This strategic attitude is characterized by a stronger company familiarization with international activities and by an understanding of the existence of differences among the different country-markets. Although the company develops a variety of multilocal strategies adapted to each market, this approach has high country-specific adaptation issues costs.

— **Global approach:** Strategically, international markets are considered as a single market; each country is not individually important in itself, but for its contribution to enterprise total strategy. One premise of this strategic approach is the interconnection and interdependency of the different international markets. This is why, what happens in one of the markets affects the others. The global approach to world markets access comprises activities of strategic extension, adaptation creation, integrated in a global approach. Global strategy deployment produces synergy in the use of resources and efforts for external operation. Different markets interconnection, considered here as a unique global market, demands for coordination of activities, as well as for sharing and spreading information generated in each market, so that it may be used by the others. Within this strategy, the company can develop some degree or standardization of its marketing mix variables, which implies the application of identical marketing policies without individual modifications or adaptations. This standardization will never be absolute, it is only degrees of standardization. In some cases, other company chain of value activities can be restructured like, for example, the productive process, which may be centralized in a country in order to achieve economies of scale. This geocentric approach allows the entrepreneur to distribute the productive links in different countries, by considering the comparative advantages of each one, through a world integrated productive system. Adaptation issues are considered in this approach, since the strategy, developed at a global level, is also sensible to the implantation local needs of each country-market. Also, the cost inefficiency implied by sustaining different strategies that vary from country to country, is solved with the integration of every market selected in a global strategy.

— **Regio-centric approach:** The strategy may be regiocentric when it selects particular regions as operative areas for the design of a generic, integrated strategy for them. In this case, the company designs panregional strategies that consider the market objective made up by different countries, as if it were a single market for strategic purposes.

## 5. EXTERNAL MARKETS EXPANSION STRATEGIES

### 5.1. Importance of Market Number and Significance of Actions

There are two defined strategies that take into account the number of markets penetrated. The first one is the market diversification strategy, through which the company gains access to numerous markets, and the concentration strategy, in which the organization concentrates its efforts and resources on a few markets.

Considering that entrepreneurs have limited resources of human, monetary, productive and commercial character, a series of factors to select the expansion strategy for a particular company or product have to be evaluated. The words "numerous" and "a few" in relation to the number of external markets accessed, are relative concepts whose meaning varies from company to company, according to a series of factors: manufactured products, organizational structure, economic importance, sector to which they belong, among others. What may be numerous markets for a small and medium-sized enterprise, may turn out to be a few for a transnational company.

The organization develops an intensive expansion marketing focus when applies a concentration strategy. The company develops an extensive expansion marketing focus when applies a diversification strategy.

## 5.2. Market Concentration

Features of the concentration strategy:

— There exists an intensive company assignation of efforts in a few markets and a more efficient use of resources so as to prevent them from being dispersed.

— A higher level of commitment and operation consolidation in each selected market is promoted.

— A selection of the few markets that the company considers "key" for international operation development is made. In general, the company turns to more dynamic and internationally stable markets. Those markets sale levels develop an increasing tendency to company participation in the markets selected.

— When the international operations risk is concentrated on a few markets, there appears a company's greater dependency on that small number of markets. The fact that the enterprise is exposed to the different selected markets ups and downs makes it more fragile.

— It brings about more knowledge about those markets, and a greater learning capacity about commercial practices, consumer's behaviour and markets competitive environments.

— It is advisable for use when the new markets access, administration, sales and distribution costs are very high for the entrepreneur. Concentrating on a few markets makes it possible to generate economies of scale in sales and distribution activities.

— It has proved to be very efficient in goods that need to be adapted as regards product variables and market communication, which is why it is not advisable to diversify expansion in numerous countries because adaptation cost would be too high. It is efficient for the marketing of goods that have a repetitive purchasing process and that allow consumer's loyalty.

— It is useful for the products that need a direct or indirect company's strong control and participation in the different stages of the marketing process (through pre- and post-marketing services). In general, it is used in middle stages during the company's internationalization.

## 5.3. Market Diversification

Features of the diversification strategy:

— Market penetration is less deep than in the concentration strategy.

— This strategy gives greater flexibility to the company due to a lesser assignation of resources to each market, which reduces vulnerability in those markets. Thus, it may be efficient to access markets with a high degree of insecurity and instability.

— It can be applied when the implementation of distribution activities in each new market or in situations where the company may divert distribution to third intermediaries in the destination market.

— There are not high costs of product adaptation to each new market due to cultural, economic, or legal issues.

— The company does not possess too much information about the variables that govern the function of each market. It has only superficial knowledge.
— It is useful for products in which quick delivery is a competitive advantage to gain access to country-markets. Also for those cases in which economies of scale are produced in the productive process, when the number of penetrated markets increases, with very competitive prices at international level.
— In general, it can be implemented in internationalization exploratory stages, as well as in more advanced stages when the company is more consolidated in the international markets.

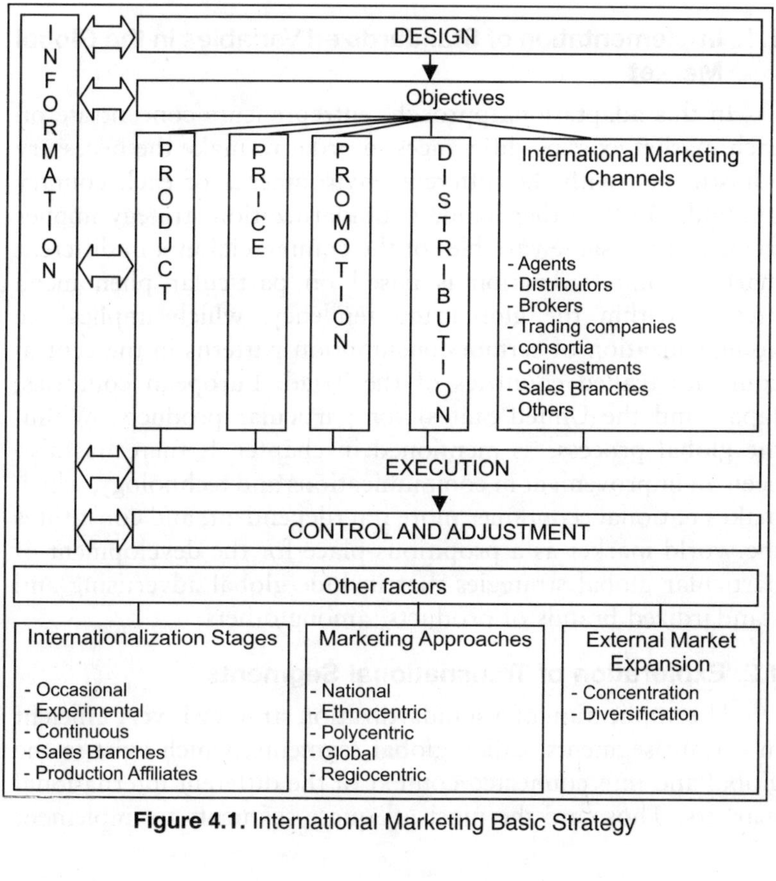


**Figure 4.1.** International Marketing Basic Strategy

# 5

# Basic Decision Variables of the Commercial Mix

## The four Ps of International Marketing (Product, Price, Promotion and Distribution)

## 1. STANDARDIZATION AND ADAPTATION

### 1.1. Implementation of Standardized Variables in the Global Market

In this adaptation approach, entrepreneurs concentrate on each market existing differences in order to make the necessary adjustments, with the different environments of each country in mind. On the other hand, a standardization strategy implies the use of the same variables of the commercial mix in different markets. Standardization is based on particular phenomena present within the globalizing tendency, which implies the homogenization of certain consumption patterns in the central countries (called countries of the Triad: European countries, Japan and the United States) for particular products. Within the global process, as mentioned in chapter 1, there has also been an improvement in communications and technology, which makes national economies more interdependent, and constitutes the world market as a propitious place for the development of particular global strategies that include global advertising and standardized brands of products, among others.

### 1.2. Exploration of Transnational Segments

The application of a standardization strategy is very efficient in certain segments, called global segments, which exist in the global and interconnected context of the different international markets. Those are the most adequate segments to implement standardization. These segments, also known as transnational or intermarket segments, consider consumers' preferences, habits, tastes and requirement similarities in different country-markets. It is a segmentation based on similar needs and equivalent expectations among consumers of different countries that, accumulated among all these international markets, result in an aggregated segment (or summation of national segments) of great interest, from the point of view of marketing.

However, standardization can go beyond the directioning of that strategy to global segments. The attributes of the company product are indifferentiatedly imposed to the different markets, disregarding of the countries heterogeneity. The enterprise may accompany these strategic actions with the development of a strong global positioning. This implies the creation of a sole image in consumers' minds (globally considered) consistent, reinforced and homogeneous in all the markets selected.

### 1.3. Standardization Advantages for International Activities

Standardization has a series of advantages that come from cost savings, as a result of using standardized variables: economies of scale, economies of research and development, marketing economies, etc. Another advantage that this strategic approach has, is the building of company and product images reinforced at a global scale, with the important demand of strong investment in international promotion, in order to reach that positioning.

Another benefit is that the enterprise can efficiently exploit creative ideas that can be shared by the different markets in which the standardized product is commercialized. One of the main obstacles to standardization is the differential aspects that make up international environments (existence of regulations, consumption patterns, particular economic issues), which vary from country to country.

End use products affected by the cultural environment may appear as less prone to standardization. Products for industrial use or that imply planned purchases and great technological development, however, have greater possibilities for standardization. These are general considerations, which is why the enterprise has to concretely evaluate its product and the industrial sector it is in (whether it is a global sector or not), apart from the chosen market features, in order to verify the viability of this strategy. Some variables are proner to become a part of a standardization strategy like: product presentation, promotional material, brand, advertisement message and some packaging characteristics.

### 1.4. Consideration of External Markets Local Needs and Expectations

Adaptation means adequation of the marketing variables for each market according to their specific requirements. This adaptation may, in turn, be obligatory, when the product has to have certain minimum requirements imposed by destination market regulations (packaging rules, labelling rules, prohibition to use some components and preservatives). Voluntary or discretional adaptation is that which is made not for legal issues, but due to other reasons (economic, technological, cultural, financial, etc.), and the company tries to adequately satisfy the local needs. The proper limit in variable adequation is going to be given by the funds spent by the specific adaptation activities of the different product components (container, brand, presentation, materials, quality, etc.). In the extreme case of total adaptation, when a company designs a specific product for each country that it penetrates, high adaptation costs may leave it out of the market.

### 1.5. Existence of Differentiated Commercial Spaces

A factor with great adaptation incidence is the cultural issue, which generates differential consumption environments in destination markets with peculiar features (certain purchasing behaviour patterns, economic status, valuation of certain product functions or attributes, buyer's level of instruction, etc.). Another important factor is the legal aspect that appears in the different markets through the existence of paratariff barriers that imply the compliance of certain rules that demand obligatory product adaptation. In this case, failure to comply with those adaptations brings about no authorization to enter the product in the destination country. Generally, the control of the requirements imposed by the external country legislation that affects the product is carried out by the customs body of the importer country. The economic issue is also important to evaluate product adaptation. The different levels of development that exist among the different countries related to consumers purchasing power, varies from market to market. So, all product variables will have to be coherently adapted according to the consumer's purchasing power. In an enterprise designed strategy, certain variables have a greater tendency to a certain degree of adaptation; for example international prices and some distribution issues, among others.

The fact that the enterprise has to achieve an adequate balance between standardization and adaptation, bearing in mind that both approaches can never be completely carried out, is something important to consider. As a result, the enterprise always performs some degree of standardization for some variables and some degree of adaptation for others.

## 2. INTERNATIONAL PRODUCT

### 2.1. Main Features

The product has a series of tangible and intangible attributes which aim at satisfying consumers' and users' wishes and needs, and contributing to the compliance of the entrepreneurial objectives.

As regards product attributes, a division is made among:

— **basic product**, which is the tangible product essential concept, also called product heart;

— **extended product**, which comprises the different attributes, like brand, packaging, style, quality and aesthetic aspects;

— **sublimation products or supporting components**, which are the different supporting services that add value to the tangible product like technical service, training and instructions, delivery and installation, and legal warranty, and other postmarketing services.

In a wide sense, services, places, and ideas are also recognized as product. The product is a complex mixture of components, some of which can be directly perceived by the senses (colour, shape, materials, etc.) and others which cannot be directly apprehended by the consumer, but for their mental preconceptions (security, status, etc.) in response to the positioning developed by the enterprise.

This controllable variable interaction with the rest of the international marketing mix variables (communication, price and distribution) makes any modification in one of them affect directly or indirectly the others.

## 2.2. Types of Products and International Lifecycle

As for products, they can be divided into two groups: entrepreneurial consumption products and end use products.

### *2.2.1. Entrepreneurial Consumption Products*

Entrepreneurial and organizational consumption are those aimed at organizations:

— state or private;

— industrial, commercial or service;

— profit or non-profit;

— big, medium or small-sized;

— urban or rural;

— internal, external, or mix market oriented.

These structures buy the product to develop their activities (industrialization, services provision, etc.). Products may be: supplies, raw material, premises, materials, spare parts, accessories, among others.

### *2.2.2. End Use Products*

They are those used or consumed by individuals or families with no commercial objectives. They comprise: massive consumption products (which have a short purchasing process, low unitary price and are present in most distribution channels adequate for their marketing), comparative products (those with a longer selective purchasing process, in which the consumer compares among different models, brands and qualities; they have a higher added value, use less distribution channels than the massive ones) and selective products (of high value, they possess a heavy load of symbolic and psychological attributes, like *status*, social class subculture, brand, reputation and are distributed in limited distribution channels).

### *2.2.3. Differential Issues between Final and Entrepreneurial Consumption Products*

In the end use and organizational consumption classification of products, differences are established on who the user or consumer of the product is as well as on how the process is performed. Organizations have a more rational and planned purchasing process, according to a purchasing budget. In some cases, they stipulate standards or requirements that products must have, and give importance to some aspects of the amplified product such as: postmarketing services, use instructions and warranty. The purchasing process can be produced in the enterprise or the seller's address.

On the other hand, end use product purchasing behaviour process is less rational, more emotional, less restricted to a purchasing plan, with the exception of economic recession times, during which consumers' purchasing power is greatly affected. Presentation (packaging, design, colours) and point of sale features (decoration, distribution, access inside the shop) are very important. For these products, the purchasing process is produced in the point of sale visited by the buyer.

## 2.3. International Product Lifecycle

### *2.3.1. International Lifecycle Stages*

A product lifecycle is similar to a person's life and is divided into stages: introduction, development, maturity and declination (birth, growth, adult age and death for a human being). This lifecycle, as well as the stages within it, can be short or long, depending on the product.

Internationally, a product lifecycle stage in a particular country-market does not necessarily coincide with the same stage for that product in another country-market. The enterprise has to know that a product may be in a state of maturity or declination in one country and may be unknown in another country because it might be in the introduction stage. Also, there may be homogeneous regional lifecycles which may include two or more country-markets.

In general, the product is unknown to the market in the introduction stage. After launching it, if there is little competition in that market, sales volume increases slowly. At this stage, the company spends a great part of its budget, falling in some cases in bankruptcy, to give the product differential attributes that can make it popular among consumers.

In the growth stage, sales and benefits increase at high speed, but at the end of this stage, sales start to decrease their growing rhythm due to the introduction of new competitors who feel attracted by the market for that product.

In the maturity stage, sales reach the maximum point and stabilise, to adopt later a decreasing tendency. The product is highly popular and accepted everywhere in the goal-market, so, companies start to use strong differentiation strategies towards the products presented by their competitors, to get a greater participation in this market, which has reached a saturation point. In the last stage, the product may disappear or be replaced by other with better attributes (to start a new lifecycle, with its corresponding stages). Product obsolescence due to technical features or fashion, among other characteristics, may be a reason for product declination.

The concept of product lifecycle, just expressed, must not be confused with the concept of product useful life, connected with durability; the maximum state of conservation of its attributes for consumption. This last concept is closely related to product economic life, which is the convergence of quality levels and economic life. Besides, life is also related to the use of certain attributes such as preservatives, packaging safety materials, among others.

### 2.3.2. Product International Marketing Lifecycle

Product lifecycle is not the same as product international marketing lifecycle. In order to explain the second cycle, we have to consider that there exist two groups of countries in the international environment: the ones that generate knowledge or ideas and commercialize them, and the ones that commercialize products.

This international cycle consists of a first stage in which the country, generally developed and with a big internal market that acts as a testing field, introduces a new product in the market as a consequence of great R+D (Research and Development) investment. In this first stage, this country monopolizes exports of the innovating product to the other countries.

Other countries start to manufacture the product in a second stage, as a consequence of licences granted by the country that originally developed it, or as a consequence of disloyal commercial actions, such as forgery. As a result, exports from the first country decrease, because the product is not imported by those second countries that produce it internationally.

In a third stage, these countries generate economies of scale and, as they use intensively abundant resources in their local markets in the productive process (for example, low cost labour force), they get very competitive final prices. In this way, they start to export and this is why external sales decrease even more, because there are new competitors in the different export markets.

In the fourth stage the product is imported from the countries incorporated after, by the country that developed it in the first place; so, this country introduces a new product to the international market, and a new cycle with its stages is started for this new product. It is clear that certain countries concentrate technological development and innovations in a first stage and then, in subsequent stages, they start to disseminate them in other countries. These countries manufacture the product and market it more efficiently than the innovating country, which impels this country to constantly create different innovations.

## 2.4. Product Design

### *2.4.1. Importance of Product Wide Conception*

Product integral design must be an objective, so as not to lose sight of the desired positioning and remark its main attributes. When positioned, one or two main attributes stand out and the other qualities arise as a result of the connection with the image in consumers' minds. The relationship between the benefits perceived by the consumer and the price paid for the product attributes (this relationship is called product value) must not be neglected in the design. Quality/price relationship has to be improved, so as to be sensitively oriented to consumer's or user's satisfaction of needs and wishes. The organization has to use materials and aesthetical conceptions in accordance with the prevailing market technology, with the different product applications required by the user in mind.

### *2.4.2. Main Issues that Affect Design*

For product design different factors have to be considered:

#### 2.4.2.1. As regards Competitive Environments and Consumers

— Functions and earnings produced by the product.

— Economic life (which allows a reasonable period from product production to product consumption, which is related to durability).

— Purchase and use patterns existing in a particular market, and product compatibility.

— Different materials used and quality requirements (as regards quality, it has to be uniform in all the components used to manufacture the product, and besides look for an adequate relationship between quality and product economic life).

— Product style or presentation preferences.

— Product reference with certain fashion trends.

#### 2.4.2.2. As Regards the Enterprise

- Cost of different materials.
- Product design, packaging, aesthetic-functional, and communicational aspects costs.
- Adequation cost of packages and packaging.
- Different extended services cost.
- Quality system upkeep costs.
- Reasonable level of earnings according to the company objectives.
- Strategic approach adopted as regards external markets (ethnocentric, polycentric or geocentric).

#### 2.4.2.3. As Regards Governmental Rules

Total adequation to rules and regulations of the country of origin, as well as that of destination in the following aspects:

- Packaging rules.
- Labelling rules.
- Regulations on prohibition of materials (preservatives, colouring, additives, use of certain chemical products).
- Environmental rules (ecological care).
- Inscription in origin or destination markets in certain producers registers.
- Production process quality parameters requirements (for example, verification of decontamination, and of compliance with sanitary and sterilizing requirements, etc.).
- Obligation of certain controls and interventions from verification official bodies on certain aspects of the products (phytosanitary, measurement of certain chemical compositions).
- Legal documentation requirement, crediting any of the previously mentioned points.
- Legislation in force that regulates different product aspects with the application environment in a regional market (Mercosur, European Union, etc.).

## 2.5. Product Strategy

### 2.5.1. Factors that Affect Product Strategy Selection

There are different product strategies to enter international markets. The most adequate entrepreneurial strategy will be chosen considering:

— Company strengths, from the differentiating attributes point of view. Company weaknesses in comparison with competitors' existing offer also have to be evaluated.

— Existence of opportunities and threats in the market.

— Economic, cultural, and legal differential environmental features of the international markets.

— Product lifecycle stage existing in the external markets (introduction, growth, maturity or declination).

— Product features: The approach will be modified according to the type of product: end or industrial use. The strategy will also vary if it is a product with few internationalization possibilities, that is, with a strong local base, or with good qualities for export, or if the product has global features, or belongs to a global sector (that is, it develops its activities with global scale and approach).

— Whether it has an innovating attribute that makes it attractive to country-market objective.

### 2.5.2. Different Product Strategies

According to different authors (Stanton, Kotler, Ledesma and Keegan) main product strategies classification is:

#### 2.5.2.1. Geographical Expansion

Composed by five substrategies:

— ***Double extension***: It refers to the adoption of an ethnocentric approach towards the product and communication variables, that is, product and promotion policies for the international markets are going to be the same as the ones applied in the national market.

— ***Product extension and communication adaptation***: In this case the same product policy is applied for the domestic and external markets, but communication policy will be adequate to the requirements of each external market. Those adaptations can arise as a result of legal issues that regulate promotion activities in destination, message adaptation to the media used, different marketing infrastructures existing in destination, or different levels of education existing in world markets.

— ***Communication extension and product adaptation***: Every communication strategy component for the different foreign markets is the same as the ones deployed in the local market of the country of origin. The enterprise expands its promotion domestic policies to different countries in a global level, but there are partial or total variations as regards the product, in accordance with features and needs of each international market.

— ***Double adaptation***: It refers to the use of a polycentric approach for both variables, and is applied in both, the product as well as in promotional activity, with destination markets legal, cultural, or economic criteria in mind.

— ***Innovation***: It implies the development of creative strategies for the external markets selected. Extension strategies prolong domestic policies to the external markets, and adaptation strategies, take product or communication implemented in the national market as the base upon which all the necessary modifications are made. Innovating strategies do not consider any national policy either to extend it or to adapt it. New, unknown products or communication activities inexistent in the national market and implemented only for international marketing are conceived. Innovative products are notoriously different from the existing ones at the time of their appearance in the market of origin.

#### 2.5.2.2. Concentration

A strategy of products is concentrated when the enterprise commercializes a few products in a few markets.

#### 2.5.2.3. Country-market Development

In comparison to the previous strategy, the enterprise commercializes a limited number of products in an important number of markets. That is, it diversifies the international markets to which it gains access, with a reduced line of products.

#### 2.5.2.4. Segment Development

In this strategy a great number of different company products is marketed in a few external markets. In this case, the organization widens its product line for limited country-markets. Going from a limited number of products per market, to a widened number of goods offered, the entrepreneur can generate economies of scope, which means sharing certain information (on international experience, international marketing strategies implemented, research and development) in a wider number of products per market.

#### 2.5.2.5. Diversification

Also called diversification of products and markets, or total diversification. In these cases the enterprise diversifies its efforts in a great number of products and markets. It is not very advisable for the small and medium-sized enterprise.

#### 2.5.2.6. Lifecycle Modification and/or Creation

It consists in the generation of a new attribute or the redesign of product positioning, which originates a new product lifecycle, avoiding its arrival to the last stage in a country-market.

#### 2.5.2.7. Lifecycle Jump from a Country-market to Another

It applies to a product in a particular external market in the declination stage; the company transfers internationalization efforts towards other market, where the product is either unknown or in the lifecycle first stages. Thus, a lifecycle renovation is produced in an intermarket strategic approach.

#### 2.5.2.8. Obsolescence Planning

This refers to the company planning to accelerate product stages in the market in order to strategically shorten the period during which the product is required by the market. This strategy may be complemented by the previous strategy, that is, the launching of a "new" product (in the wide sense) in the external market.

#### 2.5.2.9. Standardization

The same product is offered to all the markets and there is consistency with a geocentric business philosophy. As regards this issue, a universal product is the one marketed with the same attributes in every market; however, modifications such as labelling or instructions language can be made. In the case of a modified product, the product is essentially the same, since modifications constitute just a small proportion of the total. In the case of a new product for a market, adaptations and modifications take a substantial percentage of the whole product. For these last products, their main feature is originality. However, there is also a wider conception that considers new, every product that modifies any of its attributes, beyond modification proportion and importance.

#### 2.5.2.10. Line Reduction

In the case of product line reduction for a particular market, less products are offered (that is, less article variety) in this market than in the rest of them.

#### 2.5.2.11. Reduction or Extension of Product Number of Models or Lines

It is also called variation in the depth of the product mix for a market (mix is the group of products that the company presents to the market). This modification in the number of models offered in a country takes into account, among other factors: market size, number of segments detected, economic and cultural development and existing level of competition.

#### 2.5.2.12. Simplification

The enterprise offers a product in a particular market with less attributes and provisions than in the rest, generally considering special purchasing power or cultural conditions typical of that market.

#### 2.5.2.13. Segment Positioning

— ***Leadership strategy***: The company product has the first position in the market, which is accepted by competitors, and so its actions as regards product are relevant to establish their policies. This leadership strategy can be supported by the constant generation of new attributes that place the product in a dominant position as compared with its competitors.

— ***Confrontation or challenge strategy***: The company wishes for the leadership and all its strategies are directed towards that end. As a leader is not going to remain immutable when a rival presents a market quota attack, the company that applies this strategy has to act with great flexibility from the reaction and defence point of view.

— ***Simulation Strategy***: Own organizational activities are adapted to the strategy deployed by the competition. Its main goal is not to generate controversies within the competitive environment.

— ***Specialized strategy***: Product programme development is deployed in relation to a very specialized market niche.

### 2.5.2.14. Strategies with Productive and Commercial Approach

From the productive and commercial point of view, there are different product strategies such as:

— ***Tertiarization:*** It means diverting total or partially product elaboration to other enterprise. The company that diverts these manufacturing issues will later commercialize the product in the market of destination. The subhired enterprise may be located in the country of origin or destination, and will produce parts, components, containers, or the whole product for the outsourcing company.

— Implementation of an adequate harmonization of national and imported components in order to manufacture the product for export. This approach is necessary when the product is directed to a particular country-market that requires components, quality or materials unavailable or costly in the national market.

— Import of certain pieces, components, materials, inputs or containers, through procedures of temporary admission or import, to incorporate added value in the national market and then export the finished product. The advantage of this strategy is that the imported product does not pay rights and other import duties, which sensibly decreases product all-in costs. The imported merchandise may temporarily remain in the customs area of the importing country during a limited period of time, so as to incorporate it to the productive process, and has to be exported once integrated in the final product. It is necessary to comply with regulations provided by the state agency of application.

— ***Chain of value dispersion in several countries:*** In these cases, a part of the product is produced in a country and exported incompletely to another country where a production (own or in coinvestment with another company) affiliate incorporates added value through some productive processes. Thus, components and processes are incorporated in the country-markets where the company gets comparative advantages, and a final competitive price is reached in the international environment. This strategy can only be used by the small and medium-sized enterprise in more advanced internationalization stages, because of the high budget and the coordination of productive and logistic processes required for implementation.

— ***Industrial integration for export:*** Two or more companies join in an associative project, through contractual or partnership links to manufacture a product for export. This is an example: a company A and a company B join in a strategic partnership; A manufactures iron legs for tables, and B produces wood board for tables. So, they integrate both productions to export finished tables. In this way, finished products can be exported through this complementary integrated company structure. Besides, it is likely that integrated product export could get more government promotional incentives (export refund), than parts exports.

## 2.6. Differentiation and Segmentation

It is important to distinguish between these two terms which are commonly confused in practice. When the company looks for differentiation, it develops a series of activities competitor-oriented and this differentiation may be, for example, at tangible attribute level or at service or intangible attributes that have product value level. When the company segments, it takes the heterogeneous market and partitions it in smaller units (segments), which are the aim for its strategy. This division is made by considering one or more consumers' features: demographic (sex, age, etc.), socio-economic (social status, employment, purchasing power, etc.) or behavioural (loyalty and purchase frequency, etc.). In the case of industrial use products, there may be a different segmentation criteria according to: company size and/or order, industrial sector, as well as other factors like technological development, product use, organization structure, and financial solvency. As a result, segmentation consists in entrepreneurial actions consumer or user oriented.

## 2.7. Brands Power

### *2.7.1. Brand as Symbolic Communication for Product Identification and Distinction*

A brand is the name and a group of symbolic elements (logo or non-vocalizable part called "brand representation"), which identify a company's product and differentiate it from the competition. It is a codification system, in the wide sense, that allows the consumer, through brand (code) identification, to build mental images of the most relevant attributes of a particular product, generating certain attitudes towards it (purchase, rejection, brand comparative evaluation, etc.). As regards international market brands, they have to be registered in each of the country-markets the entrepreneur wants to gain access to. This is a precaution and legal protection measure of the brand ownership rights in the markets where products are to be commercialized. In some countries there are rules which establish that the first to register a brand is the only one who can use it, even when the registering company is not the original brand developer. This is a very relevant fact, because a brand may be one of the most valuable company assets, considered as "brand capital". In some countries with a different writing system (eastern and Arabic markets), it is convenient for the company to register and position the brand using criptograms for the design of the name.

### *2.7.2. Brand as a Positioning Element*

The brand is a strong positioning element of the product features in consumers' minds, it has a power of synthesis that allows the sole evocation of its symbol or word to deploy multiple ideas about the product and its distinctive features in consumers. The use of an adequate communication strategy is of substantial importance for the desired positioning of a product and its brand. It is not sufficient that the product be differentiated from the rest of the existing products in the market. Strong promotional actions are required to make the brand known. A product with brand must have a strong promotional base so as to become internalized by the consumers of that brand together with its positive features.

Brands are identifying codes because they concentrate product features in consumers' minds, and stimulate the purchasing actions of some goods and the rejection of others. It is vital for the product with a brand to keep a uniform quality level, so that it can have the same degree of performance to satisfy clients and users. Thus, a strong connecting power is created between the brand and product attributes.

### *2.7.3. Brand Policies*

There are different brand policies. There are family brands, when all the company products share the same brand, and individual brands, when each product offered has its own brand. In this last case, a reference can be made to a family brand that includes all the individual brands, which is called brand extension policy. In family brands use, the name of the brand must allow the inclusion of new products to the line offered by the enterprise, that may use that brand.

Individual brands can be determined by the company not only at product level, but also at product version, model or presentation levels. This is possible when attributes, features, or qualities of the different products are heterogeneous. This strategy allows the entrepreneur to generate a second brand for a product, directed to a segment different from the original brand segment.

The enterprise may also use its own brand, or sell the product without brand. In this last case, the product will reach consumers with some of the intermediaries' brand (for example, importers distributors' brand) or without any brand at all (this last case is called generic or indifferentiated product). Other example of intermediaries' brands are those that trading companies can impose on exported products that they get from internal market companies, or the regular brand designed by an export consortium for its members' products.

### *2.7.4. Brand Global Force*

In the global context, the use of the same brand in every international market (global brand) reinforces the company image and creates a transnational positioning. This global brand policy goes together with a standardization of certain promotional activities, so as to implement a brand dissemination strategy. The use of a global brand is very appropriate, especially in integration markets (regional markets) where economies of scale and of marketing can be accomplished.

### *2.7.5. Other Issues Relative to the Brand*

The use of a brand policy implies that the enterprise may reach an efficient product availability in the points of sale all throughout time. The product with brand has to be adequately supplied to the marketing channel intermediaries, as it is required by the market.

As regards international markets, and following CZINKOTA and RONKAINEN, some potential action lines on the subject of brands are: the use of the brand translated to the language of the destination country whenever possible, and transliteration, in which no negative connotation brand is verified in the destination market. Other approaches on the subject are transparency, which looks for a new brand without meaning or reference to real life words, and brand transcultural approach, in which a unique brand name in foreign language is used for all the external markets, with direct mention of the product origin.

If the company uses Internet and has a site for marketing or promotion, an e-brand will have to be registered (also known as electronic brand or domain), which is the name that allows virtual surfers to connect to the company web page. If the enterprise is already internationally known, it is possible that this brand may coincide with the company real name or brand. However, the company may use the same domain name, but registered with the final national country identificator (for example: *.br* for Brazil, *.de* for Germany). The enterprise that makes use of the net structure with commercial ends may design different specific virtual brands that adapt to particular features of specific segments, in order to carry out its e-business activities efficiently. This topic is going to be analyzed detailedly in chapter 7.

## 2.8. Package and Packaging

### 2.8.1. Package Functions and Features

A container can be defined as one of the components of product international policy that has to meet the following features:

- *Protective:* It makes sure the product keeps its quality level for use.
- *Containering:* It contains product and allows a harmonious relationship container-contained.
- *Communicational:* It transmits information on the different attributes of the product like: colour, shape, design and symbols, smell, taste, etc. It is part of the positioning strategy from the visual point of view.
- *Portable:* It allows product transportation and handling for use.
- *Commercial:* In self-service system points of sale, this becomes a strong promoter for consumers' purchasing process. This is why product attractiveness and design balance are so important to differentiate it from

the competition. As with the brand, the container individualizes the product and distinguishes it from the ones presented by competitors.

A container may be primary when it is in direct and close contact with the product, and secondary when several primary containers are grouped for exhibition. The tertiary container is the grouping of secondary containers in bigger modular systems (unitization).

### *2.8.2. Factors that Affect International Package Design*

As regards container design legal factors (size, message, material or shape requirements, according to destination country legislation), economic factors (lower all-in cost in design activities and use of containers), cultural factors (colours, design, presentation, use of certain symbols, inclusion of accessories for product handling and use, etc.) and ecological (environmental care, recycled and biodegradable materials, etc.) have to be considered. An interdisciplinary analysis, which implies the construction of a prototype, and a testing process that creates similar potential conditions to which the product would be subject in the different places of the international route (in transit, at a store, in the sales place, and at the place for use or consumption) has to be made in the design.

Certain containers design originality, which represents an innovating and original ornamentation, may be registered as intellectual property rights (as a registrable model). Also, the pertinent register and inclusion of a bar code, to speed up marketing systems and the generation of sales statistical information with the use of scanners is substantial for international trade.

As regards the materials used for package and presentation design, entrepreneurs must perform informal information explorations about the competition in the market of destination. A balanced compatibility and coexistence between container and content has to be achieved. The entrepreneur has to pursue a system of total quality in container integral design, as to the materials used, the container functions, the stipulation of the manufacturing requirements provided by the supplier, and buyer's requirements. The container must comply with its purposes, with minimum costs and in total accordance with international regulations.

### 2.8.3. Minimum Label Requirements

The label may be included in the container, or stuck to it. It has a communicational aim of:

— Brand, model and product manufacturing company information.

— Product differential attributes.

— Any measure reference to content: gross weight, net weight, number of cubic centimetres, extension, number of units.

— Description of the different components, ingredients and additives.

— Product origin.

— Importer company information.

— Product quality determined by specific rules.

— Use conditions and precautions.

— Steps for an adequate product conservation.

— Number of manufacturing lot.

— Dates of manufacturing and expiration.

— Some other conditions relative to the product (such as organic or ecological issues).

Label main feature has to be veracity in the information provided. In this way, effects or proprieties that the product does not have, are not demonstrable, or may lead the buyer to misinterpretation, will not be attributed to it. The label must be printed at least in two languages, the language of origin and that of destination. In some regional markets like the European Union the use of multilingual labels is quite common.

### 2.8.4. Product Packaging and Protection

Packaging is not in direct contact with the product and its objective is to reach optimum safety and protection conditions, for a series of containers within an international logistic chain. The main steps in this chain are:

1. Departure from factory stores or warehouses and inland transportation.
2. Loading in origin, international carriage and discharge in destination.
3. Internal transportation and storage in the selected country market.

Packaging has a function of safety and safeguard of every product attributes and of containers packed, and it has to be designed in total adequation to the means of transport. In some safer transportation ways, such as waterway carriage, packaging has to be designed to protect the merchandise in risky activities like: handling, loading, trimming, placing, stacking, storage and discharge. Besides, in the case of sea transport, the different risks to which the merchandise may be subject during the international trajectory must be considered, such as wetting, salinity, theft or petty theft, etc. In the case of other safer carriage ways, like air, packaging conditions are less demanding and the cost is lower. However, there may be certain goods that need special packaging care, for example, dangerous merchandise that requires particular packaging.

### 2.8.5. Information Provided in the Packaging

Packaging has to consider certain minimum shipment data: place of departure, place of destination, manufacturer's or exporter's name, importer's name, country of origin, gross and net weight, other packaging measures and bulk marks to individualize it.

Container and packaging adequate design is the exporter's responsibility so, merchandise in subpackaging or subcontaining conditions has to be avoided. It is estimated that one-third of food products arrive at destination in bad conservation conditions, due to deficiencies in packaging or container.

Packaging has to have safety marks that point out specific goods storing or handling conditions to indicate: conditions of fragility, protection against exposition to certain temperatures or humidity, place by which it has to be loaded by forklifts, possibility of staking several bulks, use of chains for loading, and what side of the packaging has to look up. These symbols, called "pictograms", are used internationally and, when in doubt about which to use for a particular shipment, entrepreneurs will be able to get advise from carriers.

### *2.8.6. Unitization and Containerization*

Unitization is the integration of different products in modular systems that may be manipulated as a unique load. This unitary charge consists in the stacking of the products packed on platforms of different materials, called "pallets". This merchandise is made safe and adjusted with different materials such as springers, thermocontractile wrapping material, etc. Palletization allows loads to be transported and loaded in the vehicles or means of transport as if they were units, which allows better costs and handling times for the exported merchandise. The use of forklifts called "transpallets" is quite frequent to carry and handle the palletized merchandise. In general, these pallets have standard sizes determined by the ISO (International Standardization Association), and the most commonly used are 800 × 1,200 mm (31.50 × 47.24 in.). Palletization or unitization systems allow the uniform module of load to integrate harmoniously to the containerization (use of containers) system. These topics will be discussed again in supplement II of this work.

## 2.9. Services

Apart from tangible qualities, the product has a series of totally **intangible** attributes. All those services that add value to the product and that are centred in consumer-oriented attention are included in this last group (whether in premarketing, marketing or postmarketing).

Main services include:

— Demonstration and advising.

— Warrant.

— Reparation and replacement of faulty pieces.

— Time and delivery compliance.

— Training on use instructions.

— Installation and starting up (in the case of machinery).

— Those related to answering complaints and claims.

These services try to satisfy consumers' needs in a period that goes beyond the purchasing process, providing safety, follow-up and containment to the buyer, assistance in case of difficulties or doubts that may appear after the purchase.

## 3. EXPORT PRICE

### 3.1. Importance of Price in the International Marketing Strategy

#### *3.1.1. Meaning of the Word "Price"*

Price is the monetary valuation about the tangible and intangible benefits perceived by the consumer or user. There is a great interrelationship between this variable with the rest of the commercial mix components. Due to this relationship, any change in the product distribution or promotion affects the fixing of the international price.

There has to be consistency among the marketing mix components, and the fixing of international prices has to be carried out in total agreement with the objectives of the international marketing strategy designed. For example: to penetrate a particular country market, the company has to adapt its product according to the statutory rules of that destination market (such as sanitary and packaging requirements). These adaptations are going to affect directly export price.

#### *3.1.2. Factors that Affect International Price Design*

In the determination of international prices, entrepreneurs have to consider these important factors:

— A technique that allows to form an adequate price, not only for the external buyer, but also for the different company objectives (profitability, sales level, earnings expected, competition ejection) must be used.

— A differential price for each country or segment of this market must be formed, considering: government regulations, cultural parameters, purchasing power, distribution channel structure, currency rate. The price may be used as one of the variables that create buyer loyalty for a specific brand.

— Intermediaries that take part in the distribution system different margins, which vary from country to country, have to be considered in the determination of a wider price (nearer the consumer or ultimate user).

— A correct imputation of its components in the determination of the export price and a correct discrimination among those items that are only charged to internal market price (local advertising in the country of origin) and those relative to international market (export costs) has to be made. However, there will be some components common to both markets, this is why the entrepreneur will have to make a correct assignation of them.

— The enterprise has little discretional power over the variables that play a role in the determination of prices (costs, competition, demand and, in some cases, the State). It may control only costs, which is why an audit of the variables that affect final price will have to be performed, considering different strategies to cheapen the most expensive items and reduce export price.

— If it is possible, demand structure for the exported product and its sensitivity to price fluctuations will be studied. Other relevant information is to learn what the market price offered by competitors is for identical products, and what differential services they render. These data imply a market research to obtain information on the most relevant variables. Whichever the method used, a fixing of prices has to be made weighing up the main factors prevailing in the market of destination.

— In price formation it is convenient to consider not only the product physical and tangible attributes, but also intangible and psychological attributes perceived by the consumer.

— A very important piece of information to take notice of, is the foreign country-market economic system, and its features, like: existence of inflation, price controls, foreign exchange and financial policies. Regional agreements that link the countries of origin and destination, and that add tariff advantages for intrazone commerce have to be considered in export price design.

— Product price has to be considered not only individually and separately from the rest of the non-exported products, but also in its contribution to the improvement of the company's total earnings and to the best allocation of fixed costs shared by the national and external markets.

— It is convenient to consider the cost of the different services included in a product (warranty, reparation, advisory, etc.) in the formation of the final price offered to the external markets.

— Price is one of the main components that makes part of the company image and is complemented with other attributes, such as quality, quick delivery, adequate package and packaging, and safety in the delivery of the shipment, which, as a whole, condition buyers' purchasing choice.

— The behaviour of ancillary products prices in destination has to be analyzed when fixing prices.

— There exists a technique in the determination of prices for the international markets, that goes beyond a simple numerical calculation and implies certain entrepreneurial intuition and flexibility in each one of its components.

— A correct policy of discounts, considering: payment forms, marketing functions assumed by the buyer, volumes acquired, and regularity of orders, has to be considered.

— It is possible that the company's commercial philosophy considered the offering of a price, as close to the buyer as possible. To do that, it has to use an international price clause (or incoterm) including most components and export expenses (international carriage, insurance, etc.).

## 3.2. Strategy to Fix International Prices

### *3.2.1. General Strategies for Price Determination*

According to the price in force for similar or identical products in the market of destination, the company may fix a low penetration price when it wants to obtain a market quota and progressively evict competitors in its market shares. This is an aggressive policy and may be used in product introduction stage in the market. It may also be used for a product protected by some intellectual property right (like a patent) which is not in the hands of the competition. In this case, the company wants to perform product total coverage and spreading in the market of destination, with an attractive and accessible price.

A policy of high prices compared to the existing ones in the selected market may also be used. The product is commercialized at a higher price than the one in force in the external market because it has certain features: popular brand, high technological development, quality of design or materials used. In some cases, this policy is used to position certain intangible psychological attributes desired by the consumer: status, vanity, social class subculture, etc.

A unique price for all the international markets, which is the same as the internal market price (which would imply an ethnocentric strategy) may be used. In this case, the entrepreneur extends the local price abroad, disregarding local peculiarities of each market, as well as internal and export costs.

The entrepreneur may quote a differential or market adapted price. This is a polycentric strategy that forms price "dexterously", considering each country-market peculiarities. Yet, within each foreign country, there may be different differential prices for each buyer, segment, or geographical zone.

Other alternative is the fixing of a price base for export common to every market, upon which all the adaptations for each specific market will be made. Other option is fixing a new price for that market, because the enterprise does not commercialize this product in the domestic market and, consequently, there is no base price to make adjustments in order to determine the export price.

In some cases, a price near the production costs in order to achieve different objectives, such as aggressive differentiation due to monetary issues as regards its competitors, or to sell off production surpluses, may be fixed. Competitors may react lowering their prices, and a price war may break out, in which a general homogeneous and low price, with very reduced margins of earnings for the intervening companies is achieved.

The company approach may be cost, demand or competition oriented. Orientation to the competition may follow a strategy of price leadership (which is going to be considered as a price of reference in a particular market) and imitation price, which is the one that adapts according to competitors' actions while the company performs follow up of competition prices.

When the price is demand-oriented, the most important variable is how much are consumers willing to pay for a product. In the case of a cost-oriented price it will be determined by the summation of different costs (productive, commercial, financial, and export) plus a margin of profits. The disadvantage of this last method is that it does not take into account the competition, the requirements and needs of the demand, so it is advisable to use it at its purest form, because it may give rise to non-competitive prices in the destination market. If it were used as a promotional strategy in the initial market access stages, the fact that this price policy is very difficult to reverse in subsequent periods has to be considered. The entrepreneur has to conceive costs as the inferior limit when fixing prices, that is, consider costs as a restriction below which prices are not going to be considered.

The enterprise may use a strategy of total costs for the formation of export prices. The entrepreneur fixes the monetary value of the product directed to the external markets, considering fixed costs (those that do not vary with the volume produced such as: rents, machinery depreciation, etc.) and variable costs (those that vary when there are fluctuations of production volumes such as: raw material, containers, etc.). However, some entrepreneurs use a strategy of variable costs for exports, charging all fixed costs to internal market national sales. In this last approach, more competitive external prices are accomplished, but there exists the possibility that the company could be investigated on dumping issues grounds. Dumping is when a product is sold in the external market at a price lower than in the market of origin, and causes damage to the industry of the country of destination. Dumping is internationally considered, within the frame of the World Trade Organization, as a disloyal commercial policy. The importer market may apply antidumping rights to correct the damage caused by that entrepreneurial strategy.

The enterprise may fix marginal prices, that is, what the price of an additional unit for that market would be, which is why it has to calculate marginal costs. This method presents great complexity in companies that use a great number of components with variation in the degrees of its use, in the product manufacturing process. So, it is not an adequate method, because it requires precise information about costs, and implies a great difficulty to estimate them, especially for small companies.

The company may fix certain costs objective that are going to determine the price offered to a particular market; and from that cost objective, the enterprise will start to negotiate with suppliers and reduce internal costs to see how it may achieve a more competitive price. A referential price in force in the country of destination may be also taken into account, and start to disaggregate the different components that make up that price (international carriage, insurance, commercial commissions, etc.) until costs in origin are reached; then, it will be analyzed whether these allow the entrepreneur to have a minimum margin of benefit. This disaggregating policy may be used in products that have international quotation such as commodities. This approach is the opposite to the adding up method (in which the different components that make up the cost are added to obtain the final price); this strategy of addition or aggregation of different costs and benefit is called "escandallo".

In some cases, the company may establish high prices in its introduction in a particular market and adequate them as it tests market acceptance. The entrepreneur gradually produces a decantation of the price as it acquires information and experience in that market.

It is very difficult to get a total standardization for the variable price, because competitive environments, consumers' purchasing power, and state policies that may influence the fixation of prices are different in each country-market. If price global policy wants to be implemented, product positioning will have to be adapted to meet the requirements of each market.

In the price formed, the incidence of the different product optional and accessory components that allow to get differentiation according to the buyer's specific requirements will have to be considered. Entrepreneurs may have a policy of multiple prices, depending on the features of the product required, payment form, services included, marketing undertakings in charge of the buyer, etc.

When fixing a price for a particular country, the product lifecycle stage in which the selected market is, has to be considered (introduction, development, maturity or declination). For example, in a maturity stage, the enterprise is going to look for a competitive price that distinguishes it from the competition, and in a declination stage, it is going to produce an important decrease in the prices offered so as to make the offer more attractive.

In exporting countries with a weak national currency the price may stand out as one of the main benefits and attributes of a product, thus becoming the most relevant differential variable. On the other hand, in countries with a strong currency, offer abroad will be based, especially, in the different services implied by that price (postmarketing, delivery speed, warrant, financing, etc.). In country-markets where there is a high inflationary rate, prices in force will suffer frequent adjustments made by the companies in order to cover replacement value.

### *3.2.2. Strategies for Price Reduction*

The entrepreneur has to fix strategies for exported product price reduction through the implementation of certain activities like:

— Use of imported components to substitute national ones.

— Outsourcing certain production processes (total or partial).

— Performing temporary imports of certain components to add them to the exported product.

— Performing a vertical integration with suppliers.

— Improving company productivity through the incorporation of technologically advanced machinery, or change in manufacturing methods.

— Reducing the range of products offered or eliminating product costly adaptations that may be really unnecessary. In these cases there is a tendency for a reduced offer of products with a high degree of international standardization, which directly results in the reduction of costs.

— Integrating some associative projects like consortia, exportation cooperatives, to reduce certain costs (especially all the fixed ones) and get scale and marketing economies.

— Selecting other more economical alternatives of international carriage, evaluating factors like safety, speed, loading capacity and cost of the different modes.

— Performing relocation of certain productive activities in some markets where comparative advantages could be obtained (production affiliate and productive coinvestment). In particular markets, besides, governmental incentives for the development of production premises may be obtained.

— Analyzing product material quality to assess product economic life, and evaluating whether economic quality is correct. In case it is excessive as regards product life, it is advisable to diminish it.

— Replanning of the company chain of supply by the different suppliers and redesign of the international distribution system, considering in both issues, alternative of elimination or substitution of intermediaries to make the product cheaper.

— Detailed analysis of administrative, financial, productive, and commercial aspects of great incidence in the final price, that may make the product more costly.

— Use of free trade areas with commercial or productive objectives.

### 3.3. Components of the Export Price

The components that make up the exported product vary according to the incoterm (or price clause) used and may consist in a percentual or fixed amount calculated upon the final quoted price. Some of the main items are:

— **Production costs:** They have to include those product costs which are the result of adaptation to legal, cultural or economic requirements of the market of destination.

— Administration, international marketing and financing costs: The following costs are going to be considered: expenditures related to the company export department, international market exploration, obtention of credits to export or manufacture exportable products, bank commissions from financial instruments used (letter of credit, international transfers or documentary collection), international participation in trade shows, among others.

— **Export costs:** This series of expenses include:

- Documentation necessary to export: export commercial invoice, packaging list, certificate of origin and sanitary certificate, customs papers, transportation papers, etc.
- Manuals, labels, etc.
- Internal carriage and insurance.
- Sampling abroad.
- Port taxes and expenses.

- Commissions per commercial contact made.
- Different intervening professionals' fees (customs agents, consultants, etc.).
- Container loading and consolidating costs.
- Export taxation (rights).
- Various inspections costs (phytosanitary, quality, etc.).

— **Export incentives:** If the company received some government incentives, such as refunds or drawbacks, those components should be deducted from the price to make it more competitive.

— **Wished earnings:** They may consist of a fixed or percentual amount on the quoted incoterm or a combination of both.

— **International carriage:** International freight charge, which will vary according to use (water, air or ground) and conditions agreed with the carrier.

— **International insurance:** Insurance cost will vary according to coverage, potential risks, product features, means of transport used, distance covered, among other factors.

— **Interests for external financing:** Components of deferred collection of export operations financing.

— **Expenses in destination:** They are of different kind:

- discharge, port, documentation management and customs tax collection (import tariff barriers).
- internal carriage and insurance.
- intermediation commissions in their different levels (wholesalers, retailers, bonded warehouses, etc.).
- different taxes and duties in destination.

## 3.4. Incoterms

### *3.4.1. Importance of Incoterms and their Functions*

These are price clauses pre-established by the International Chamber of Commerce. These international commercial terms are based on world commercial practices and uses. Every certain number of years, these clauses are updated and they are not compulsory, but they are accepted and recognized by most external world operators. Incoterms 2000 constitute the last published version in force on the edition date of this work. It is important to remark that some countries, like the United States, have their own commercial clauses, similar to the incoterms.

Incoterms objective is to determine:

- — distribution of buyer and seller operation risks, that is, where responsibility upon the goods is transferred from one party to the other.
- — different costs included in the quoted price (for example, whether it comprises international carriage, international insurance, discharge, etc.).
- — implicitly, what documents each commercial operation participant has to manage.

### *3.4.2. Incoterm Individual Features*

Incoterms are divided in 4 groups E, F, C, and D, arranged from those with less sellers' degree of responsibility and expenses to those with higher expenses level and risk transmission nearer the buyer.

#### Group E

***EXW*** **(*ex works*):** The seller makes the goods available to the buyer at the factory door, in its surroundings or in its warehouses (in origin). The sale performed is assimilated to an internal market sale. It is the seller's responsibility to deliver the goods at that place with adequate exporting packaging. The goods are going to be exported and imported by the buyer, who will manage every necessary step and document. In the price, the incoterm EXW will be accompanied by the market of origin city name. It is used by any type of carriage.

#### Group F

***FCA*** **(*free carrier*):** It is used by any carriage modes. The merchandise is cleared for export by the seller and made available to the carrier at a point agreed with every necessary exporting step and document already complied with. Any other expense (international carriage, international insurance and destination expenses) will be the buyer's responsibility. FCA incoterm is always accompanied by the name of the city of origin.

*FAS* (*free alongside ship*): Goods are delivered by the seller *alongside the ship or in lighters* for the buyer to load. It includes all the export procedures and documents already complied with. Other procedures and documents are buyer's responsibility. The incoterm FAS is accompanied by the name of the port of shipment city and is used for waterway carriage.

*FOB* (*free on board*): Commercialized goods are delivered by the seller on board of the ship, with all procedures for export accomplished. All the other procedures and documents are managed by the buyer. FOB is used for waterway carriage and it is accompanied by the name of port of shipment city.

**Group C**

*CPT* (*carriage paid to*): The seller makes goods available to the carrier in the point agreed, cleared for export. But, unlike the FCA, the cost of international carriage is included in the price. All the other components (international insurance and expenses in destination) are paid by the buyer. The incoterm is accompanied by the name of the city of the market of destination and is used for any means of transport.

*CIP* (*carriage and insurance paid to*): It is used by any means of transport. The goods are delivered by the seller and made available to the carrier in the point agreed, with all the export procedures accomplished. But this incoterm includes, unlike the FCA, international carriage and insurance cost. All the payments in destination are made by the buyer. The incoterm is accompanied by the name of the city of the market in destination and is used for any mode of transport.

*CFR* (*cost and freight*): It is used for waterway carriage. The seller delivers the goods put on board of the ship cleared for export. Risk of damage or loss is transferred to the importer once the goods on board of the ship pass the ship's rail in the port of shipment; besides this, the price includes the cost of international freight. All the other documents and expenses are transferred to the buyer. It is only used for waterway transport. The incoterm is accompanied by the name of the port of destination city.

*CIF* (cost, insurance and freight): Goods are delivered by the seller on board of the ship, with all the procedures for export accomplished. At that place, goods risk is transferred. The costs include international freight and insurance cost. All the other procedures, expenses and documents are the buyer's responsibility. It is used for waterway carriage. The incoterm is accompanied by the name of the port of destination city.

**Group D**

*DAF* (*delivered at frontier*): The marketed goods are put by the seller at an agreed point between the exporter and importer countries frontier. All the other procedures, costs and documents, are the buyer's responsibility from the moment the goods are delivered at that place. It is generally used for ground carriage. The incoterm is accompanied by the name of the market of destination city.

*DES* (*delivered ex ship*): Goods are delivered by the seller on board of the ship in the port of destination. All the other procedures, costs and documents, are the buyer's responsibility. It is used for waterway carriage. The incoterm is accompanied by the name of the port of destination city.

*DEQ* (*delivered ex quay*): Goods are made available by the seller, discharged in the port of destination quay. All the other procedures, costs and documents, are the buyer's responsibility. It is used for water carriage. The incoterm is accompanied by the name of the port of destination city.

*DDU* (*delivered duty unpaid*): The goods are delivered by the seller at the place agreed in destination, duties unpaid. All the other procedures, costs and documents, are the buyer's responsibility. It is used for any kind of carriage. The incoterm is accompanied by the name of the city in the market of destination.

*DDP* (*delivered duty paid*): It is delivered by the seller in the point agreed in destination with duties paid. All the other procedures, costs and documents, are the buyer's responsibility. It is used for any kind of carriage. The incoterm is accompanied by the name of the city of the market of destination. It is optimum for the house to house system.

## 3.5. International Quotation

### *3.5.1. Importance of an Appropriate Offer Preparation: Main Components*

The offer or quotation is one of the main commercial documents in which the seller, either by himself or at the buyer's request, communicates product attributes, as well as the main terms and conditions on a potential commercial operation. One of the relevant variables within an international quotation is price, which is the monetary valuation of everything included in the offer.

Some of the offer relevant elements are: a correct description of the merchandise (in its commercial, technical, and customs forms), merchandise tariff item (according to tariff classification rules), means of transport used, merchandise insurance issues, product container and packaging issues, operation payment terms (payment instrument used). Other important element is to establish a date for the validity of offer conditions.

This document has two substantial elements: number offered and price. The number may be specific, or with quantitative limits (minimum or maximum), or it may provide supply during a period of time (i.e. 1,000 monthly units). Total, as well as unitary prices have to be made clear, in relation to the offer numbers, attributes and conditions. The international offer must have the following elements:

— Incoterm used.

— National or foreign currency in which the merchandise is quoted.

— Number of monetary units.

Example: FOB Buenos Aires US$ 10,000.00.

The legend "Incoterms 2000" could also be added to the offer.

### 3.5.2. Other Relevant Offer Factors

Other issues that influence quoted price are: discounts for big orders, fixation of delivery maximum deadlines, special merchandise packaging issues, postmarketing service inclusion, and labelling or presentation modifications. Some contractual issues, like the granting of exclusivity or the fixing of a long term agreement, affect the price the seller offers the buyer. Any of these items may be modified through a counteroffer made by the potential buyer.

If the point of discussion between commercial operators is based solely on price (that is, the foreign counterpart considers it too high), it is necessary to remark more product attributes (quality, services, payment form, etc.), without centralizing discussion only on the price variable. In some cases, foreign companies do not accept the price offered in a first instance, so as to check the seller's negotiating force and the seriousness of the offer.

In the instance of price reduction requests, the company seller does not have to consent immediately, it has to look for a win-win strategy, in which both parties make mutual concessions (for example, the buyer gets a price discount, but, in compensation, warrant time is shortened).

If the price offered by the seller is not accepted, and due to particular issues, like distrust or lack of interest, the buyer does not make a counteroffer, the exporting entrepreneur should ask what he or she considers an "adequate" price would be.

The seller must make a reasonable evaluation of the negotiated conditions, using information previously obtained like: prices offered by the competition, price of final sale valid in the market for that product, usual margins for channel intermediaries in the market in order to make an offer abroad or answer a counteroffer with prices modified by the buyer. The company's responsibility and course in the national and/or international market, as well as the different antecedents in the compliance of commitments have to be pointed out, timely, when negotiating the international price.

Price is a monetary consequence of many variables, among which could be included: product different attributes, operation specific conditions and issues related to the company image and prestige. So, it is important to open the discussion to other issues indirectly related to price when offering a quotation abroad. The entrepreneur has to discover the different motivations of the buyer as regards the product offered when interacting with this company, so as to awaken and keep the interest on the likely commercial operation and satisfy the needs of both parties, in a profitable commercial agreement.

## 4. INTERNATIONAL COMMUNICATION OR PROMOTION

### 4.1. Importance of Communication

#### *4.1.1. Functions of International Promotion*

Communication consists in a series of activities that, together with international marketing strategy objectives, aim at:

- — educating;
- — persuading;
- — informing;
- — reminding.

About some attributes of:

- — product;
- — service;
- — idea;
- — company features.

#### *4.1.2. Communication Constitutive Elements*

This idea of communication implies the existence of an addresser (the one who produces a message), an addressee (the one who receives the message), a message (transmitted from addresser to addressee), a code (a shared system of symbols and meanings used to produce the message), a context in which the communication process is produced (which may be constituted by two or more environments), a point of contact (the moment when the message is transmitted) and a feedback process (through explicit or implicit answers that generate communicational transmission).

Within the context there may be physical noise which could make the message emission or reception difficult (channel distortions, interference in the transmission of the message, etc.). Also there are more significant levels of noise that influence negatively in the process of communication, which is called conceptual noise. When the message is produced, the addresser may have little sensitivity to the addressee's peculiar attitudes, beliefs, academic training and codes. It is very likely that when the addresser creates and emits the message, he or she may not consider the differences in environments between the addresser's and the addressee's. As it has been mentioned, one of the main environments that differentiates country-markets are cultural environments. Different behaviours, preferences, customs and idiomatic expressions that exist in the external markets, generate conceptual noise, which makes it difficult for the addressee to understand the addresser's message. This noise threatens clarity and precision in transmission.

As regards the code, this is composed by symbols, images, words, which may have a different level of signification in the addresser's and addressee's environments. As regards words, there may also exist idiomatic differences between the markets of origin and destination, that require adaptation of the message to a language shared by the two markets. A process of message codification is produced by the addresser and a process of decodification by the addressee, which requires a common language (and an international common language). In communication activity, codes develop as an interactive and continuous process of construction and interpretation of message meaning loaded with a strong symbolic relevance.

The point of contact is the time when the message is transmitted (maybe the encounter between addresser and addressee in a trade show, a potential buyer's reading of a company leaflet). The point of contact reappears when the message is answered, and all throughout the communicational process, successive points of contact generate, sometimes juxtaposed.

It is important to remark that external buyers run their commercial activities by perceptions; their reality is their perception of reality. It is a duty of communication to concentrate efforts to obtain an influence upon buyers' decision process and make them choose the product of the company, among several offered in the market.

## 4.2. Factors that Influence International Communication Actions

### *4.2.1. Main Aspects to Consider from the Communicational Point of View*

International communication must take into account the following factors:

- — Internationalizing company (the one that will conceive the message to be communicated) strengths and weaknesses.
- — Addressee features (consumer, user, society, etc.).
- — Type of product and lifecycle stage in the external market.
- — Actions of communication of the different competitors in the market of destination.
- — Market of destination legal issues that influence the process of communication.
- — External market infrastructure issues (and others related to the economic environment).
- — Communication strategy used (geocentric, polycentric, etc.) and promotional objectives pursued.
- — Different alternative of funds available for communication assignation.

### *4.2.2. Detailed Analysis of International Communication: Main Aspects*

#### 4.2.2.1. Influence of Differential Environments

In the international promotion process, the entrepreneur has to perform an exhaustive analysis and recompilation of information, in order to detect and understand the existing differences between the environments (of the country of origin and that of destination), that make part of the communication context. Communication always has to have the market of destination as a reference criterion. Actions have to be deployed considering addressee's singularities and the prevailing factors in their environments.

The different cultural environments (composed by linguistic elements, symbols, uses and practices, cultural heritage, levels of illiteracy, etc.), which make up the context where the international promotion action is deployed have to be considered. Even in the same culture, there may exist cultural notes or subcultures. The enterprise must be sensitive to the cultural environment so as not to communicate messages that may result harmful or offensive of customs and beliefs in a particular market.

As regards the legal issues of the market of destination, there may exist regulations that limit the use of certain forms of communication as, for example: broadcasting of messages advertising particular products allowed only at certain hours, or prohibition of comparative advertising between products of different companies. This type of regulation may constitute a real barrier to promotion and may promote total redefinition of the communication strategy in a particular country-market.

The degree of similarity that the communicational strategy in destination may have, in relation to the one used in origin, is going to be given by the psychological vicinity between both markets, that is, the existence of similarity between cultures, commercial practices and legal and economic environments.

#### 4.2.2.2. Relevance of the Correct Definition of Addressee and Message Intention

The information addressee (or market objective of the promotional action) may be an industrial user that may have a more rational message demand, or a ultimate consumer, who, in some cases, may demand the production of a message with emotional features. Some actions of communication may have a massive, impersonal audience as objective, and other promotional activities may be more personalized. These issues are going to be closely linked to the strategy of market segmentation implemented and the product and company positioning strategy.

Some messages may have a direct or indirect commercial objective (with a primary objective to promote international marketing) and others may have a non-commercial objective (for example communicating certain ideas or beliefs). Promotion structure may be directed to the intermediaries, when the manufacturing company grants discounts and bonuses, which generates, in turn, more purchasing processes. Also, the intermediaries that benefit with those advantages, become promoters of a new purchasing process in the different subsequent channel levels, until the ultimate consumer. This strategy is called push.

On the other hand, international communication actions may also be directed directly and intentionally to the ultimate consumer, through a pull strategy. In this approach, the organization grants promotions, prizes, discounts and presents aimed at the ultimate consumer that motivates the purchase. It is ultimate demand, the propeller for the different channel intermediaries to get the product, so as to satisfy the demand promoted by the company actions.

#### 4.2.2.3. Message Scope

The main objective of communication is to promote the different attributes of a product like: quality, brand, price, packaging, technological level, design, etc. Promotional activity may be performed in a wide sense, when most differential features, principal as well as secondary, of the product are remarked, or in a restricted way, when only one or two of the main attributes are made known, and the rest of them will appear associated with these. A tenacious international communication strategy allows the generation of consumers' recognition about a product main attractions, and the conditions of loyalty to the company brand, awakening purchase and repurchase desire of the promoted product.

Communication may also position certain company issues—process known as "corporative communication". In these cases, the company looks for a message whose attention is centred in its own organizational image. Through promotional strategy, it tries to point out company differential features like: reliability, prestige, company responsibility, and competence with the objective of producing a good impression in the different addressees upon the history and present activities of the firm.

#### 4.2.2.4. Communication and Product Lifecycle

As regards product lifecycle, certain stages, like introduction, demand a greater presence of some communication forms, such as educational or informative advertising; in the growing stage sales promotion is more forceful, and in maturity stage, advertising for differentiation and memory. These rules are not general, they vary according to the product, market features and competitive environment.

#### 4.2.2.5. Communication and its Relation with the Resources and Means Used

As regards company strengths and weaknesses, it has to evaluate which is the best channel for the desired communication, which is the level of resources that may be assigned to the promotional action, etc.

Entrepreneurs ought to develop international promotion in total agreement with the objectives of the international marketing strategy. Communication uses promotional instruments of its own, that belong to the theory of communication, for strategic objectives to develop external markets.

#### 4.2.2.6. The International Approach and the Communicational Approach

The communicational strategy may be ethnocentric, when the same promotional mix components are used in the internal as well as in the external markets; that is, promotion in the national market extends to the penetrated countries. This strategic attitude may be polycentric, when the enterprise performs adaptations in different aspects of promotion, considering political, legal, economic, commercial, and cultural issues of each country-market.

The geocentric approach is applied, within a global strategy, considering the different countries as one promotional market, with extension, adaptation and innovation practices in communication activities. Within this global strategy, the communicational variable standardization approach may be applied, which implies the use of certain universal elements of total or partial communicational dissemination in every market.

#### 4.2.2.7. Panregional Approach to Communication

Within the regional markets, the enterprise may establish a platform of panregional promotional actions, considering the different country-markets that compose the commercial block, as if they composed a unique market, accomplishing economies of marketing (for example, through a unique advertising campaign) or economies of scale in the unique design of promotional elements (samples and promotional presents, elements of global merchandising). These economies generate lower unitary promotional costs, that are going to be charged to the price of the marketed product.

To establish a communication panregional strategy, the entrepreneur will have to assess the degree of homogeneity that the different countries member of the integration have. In the case when the regional block is composed by very heterogeneous country-markets, points of similarity will have to be found so that they could be used in the application of the communication strategy. Both global as well as panregional strategies allow the company to take advantage of creative ideas for communication, and share them among the different markets accessed.

It has been noticed that there is more than one strategic possibility to select for the compliance of the company with the strategic promotional objectives.

#### 4.2.2.8. Bond between International Communication and Infrastructure, and Activities Developed in a Country-market

As regards infrastructure existing in the market of destination, entrepreneurs have to gather information about the different promotion systems existing in that market, and select the most adequate for the strategy. The existence of marketing agencies, advertising companies, television channels, promotional events, massive and specific publications, among other operative facilities of the country of destination, useful to transmit the company different messages, is important. As regards the number of means used, it may be an exhaustive strategy, which makes use of the greatest possible number, or one concentrated on a few means. The degree of technological progress in that infrastructure and its degree of advance, as compared to that used in countries of great economic development, will also have to be analyzed.

#### 4.2.2.9. Communicational Saturation and Pollution

The enterprise has to know that, in some markets, there is a strong promotional activity which saturates them with messages, and an environment of overcommunication is created; for example, those markets where there is an excess of promotional campaigns, constantly renovated, or those in which there is a visual pollution (and, in a wider sense, communicational pollution), which implies a constant impact of promotional images that affect negatively the behaviour of a particular society. As a result, the consumer becomes indifferent to the different promotional actions of the companies, and, besides, product differentiation becomes confusing and hard. Those effects require the presentation of clear, precise messages, mixed in an ingenious and creative communicational strategy. This implies a clear brand and main attribute differentiation of the product in order to meet consumers' preferences.

#### 4.2.2.10. Associativity in International Communication

As regards economic resources which the company has for promotional actions, different strategies to perform in the case when the company has a low promotional budget available may be proposed. If the enterprise participates in some partnership to gain access to external markets, such as a consortium or an export cooperative, it may look for an associative communication, for example through a unique catalogue that promotes the complete line of products offered by the consortium, or through the participation of the associative structure representative in events, like trade shows or commercial missions. Thus, each partner of the project faces less unitary costs in international communication, since it shares them with all the members of the association.

Other valid strategic actions are joint promotional actions between the exporting company and the one that commercializes the product in destination. In this case, both companies participate in the promotional activity, and share international communication costs, according to the conditions agreed by the parties. In other cases, the exporter grants the company in destination incentives for promotional activities, that this last will develop in its market, as, for example: price discounts, supply of promotional material, etc.

#### 4.2.2.11. Other Issues to Consider

A very significant aspect is the consideration of the different aesthetic issues that affect the communicational approach adopted, with the use of creative techniques of message generation and conception of promotion as a way of artistic expression. Other important aspect of communication comprises the ethical dimensions, that try promotional activities to be responsibly implanted so as not to affect the rights of the others, trying not to send confusing, deceitful or exaggerated messages purposely misleading.

## 4.3. Different Components of the Communicational Mix

### *4.3.1. Advertising*

#### 4.3.1.1. Advertising Definition, Media and Means

Advertising consists in communication paid actions, done by the company in the media oriented to an impersonal public. The most adequate media, categories and means to develop advertising activities have to be determined. The media are numerous: television, radio, public ways, internet (called "virtual advertising"), posters, advertising, etc. Categories are marked by the features that define the different groups in a medium (for example, within the medium radio a category could be sports programmes) and means are the actual instruments used to make advertising (for example, radio programme XX). The following factors have to be evaluated for the election of a particular advertising means: degree of coverage, importance of the means and whether it is specialized or general. Other issues to evaluate are sponsors' features (or company that exploits the advertising business), its experience in the market of destination, services that offers and differential features as regards its competitors. Apart from this, it is convenient to know that international advertising is significantly costly, and so it may become inaccessible for the small and medium-sized enterprises.

#### 4.3.1.2. Style, Image, Subject and Public of Commercial Ads

International advertising seeks to plan certain aspects of the company line of thought, beyond the national frontiers, by sending messages to a multiple and anonymous public. Advertising strategy should reflect the company style and that of its products, targeting messages correctly and avoiding communication distraction.

In advertising there is a message that tries to communicate a correct image of the product and an expressed and impersonal public presentation of the product main features is looked for. One of its objectives is to provide information about the product, that may have an influence on consumers' or users' beliefs and encourage for consumption. Advertising may be done comparatively, when the product is compared with the competition product, but in certain country-markets this approach is banned by specific regulations.

Beyond the reach of the media used, advertising actions are oriented to a multiple depersonalized audience and product purchase is not an immediate aim, as it happens with other ways of communication. As regards the advertising theme, this may have emotional or rational elements according to the market product and segment to which the message is directed. Besides, the message content has to take into account the social differences of the different cultures. As regards the legal issues, certain countries establish restrictions to the advertising actions, such as censorship of some messages or specific timetable restrictions for the broadcasting of such messages.

Advertising always aims at consumers' or users' attention for a particular product, so that they give the purchasing of the product preferential treatment. The continuous broadcasting of advertisements that a company produces generates, in those who receive them, an unconscious process of recollection, which internalizes and affects subsequent purchasing attitudes.

#### 4.3.1.3. Adaptative Approach of Advertising Activities

The advertising strategy has to fix clearly what the objectives are, what concepts or ideas are desired to be communicated. Some messages may contain verbal and non-verbal, communication elements, may also remark visual or auditory dimensions, or may be multidimensional. The entrepreneur has to consider adaptations according to existing linguistic, economic, competitive and socio-cultural differences between the markets of origin and destination. These adaptations are necessary to avoid message misinterpretation.

In some cases, a global approach in the advertising campaign that considers universal elements surviving in the different markets may be established. The message may concentrate on the circulation of product physical attributes or intangible issues, such as the services it provides or the psychological value attributed. However, it is convenient to consider the use of advertising agencies services or sponsors located in the market of destination (that is, an advertising policy with some degree of decentralization), for a better adaptation to the peculiar features of that country.

#### 4.3.1.4. Cooperation in Advertising Activities

Small and medium-sized companies have to have an important budget, in order to implement international advertising actions. In small-sized companies with little financing capacity, cooperative actions (those performed with other companies within a joint exporting plan) or vertical agreements, made with the external buyer to cut down on advertising costs, have to be achieved.

It is important to perform advertising shared among two or more products of different compatible companies. Beyond the approach adopted, every advertising activity has to be instrumented with sensitivity towards the consumer, and to competitors' actions in the country of destination.

#### 4.3.1.5. The Advertising Promise

Advertising may have several functions: informing about some features or uses of a product, reminding of its existence, relaunching the product in the market, differentiating it from the competition, persuading for purchase, and these goals vary according to the product lifecycle stage. Beyond the set objectives, advertising actions always comprise a promise by the company on some aspects of the product. This is implicit in the message which pursues to attract the consumer.

#### 4.3.1.6. Other Aspects of Advertising

The entrepreneur may consider an alternative to the traditional advertising activity, such as advertising in periodicals. The enterprise communicates under cover, through some news that comments on positive aspects of its activities, which generates a greater acceptance in the people. This information is presented, as if the responsible addresser of the message were the mass media.

Finally, the organization has to consider adequately the different advertising innovations, such as advertising in web sites, the use of audio-visual means, etc.

### *4.3.2. Sales Promotion*

#### 4.3.2.1. International Sales Promotion Complexity and Diversity

Acerenza defines sales promotion as "every commercial activity that includes neither personal sales nor advertising or publicity, whose goal is to stimulate consumers' purchase and intermediaries' effectivity".

Sales promotion complements the other international communication activities, such as public relations, advertising and sales force. Incentive marketing is oriented to consumers and users, and to marketing channel intermediaries. There are different forms of sales promotion:

— contests, prizes and bonuses;

— commercial exhibitions and expositions (among which there are trade shows and other international events);

— promotional presents and commercial samples;
— commercial missions and business trips;
— direct postage (via postal mail, e-mail and fax).

### 4.3.2.2. Importance of International Trade Shows and Expositions

#### *4.3.2.2.1. Dynamics and Structure of Trade Shows and Expositions*

Trade shows and expositions are space environments where supply and demand are concentrated for a limited period of time. They were started in the antique Persia and Phoenicia, with their peak at the Industrial Revolution. At present, trade show events are on the rise and diversify offer to such a degree, that it could almost be stated that every product or service has its trade show: food products, construction, information technology, transport, metalmechanic industry, etc.

Following LE MONNIER FRAMIS, professional salons are presented as an optimum instrument that allows to combine synergically the following elements: sales force, advertising, promotion, public relations and market research. They are one of the most relevant components in communication, within the marketing mix, because they allow the exhibitors to attract attendees to the event, by taking them out of their habitual working environment to expose comparatively and multidimensionally the attributes of their products. These commercial meetings allow the generation of a strong interaction exhibitor-visitor. The attendant to the trade show contest is going to have immediate access to a great range of offers that may cover his or her needs, generating a much richer product evaluation and selection process, within a more integral vision of the market. Trade show events are proposed with certain features that differentiate them from other forms of sales promotion: they make use of multiple communication features, are used as global marketing instruments, and consolidate as true communicational knots.

#### 4.3.2.3. Trade Shows Objectives

— Gaining access to a comparative analysis of the competition offer.

— Getting information about agents, distributors, and other intermediaries and generating commercial contacts and agreements to penetrate external markets. It also allows the global recollection of market data, as regards clients' preferences and their requirements in services (premarketing, marketing and postmarketing) related to the product.

— Contributing to the process of sales acceleration, which optimizes the cost-sale/client relationship in a privileged environment for personalized sales.

— Accomplishing a solid image of the organization and increasing its public relations policy.

— Being a strong promotion tool oriented to a particular market, with delimited time and space.

— Performing product and innovation tests and demonstrations.

— Improving the image and morale of the enterprise, gaining a certain position of status and prestige due to participation in international events.

#### 4.3.2.4. Types of Trade Shows

(a) According to their objectives:

— ***Commercial trade shows***: In these events, company products are exhibited, to promote business and diversify markets and products in the world environment.

— ***Image or presence trade shows, expositions***: Exhibitors attend, with the sole intention of being present as an enterprise, without any immediate commercial ends.

(b) According to the character of the organizer:

They may be public, private or mixed.

(c) According to the products offered:
- ***Horizontal or general trade shows***: Different sectors production is exhibited.
- ***Vertical or specialized trade shows***: In these competitions, products of a specific sector are exhibited and they are directed to particular entrepreneurs interested in them. In this type of trade shows, communication efforts are directed to a public objective clearly identified. These are the most useful for the small and medium-sized enterprises that want to internationalize.

(d) According to the number of countries that participate or geographical coverage amplitude:

They may be regional, national or international. The most important are the international shows, in which several countries take part with their industrial or agricultural displays assigned for horizontal or vertical exhibitions.

There are also the so-called trade shows solo in which there is only one exhibitor that displays its products in a closed space.

(e) According to the type of audience:

May be open to the public or with restricted access to particular groups or sectors.

#### 4.3.2.5. Criteria for the Selection of a Trade Show Event

In the international environment, there are numerous trade show meetings, with a sustained trend to the proliferation of specialized events. In order to participate in a professional salon, entrepreneurs, either as attendees or exhibitors, have to evaluate, among other factors:

- the type of product desired to be displayed or found;
- the importance and history of the trade show event;
- audience projected volume and geographical coverage environment of the event;

- sectors and categories of products exhibited at the display;
- importance of the trade show organizing country-market for the company objectives;
- participation cost in the trade show event and its relationship with the company promotional budget (an evaluation based on the potential cost-benefit relationship of the participation in the trade show must be carried out);
- other elements to consider like: possibility of getting some help from intermediate or governmental bodies to participate in the event, reports and commentaries about similar events previously organized in that market, etc.

#### 4.3.2.6. Costs of Exposition in a Trade Show Competition

It is important to consider the different costs, implied by the participation as an exhibitor in an international event, that is:

- Stand hiring costs (generally it is a fixed amount per square meter).
- Stand structure and architectural features (design, materials and exhibition, transit and resting places). The enterprise may provide for stand construction or hiring. Decoration, which includes displays, graphics, photographs, gigantographies, and audio-visual means, etc., is a very important aspect, and so is international carriage.
- Wages, trips and travelling expenses spent by different company representatives who participate in trade shows (executives, sellers, technicians, translators, air hostesses, etc.).
- Promotional material (samples, presents, brochures, catalogues, cards, etc.) and their international transportation.
- Communication costs relative to the participation of the enterprise as exhibitor: mailing, circulars, advertising in specialized media, special invitations, etc. Entrepreneurs

have to know that there are different sources for the obtention of information about potential invitations: company associations, industrial directories, yellow pages, relative to the country exhibitor.

— Other items are: electricity, faxing, cleaning and vigilancy, taxes and duties.

Small and medium-sized enterprises have to consider the participation as a member exhibitor of an official grandstand as an alternative. This will be coordinated by some State body of the country of origin, because in this way the budget for trade show participation will be sensibly reduced. Generally, there is a national schedule, in which the different governmental departments decide which the state trade shows salons will be, and subsidize totally or partially the participation of small-sized companies that exhibit in the national stand.

#### 4.3.2.7. Management of Trade Show Participation

An exhibitor has to coordinate participation in a trade show beforehand, through commitment with all the areas of the enterprise related to the event. A trade show participation plan has to be determined, and a check list of all the activities to be performed at each stage has to be prepared, as well as the main documents and procedures related to the access to the event. A person will be appointed as responsible for the planning and coordination of all the trade show actions so that the enterprise could succeed in the compliance with the set objectives. This person is in charge of the trade show management, which is closely linked to the company's commercial sector, and of the trade show strategy of participation design, as well as of the hiring and coordination of the different commercial and logistic entrepreneurial actions for that event. This responsible person's functions are: synchronization of transport activities, stand and other promotional elements assembling and disassembling, management of dispatch documents, selection and request of promotional material pieces, site selection and commercial lease negotiation for the trade show space, communication action planning, not only during the trade show, but also before and after it as well, evaluation system definition and preparation of a report on the results of the participation in the event.

Due to communication time limitations in the trade show and the great number of attendees to these events (it may be a very heterogeneous public), it is necessary to find a correct policy of contact, which prioritizes quality of the attendees over its number. The people in charge of the stand should adopt an enthusiastic, polite and alert policy of communication, in agreement with the company trade show strategy. Attendees' needs should be evaluated, through a fluent communicative relationship, to "catch" sales potential contacts, that may be subject to subsequent follow up actions. The enterprise may deliver manuals on public relations to the people in charge of the stand; however, building personal commercial relationships also requires creativity and spontaneity.

#### 4.3.2.8. Attitude of Personnel in Charge of the Stand

The correct selection of suitable and commercially trained personnel to be in charge of the stand is very important. These employees must have a complete knowledge of the product and its differential benefits, and they have to be informed about the main aspects of the enterprise's commercial policy as well: price lists, payment conditions, discounts, product delivery and financing. These people are going to be the face of the enterprise during the course of the event, and have to manage perfectly the promotional technique.

Personnel assigned to the stand have to use different means (tastings, demostrations, etc.) to show the different uses, functions, and technical features of the products displayed, and deliver selectively the promotional material. It is possible for the enterprise to detect different qualified contacts, which have to be registered in records with their main data, during the exposition, and interact with them in order to deploy in a stage subsequent to the closing of the event, an activity of follow up and commercial promotion. Daily meetings with all the company personnel that participates in the exposition have to be called during the course of the event to exchange opinions, debate objections and doubts, contrast the results obtained with the objectives proposed and estimate the most significant facts that occur, in order to implement the necessary tactic measures.

#### 4.3.2.9. Results Evaluation of Event Participation

Writing a final report to show the main quantitative and qualitative results that the company obtained as an exhibitor, that is, responsibility of the personnel affected to the event, different communicational strategy activities deployed, number of contacts made and detail of the ones that showed interest in a potential commercial agreement, number of sales operations made and other type of relevant information, is important. This report is useful for the enterprise to assess trade show participation profitability and analyze the adjustments to implement in future events.

### *4.3.3. Other Important Elements of Sales Promotion*

#### 4.3.3.1. Promotional Sampling Abroad

Sampling abroad is relevant for the promotion of international activities. Although a complete offer or quotation sent to the international markets may describe clearly the main conditions of an operation with regard to the physical and chemical features, and other aspects related to product design and quality, it is necessary to send samples to the country of destination, as a complement to the offer made by the potential buyer. Samples are, then, significant objects or models that represent the main product attributes and do not have commercial value. Their only objective is that the external buyer verify concretely the main qualities of the product, and that subject it to the analyses, tests and procedures necessary to corroborate its most relevant features. There are specific norms that regulate sampling, and fix the properties, procedures and maximum values that these promotional elements have to meet.

#### 4.3.3.2. The Use of International Leaflets and Catalogues

Other relevant promotional activity is the one developed through international brochures and catalogues. The difference between them is that the brochure refers to a line of products of the company, and the catalogue refers to the whole spectrum of products offered; the latter also describes some aspects of the enterprise history and evolution. Brochures and catalogues, generally, do not report about product prices, since they are going to be negotiated within each particular operation. This communication material may be sent by post or by e-mail, with a scanned file attached to the message. Design and edition quality, and the inclusion of illustrations and photographs that remark the visual part are very important. Text has to be printed at least in two languages: that of the market of origin and that of destination; catalogues and brochures may also be multilingual. In integration markets, it is possible to use panregional brochures as a communicational element.

#### 4.3.3.3. Other Ways of Sales Promotion

International sales communication and promotion can be performed through business rounds and commercial missions. Other substantial aspects of communication are: the use of promotional videos, interactive CDs and the use and design of web sites. Other sales promotion ways are sales, demonstrations and tastings, contests, prizes for sales volumes, etc.

### *4.3.4. Merchandising*

They are different elements that help to fix consumers' attention on those instruments of promotion, in the development of the company commercial activity. These elements are physically intentionally located in its purchasing environment as a result of the planning process. It has to do with real elements or figurative messages in the point of sale. Some examples of merchandising elements are: posters, promotion elements, product exhibitors, expending machines and product sample machines. Other issues that complement merchandising are: product location and preferential exhibition in the points of sale, as well as other aspects of internal distribution in the commercial points.

In a wider sense, some elements unintentionally placed outside the point of sale that attract the consumers' attention are also considered merchandising. An example of this may be an almanac, that has originally been given to a person, and is used to call occasional onlookers' attention.

### *4.3.5. Public Relations*

#### 4.3.5.1. Public Relations Activities and the Creation of Bonds

Public Relations (PRs) are all those strategic activities, aimed at generating certain image upon the most significant features and aspects of a company. This way of communication is oriented to certain groups objective, which become the centre of interest of relational actions. PRs are composed by a series of personal actions conceived to make people perceive prestige in the enterprise, and its effectivity grows when it is implemented permanently. Public relations look for the legitimation of the performance of the organization that develops these actions, to ratify its credibility within the environment of a society. In a restricted sense, relational activities may be directed to clients, suppliers, institutions, governmental intermediate bodies.

#### 4.3.5.2. Different Activities that Make up PRs

Public relations may use a varied group of actions to generate positive attitudes towards the organization. Among the most important there are:

— Company presence in different social events, charities, sports, artistic and scientific events, and sponsoring of certain activities.

— Contests, competitions, etc.

— Invitation to representative bodies or to other companies to visit the enterprise facilities.

— Issuance of informative publications and bulletins about the company activities performed.

— Events such as the opening of plants, premises; development of specific technology, and launching of new products. Organization of light meals, and lavish attention are also included.

All these activities do not pursue direct sale, but positioning of the salient aspects of a company's organizational culture.

In a wider sense, public relations may also be directed to internal personnel of an enterprise (through presents for employees, meetings with every sector of the company, suggestion mailboxes, etc.).

### 4.3.6. Sales Force

Sales force or personal sales tries to communicate, in a face to face process or through telephone or virtual marketing, information about the company products. Its objective is to generate lasting relationships between the company and the client. A restricted concept of sales force is limited to company's internal representatives, that is, sellers.

Sales force has to be flexible, have a qualified formation on the product of which information is provided, and on the main marketing techniques. The people who compose it have awaken positive beliefs about the products they offer, within commercial relationships social environments. Sales force has to be motivated, in order to promote company operations, and sellers are authorized to close deals. Employees at this function have to be tenacious, tactful, convincing, competent, and have communicative skills to adapt their message in each commercial relationship started with flexibility. In some cases, technical and commercial training may be promoted by the same enterprise, using a standardized training policy. However, company representative have to adapt their treatment and commercial orientation when carrying out promotional actions in long psychographic distance markets with regard to the market of origin. Sales force, also, may have some kind of participation in organization product pre- and post-marketing service.

A wider concept of the term considers that there also exists sales force in different intermediaries, such as agents, distributors, etc. They are not employees of the company, but free lancers framed within the commercial policy of the exporting enterprise.

### 4.3.7. Package Communication

The package, apart from protecting and containing the product, has a function of exhibition or appreciation. These communication actions of the package deploy silently through colours, typography, labels, contrasts, space, and shapes, whose objective is to awaken consumers' interest. When designing the package, it is fundamental that a visual communication designer together with the entrepreneur, consider the different aspects of product promotion. Container shape, as well as its use and a balanced combination of colours, that identify and differentiate it from the ones offered by the competition, is very important. Other qualities to consider are: legible exhibition of the brand and texts, as well as an adequate language, to attract and keep consumers' attention, and position a container-product relationship in their minds.

Through an attractive package design, the company product is individualized among all the products offered in the market. The package also contributes to the satisfaction of consumers' needs and fantasies, clearly differentiating products in the purchasing process.

The exporting enterprise uses the package as an information and communication channel, as direct as possible, with the consumer. An adequate package design for international marketing has to consider, not only technical, legal, handling and carriage aspects, but also visual and creative features from the artistic point of view. A good industrial and graphic design is necessary, so that the package becomes a sales instrument that creates links between the product and the consumer.

A SME entrepreneur has to create a package to form the product "position" in consumers' minds, through presentation style and symbols included. The enterprise should analyze ultimate consumer in destination main psychological and sociological features to get that positive and differentiated image in consumers' minds.

### *4.3.8. Communication and Positioning*

#### 4.3.8.1. Relationship between Promotion and Positioning

The product positioning process consists in a series of cumulative activities so as to get a privileged place in the addressee's mind. Positioning is developed through the different company communicative skills oriented to a particular market, and aims at dominating the main area with its product, within its category, in consumers' and users' mental processes. Some powerful positioning elements are brands and containers, apart from other important product attributes. The idea of positioning is to achieve product priority in the purchasing decision process, as regards the other goods existing in the market.

#### 4.3.8.2. Simplicity in the Message Issued

Messages have to be realistic and simplified, with an appropriate correlation between the product and the buyer's perceptions. According to AL RIES and TROUT, it is important to know that the consumer has mental ladders, and the company product must be placed in the highest steps.

As there are multiple offers, similar products that flood the market, and that affect the buyer's receptivity, the message has to be simple but convincing, without data overload, so as to get a position of power, making reference to the company product main attribute that differentiates it from the competition's. This product differentiation must look for mental blanks in consumers' mind, to position the product. Some effective international positioning techniques are:

- Widening a market buyer database. That is, within the same market, issue messages that extend consumption to other segments.
- Applying positioning to widen international geographic coverage (extending a product that has been accepted in a particular country-market, to another market).

Both strategies try to position product effectively, and are always implemented within a frame of verisimilitude and flexibility.

#### 4.3.8.3. Brand Communication-Positioning Relationship

As regards international brands, it is of fundamental importance the use of individual brands for positioning, which may allow a brand-product identification without ambiguity. However, it is generally advisable to use organization brands, that is, brands that are not individual, for those products of small size and value, for those in which the market is saturated, in the case of inputs and raw material, or when the product does not have an advertising budget to support the brand, among others.

### *4.3.9. Country Image*

#### 4.3.9.1. Country Image and Internationalization

Country image encloses multiple factors that superimpose and interrelate. This image is made up by the different symbolic representations that, on a global projection, reflect the most important features that differentiate a country from the rest, in the world environment. Country image is a perception of a country as a whole, however, it is composed by different elements:

- — A country's culture and history, and currect affairs.
- — Political system dynamics.
- — Issues of economic development and commercial policies.
- — Native inhabitants' distinctive features.
- — Physical factors: relief, natural landscapes, resources, climate, etc.
- — Relation State-society.
- — Principles of liberty and equality of opportunities.
- — Financial situation and compliance with commitments.
- — Levels of technological development.
- — Country negative aspects: war involvements, kidnapping, drug dealing, deforestation, corruption, etc.
- — Approach adopted in international relationships.
- — Main industries and services.
- — Importance of the country in world commercial activities and main products sold.

Country image is a complex association of ideas conceptualized in consumers' and buyers' minds in the rest of the world. Those perceptions may or may not coincide with the different aspects of a country reality, and deal jointly and synthetically with the global meaning of it.

In general, country image may have negative or positive qualities. It may happen that the big number of negative factors make up a totalizing universe, which may hide or overshadow the positive features. The adequate consideration of the country image by the entrepreneur is of fundamental importance, since this directly or indirectly affects upon its international commercial operations. The entrepreneur exports as a member component of a country, and a multidimensional relationship between image company-product and country image is produced.

#### 4.3.9.2 Entrepreneurial Attitudes as regards Country Image

The organization has to consider country image as an uncontrollable factor to be taken into account when devising the communication strategy. The positive aspects of country image related to the product have to be emphasized. The entrepreneur has to reach a synergic conjunction among the most valuable aspects of country image and the product qualities, to add more value to the product and give it additional features. When analyzing this image, the enterprise has to ask itself the following question: Which are the main issues in my country-environment that may be positively related to the product to be internationally promoted? After discovering the country image main quality associated to the company, a communicational strategy that may produce the linkage between this attribute and the ones that make the commercialized product has to be created.

## 5. INTERNATIONAL DISTRIBUTION

### 5.1. General Aspects of Distribution

#### *5.1.1. Relevance of International Distribution*

This variable is part of the international marketing mix and is also known as international distribution. Some authors, like LEVY, define it as marketing logistics, or distribution function, to those activities that include "planning, implementation and control of the nets that connect the company to the ultimate consumer through which marketed products and required information flow physically in such a way that maximizing service level and minimizing cost level optimize the integrated marketing strategy objective".

Distribution channels are composed by a series of levels that relate the company with ultimate consumer or user. From a total logistic approach, there are not only external channels, but also internal channels that make traffic of materials through the company structure easier. In this approach, those activities of material supply, inputs and goods for resale, which flow from suppliers to the company are also included. That is to say that logistic integrated strategy considers all material flow towards, through, and from the company.

### *5.1.2. International Distribution Tendencies*

At present, in the international commercial environment, there is a tendency to the concentration of the different distribution forces in big global chains. A phenomenon of distribution channels oligopolization is produced, and a progressive participation at international level of megabuyers, such as global distribution chains, that hoard a great percentage of world coverage. In the retailing marketing there is a great proliferation of big specialized areas, supermarkets and hypermarkets, that expand intercontinentally. There also exists a proliferation of strategic partnerships and agreements among the different levels of the distribution channels.

### *5.1.3. International Distribution Entrepreneurial Concerns*

Concerns on the most adequate distribution channel selection, within the variety existing in a particular market, may be influenced by:

— geographic concentration of the clients;

— consumption habits and preferences of the segments to which the company orients its efforts;

— existing distance between the market of origin and that of destination, and issues that may make it difficult to access that market;

— other features of the penetrated market (existence of rural populations, weather and topography peculiarities of the market in destination);

— existing distribution infrastructure (availability of means and premises that allow the introduction of a particular product in a country-market to reach the consumer or user);

— the type of product to distribute (end use, industrial, selective, exclusive, etc.);
— service level to be rendered in distribution (consumer-oriented, postmarketing, reparation, warrant, etc.);
— different distribution costs and their relationship with the company budget;
— relationship between the chosen system and the company marketing strategy;
— degree of compatibility of channel with the distributed product;
— different intermediaries features (level of market knowledge, negotiating capacity, performance, contacts and influence on different public and private entities);
— percentage of market coverage of the different distribution systems;
— the existence of governmental rules that affect distribution in destination.

### *5.1.4. Distribution as a Differentiating Element*

The small and medium-sized enterprise has to achieve differentiation in the distribution systems used, but the level of control that it can exert upon the distribution structures existing in a particular market is little. International distribution structures exert in a particular market do not suffer modifications in the short term and have to be considered as uncontrollable variables for the small and medium-sized enterprise. However, the enterprise can perform a flexible strategic planning of the international distribution variable, since there are different alternatives to distribute a product in a particular market.

The entrepreneur has to deepen the analysis to evaluate the most convenient system for the company's international objectives, that is, determine which intermediaries have greater active presence, control and dynamics in the distribution functions. The company has to look for an efficient distribution system, attempting for total channel approach, making agreements that bond coordinatedly the different intermediaries within a global vision.

### *5.1.5. Distribution as an Access Obstacle to External Markets*

International distribution may be constituted as a paratariff barrier when distribution structure complexity existing in particular country-markets, blocks or hinders specific products access. The distribution variable is rarely standardizable in the different external markets, due to the strong influence of legal, economic, technological and cultural environments in this system.

## 5.2. Distribution Functions

### *5.2.1. Distribution Activities: Main Aspects*

Distribution activities may be performed with company resources and personnel or be externalized, by directing it totally or partially to specialized intermediaries. The greatest degree of externalization of those functions will depend on specific factors, like a long psychographic distance between the markets of origin and destination, and the difficulty of accessibility to the country selected. Other factors that influence delegation of functions distribution to third parties are channel presence and control level of a particular intermediary, differentiated technology used for service rendering, extra services provided by a particular intermediary, knowledge about a particular country-market and aggressiveness in positioning within its level. Some issues to consider when choosing an international distribution structure are: seasonal or regularity of orders, geographical distance, shipment volumes and dissemination of clients in the country of destination.

### *5.2.2. Zoning and Distribution*

The concept of zoning is important to analyze in distribution. Zoning consists in detecting the concentration of a significant number of potential product consumers for a company, on the base of wealth, social and cultural rates in particular geographical units. In general, external clients are not distributed uniformly in the whole area of the market of destination. Each country-market has big concentration areas towards which the company has to direct its vital distribution efforts. These big zones generally coincide with big cities, which are centres of attraction to other cities and neighbouring towns, making up truly integrated regions from the economic and commercial point of view. A small and medium-sized company with low budget to implement international operations, will firstly have to direct its connections to these big areas, so that it could later expand penetration to the rest of the country-market.

### *5.2.3. Distribution Work Division*

Distribution has to be considered as a strategic service for an effective penetration in the market of destination. Distribution functions are characterized by a great heterogeneity and complexity of processes, which comprise a strong specialization in every activity developed. A distribution channel is composed of different intermediaries that may be divided in commercial (wholesaler, retailer, etc.) and facilitators (carriers, bonded warehouses, insurance companies, etc.). An effective distribution system needs the coordinated intervention of intermediaries that handle adequate distribution know-how, and which allow the transference of the product from the factory to the ultimate consumer. It implies a division of work among the different intermediaries that, due to the high level of speciality, reach economies of scale in the development of the different activities within the channel.

Commercial intermediaries may be intermediary agents, who are those that promote sales without taking physical possession of the merchandise, or trading intermediaries, who buy merchandise for resale.

### *5.2.4. Flows that Make up the Distribution Channel*

Selected channel dimension and structure have to be conceived within a cooperative frame among the different intermediaries. These latter do not have to be considered in isolation, but as partners in a team that generates different physical, transactional and informative flow exchanges.

Physical flow exchanges within the distribution channel involve functions like:

— management of materials inside the factory;

— stock policies;

- goods storage and merchandise dispatch;
- policies of central, regional or local warehouses;
- management of link of international carriage (selection and coordination of means) and goods insurance among the different points of stock.

The objective of physical exchange is to achieve a synergic logistic activity without fracture in its different stages.

Transactional exchange flows comprise functions like:

- negotiation among the different intermediaries of benefit margins, services cost, functions and responsibilities of each one;
- sales and promotion tactics;
- financing of operations;
- granting of discounts, bonuses, etc.;
- application of the contractual clauses that relate to the different members of the channel: minimum purchase volume, stock reserves, commercial objective compliance, rescission of the relationship among the different members of the channel, etc.

Transactions exchange aim is to achieve an adequate level of economic, financial and legal compensations for the different system participants. These objectives have to be framed within a maximization of service rendered to the different intermediaries, users and consumers, with a cost minimization of services rendered.

Communicational or informative flows group a series of functions:

- orders issuance and processing average time of its items;
- response capacity, or reaction time, on different level requirements;
- communication of consumers' preferences among the different channel levels;
- information about demand fluctuations;

— claims for quality, specifications, breakage, etc.;

— communication of reference price to be implanted at each level.

This communication exchange objective is to achieve an efficient information system, which could allow for minimum levels of security in distribution service maintenance.

### *5.2.5. Time, Place and Presentation, and their Relationship with International Distribution*

International distribution function allows for three important variables compatibility. They are:

— time;

— place;

— number (and other issues about product presentation).

An effective channel allows amounts offered by the manufacturer to be adapted to the demand requirements, through the different activities of fractioning, grouping and assembling of assortments, which adapt the dispatched product from the company in origin, to introduce it adapted to consumers' or users' preferences in the external market.

An efficient system management allows goods produced by the company in its country of origin to become available to the external market where the consumer is. This function, that covers long geographical international distances, which separate production from consumption places, is articulated through different processes like carriage, storage, etc.

Production and consumption times harmonization are also very important in distribution. These goals are reached through supplies activities, frequent orders, constitution of adequately sized reserve stocks, etc.

It is noted that total international distribution, which is a system that includes international markets penetration channel, plus the distribution channel in destination, pursue correct product positioning for the satisfaction of psychological and physiologic consumers' needs, with time, number and place issues in mind, linking two markets geographically separated. Its efficacy will be based on its capacity to balance geographic distribution, chronological and preferences gaps that exist between consumer and producer units.

### 5.2.6. Different Distribution Approaches

Channel structure will vary according to the type of product. Generally, short or direct channels, in which there are few or none commercial intermediaries, respectively, are used. This type of channel is widely used when valuable, perishable, specialized with highly technical components, or that need a particular postmarketing service goods are distributed. On the other hand, the distribution channel may be longer for products of little value, small, or of massive consumption. Industrial consumption products generally have shorter channels than end use channels.

The density of the distribution system will be given by the number of intermediaries that exist at a particular channel level. Distribution may be intensive, also called "indifferentiated" (when it uses the greatest number of intermediaries possible per level). Distribution may be differentiated through a selective approach—when only some intermediaries are chosen—, or exclusive—when only one intermediary is used—. In intensive distribution, the manufacturer serves the channel an important service of promotional support for product sale, whereas, in the exclusive channel these communicational functions are mainly assumed by the intermediary, who concentrates all the benefits of marketing the product.

Distribution physical coverage is the quotient between the number of intermediaries used by the company in a particular level, and the total of intermediaries in the same level that exist in the penetrated market. Distribution sales coverage comprises the organization sales amount at a particular level, and the total of potential sales for the market in that level ratio. This coverage measures penetration level in a particular country-market.

### 5.2.7. Non-authorized Distribution Systems

The existence of grey markets, or marketing of products by alternative channels not authorized by the company, is becoming more and more common in international distribution. These markets seriously threaten competitiveness and the equilibrium of the formal distribution structure. The existence of intermediaries that commercialize a product originated in non-authorized deviations and disloyal commercial policies may give rise different negative attitudes in the members of the channel, which may seriously affect their interactions (lack of collaboration, reduction in services, loss of interest in the product line, etc.).

#### *5.2.8. Linking of Distribution Systems and International Penetration Channels*

Following GARCÍA CRUZ, international distribution is closely related to international marketing channels that the enterprise chooses for a particular market, according to the risk and the level of commitment assumed, and the flexibility and control upon external operations. It may be a distribution through direct access (sales agents, distributor, seller or sales branch), an indirect access (through purchasing traders, trading companies) or a concerted access (through structures like export consortia and cooperatives, coinvestment, licences and franchising).

### 5.3. Distribution and Product Final Demand

#### *5.3.1. Consumer or User Oriented Activities*

The distribution strategy is directly related to the company product final demand features. All distribution channel integrated and coordinated activities have a final and last addressee upon which all the efforts fall, who is the ultimate consumer. It is necessary to design a system of intelligence that allows to get information on the market of destination. This information system must detect, as regards consumers:

— their preferences (product design, required amounts, and other features and perceptions of target-market);

— fluctuations in the purchasing behaviour and consumption pattern (whether demand is temporary, fixed or unpredictable);

— more adequate attraction and communication strategies to motivate marketing processes;

— service requirements (security, speed, adequate variety, postmarketing, etc.);
— **client concentration** in a particular market.

### *5.3.2. Obtainment of Information about Target Markets*

This information flow will be determined not only by explorations made by the company, but also by distribution channel transdirectional communications. That is to say that information about the consumer or user is not only a manufacturing company in origin responsibility, but of all the autonomous intermediaries that make up the structure. The objective is the optimization of the total use of the distribution system, improving reliability so as to reduce to the minimum mistakes in prediction and the costs due to unattended sales. However, it is important to know that demand features are estimated forecasts, and only partial information is used in an environment of great uncertainty. Demand tendency distribution for certain international products does not have uniform parameters, it is variable and asymmetric.

The distribution structure tries to soothe intercultural differences that exist between the markets of origin and destination. The use of expert intermediaries with knowledge of the market of destination and their familiarization with the commercial practices and uses distinctive of every country permit the achievement of a systemic, integrated, compensated and with adequate response capacity to the requirements that the structure demands.

### *5.3.3. Adjustments in the Distribution System According to Demand and Channel Requirements*

Final demand and channel intermediaries different requirements may encourage some logistic adjustments within the system, in order to improve global sales:

— Improvement in transmission orders and reduction of reaction times for their compliance.
— Adjustments in channel supplies costs at different levels.

— Constitution of optimum reserve stocks geographically centralized or decentralized, stock cost management and use of own or somebody else's warehouses. The main function of inventories is to soften economically and financially the distribution system, for an adequate attention or orders requested.
— Choice of specific means of transport, weighing factors like: speed, safety, convenience, compatibility means-product, freight cost and delivery costs, waiting times cost, product fragility, accessibility, use of containers, unitary volume of merchandise, importance shipments and product value-weight ratio.
— Insurance of the merchandise along the international itinerary considering: type of product, means of transport, type of packaging, risks to which the product is exposed, etc.
— Improvement of the relationship among: inventory points, carriage systems and average time of response to the buyer's order.
— Efficiency in market coverage in the case of demand physical dispersion.
— Optimization of internal transport and manipulation of shipping products. Use of manual, mechanic or automatic means, cranes and tractors, conveyor belts and frames, separation of work and reserve areas, reception, goods classification and selection, internal movements register and use of information processing equipment.
— Production reprogramming according to orders. It takes a higher operative and productive frequency and higher financial investment to comply with buyers' requirements.
— Creation of financing systems (all along the channel to the ultimate consumer).
— Planning of expedition and traffic of products that improve company contact with external markets, with

activities like: revision of delivery due dates, revision of numbers shipped and packaging conditions.

— Relocalization of storage structures or stocks networks, which allow for product availability.
— Consideration of product loss by issues like: fragility, breakage, deterioration, obsolescence, customs, seasons, etc.
— Generation of alliances to contact closely each one of the intermediaries, to optimize the efficiency of integral distribution and increase its competitive power (greater logistic competitiveness).
— Use of free trade areas for labelling, transformation, grouping, consolidation, transferring and other handling operations of the exported goods.
— Implantation of technological and commercial innovations (internet, intranet, EDI—electronic data interchange) applied all along the channel.
— Revision of the cost-service relationship in each of the distribution chain links, and consideration of additional alternatives to implement in every channel level.

The enterprise has to procure a constant improvement in intrachannel relationships, minimizing conflicts and obstacles that may be produced in its different activities looking for the organization of a balanced distribution net.

### *5.3.4. Pull and Push Distribution Strategies*

The company may have two kinds of distribution strategies to influence demand. In the push strategy, the enterprise grants certain motivations to the intermediary channels, like purchasing discounts, financing, bonuses, in order to promote purchase to the immediate next intermediaries, until reaching the consumer. It is also called mixed communication and distribution push through channel strategy, and the producer looks for final demand stimulation in an indirect way, through the different activities implemented by intermediaries for that effect.

In the pull strategy, the producer orients motivation efforts directly to the final demand with cash discount coupons, sales promotions, presents, so that consumers order the product to the different intermediaries and generate supplying attitudes in these to satisfy the demand. This is known as communication and distribution mixed strategy of pulling through the channel.

## 5.4. Relationship between Distribution and Other Mix Variables

### *5.4.1. Convergence among the Different Variables*

A company international distribution policy must be framed within the international marketing strategy objectives. The distribution system has to be optimized, and consider the different changes produced in the other international commercial mix variables: product, price, and promotion.

### *5.4.2. Interrelation of Mix Components*

The selected via of distribution is going to be in close relationship with the product and its tangible and intangible features, as well as with the target segment to which it is oriented. Modifications made in the product container or packaging may sensibly affect the carriage, storage, and goods manipulation cost, among others. When product intangible issues like psychological attributes are modified, these new qualities may reposition the modified product in a new segment which may require differential distribution systems. The inclusion of additional services (like shortest response time to order, higher delivery security, greater variety at each point of sale) creates, in turn, higher costs at the chain of distribution different levels (for example, stock increase, higher dispatch, reception, register costs), which are going to affect the product final price. There is a bidirectional relationship between the promotion and distribution variables, as it was studied in push and pull strategy implementation, as well as in the different communicational aspects that make up a distribution system.

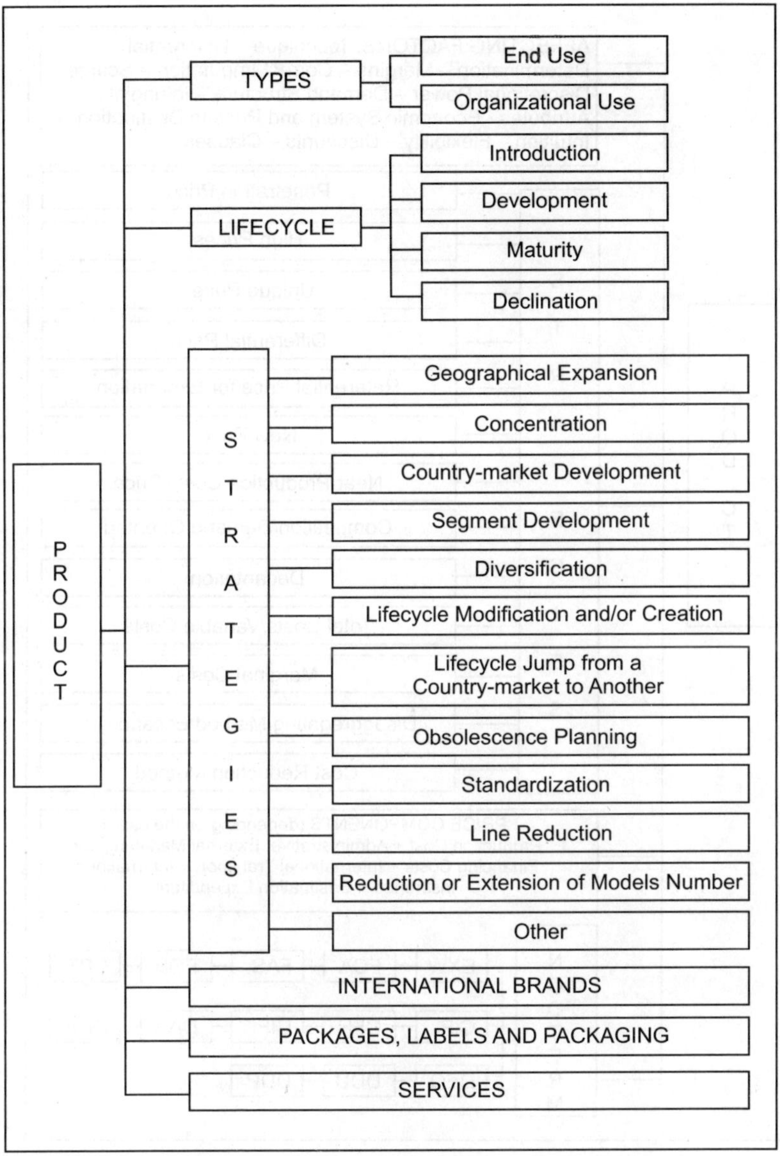


**Figure 5.1.** International Product Variable

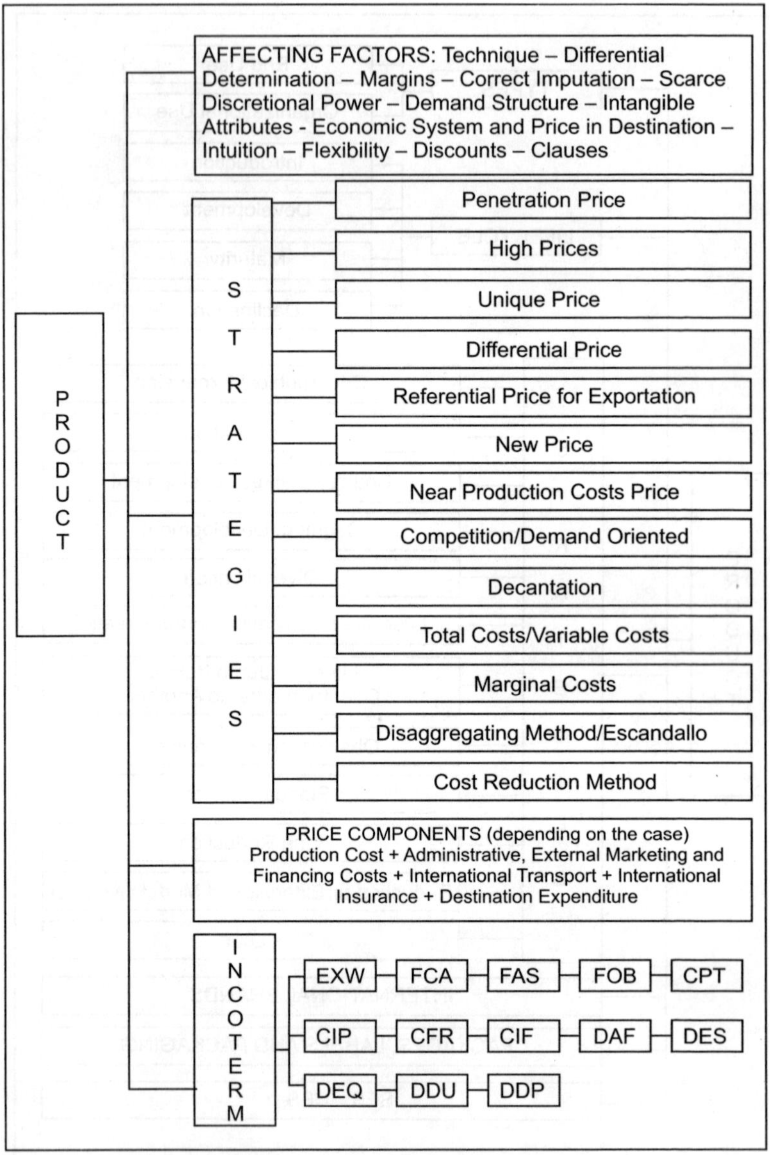


**Figure 5.2.** International Price Variable

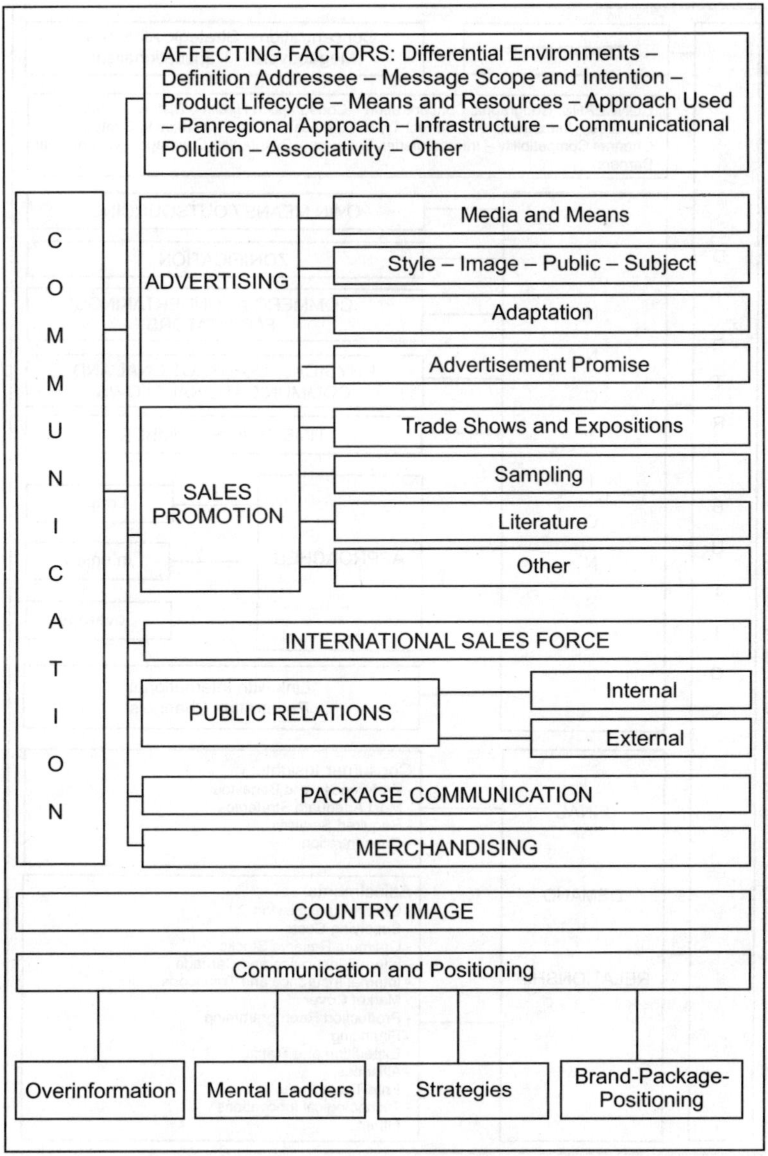


**Figure 5.3.** International Communication Variable

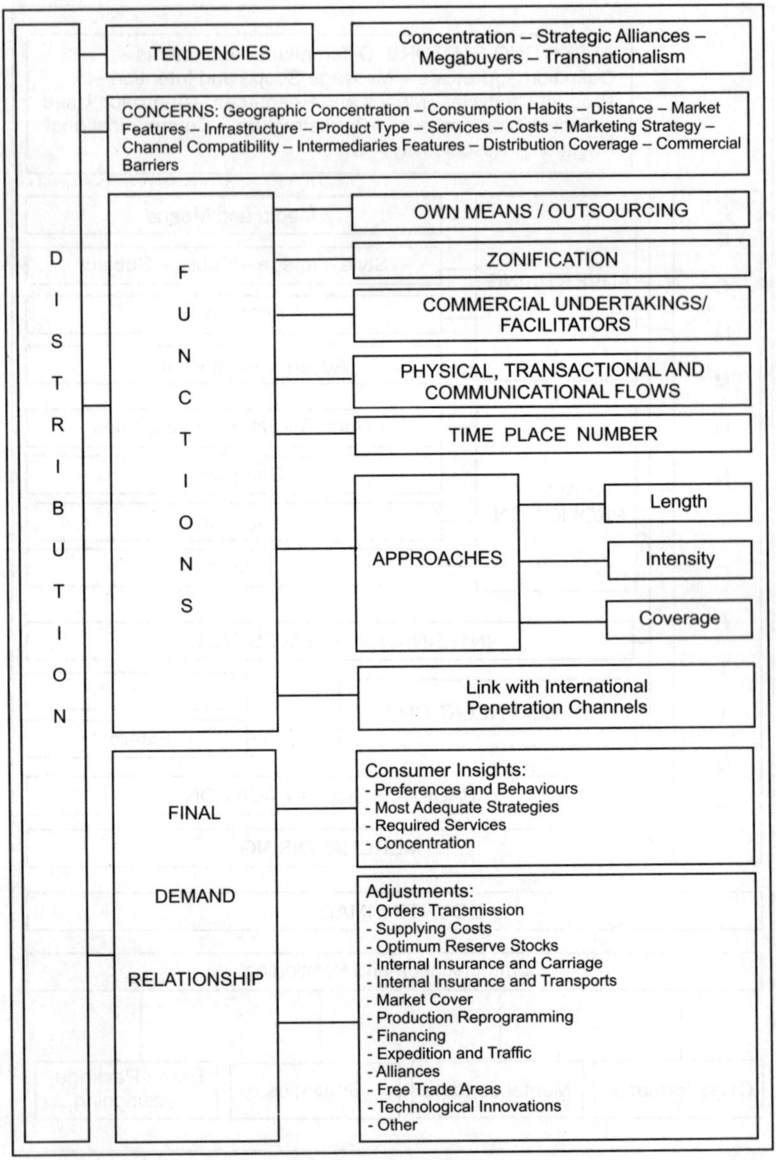


**Figure 5.4.** International Distribution Variable

# 6

# SMEs Basic International Marketing Channels

## 1. INTERNATIONAL MARKETING CHANNELS

### 1.1. Definition

International marketing channels, also called world market penetration policies, could be defined as those different company structures that perform or facilitate, totally or partially, the undertakings implied by the internationalization of a company.

A company internationalization implies a gradual and constant assumption of commitments of different kinds (financial, human, productive, among others), which allows a progressive connection with external markets, and which promotes the generation of commercial agreements in the medium and long term. The concept of internationalization can be thought of from the exporting as well as from the importing operation point of view. Unless a specific remark pointed out the opposite, the meaning of that term used in this book is from the exporting point of view (and, in a wider sense, it will also include some other ways of international marketing, like franchising, licences, direct investment, manufacturing contracts, etc.).

### 1.2. Differences between Marketing Channels and Distribution Systems

International marketing channels are different from distribution strategies in that the latter limit themselves to the creation or use of channels within the destination country (that may be direct channels, or with a large number of intermediaries like wholesalers, retailers and agents). On the other hand, international market penetration policy consists in the constitution of channels that only reach product actual entry in the destination market. In practice both concepts may be considered together (international marketing channels + distribution strategies in the destination market), as integral or total international marketing channels.

## 2. FACTORS TO BE CONSIDERED FOR EXTERNAL MARKET PENETRATION

A small and medium-sized organization entrepreneur who wants to have access to international markets with his or her product has to know that there is not only one standardized way to gain access. There are different factors that should be assessed in order to enter a product in the global markets, which will directly affect the selection of the access channel. Among the most important there are:

- Kind of product commercialized in the internal market (differentiated or indifferentiated product, industrial or for ultimate consumers, etc.).
- Market knowledge degree the company that wants to have access to the world market possesses (in some cases, it is even unknown which the most convenient market for a product is).
- Level of knowledge of the different aspects of international marketing: export operations, management of international commercial documents and means of payment, insurance and carriage hiring, and detection of business opportunities.
- Competitive environment features of the destination market. That is, how concentrated competition is, what the number of competitors is, and what their distribution participation in the market is.
- The existence of strong tariff (taxation on imports) or paratariff barriers (quota for imports; bureaucratic, customs, packing, commercial documentation and

quality regulations), that hinder access to the market through exportation.

— Market size and its features: Market size, as well as its cultural, political and economic features that make it different from the market of origin, will have to be analyzed.

— The degree of risk (closely related to the levels of income yield capacity that each operation may render) the company is willing to accept in internationalization. There are channels like direct investment or product manufacturing in the destination market, which carry a higher risk for the operator that enters international markets. However, other channels such as trading companies that buy the product directly to the manufacturer in order to export it later at their own risk, represent less risk for entrepreneurs.

— Number of resources (financial, human, productive, etc.) that the company devotes to international activity.

— Degree of control that the organization wants to keep over the international marketing process.

— Internationalization stage of the company.

## 3. TOTAL OR PARTIAL EXTERNALIZATION OF THE INTERNATIONAL ACCESS PROCESS

### 3.1. Ways to Gain Access to External Markets

Generally, the company may internationalize in different ways:

— Via export.

— Through partial or total production in destination.

— By other mixed or non-conventional ways (licences, franchising, manufacturing contract, etc.).

The entrepreneur who penetrates world markets with a product always outsources the execution of some of the investigative, financial, operative, sales, documentary, distributional, or promotional activities. It is important to emphasize that, from the operative and commercial point of view, there are differences in the **range of services** rendered by intermediaries to whom the company diverts activities, irrespective of whether it is a market of origin or destination.

From the commercial point of view, when export is carried out, the company productive process concentrates in the country-market of origin, and the marketing of the manufactured products develops in the external market. Export includes a series of operative procedures, business papers, statements and specifications in customs of origin and destination, loading and discharge operations, insurance and storage, being among the most relevant. Export can be carried out in a direct or an indirect way.

From an operative-commercial approach, in direct export there is no participation of any intermediary located in the market of origin that could facilitate or perform activities that may contribute to the marketing of the company products in destination. In direct export there may be intermediaries who may contribute with the exporting company, but they will be located in the destination market, that is, in the importer's country market.

On the other hand, in indirect export there exists, as an indispensable requisite, some intermediary's help for internationalization of the company products based in the market of origin. In some cases, it just buys the product from the manufacturing company in order to export at its own expense and risk; on other occasions, it establishes links between the external buyer and the national manufacturer to promote sales.

### 3.2. Advantages and Disadvantages of Direct and Indirect Export

If a comparison between direct and indirect export is made, what is an advantage for the former becomes a disadvantage for the latter, and *vice versa*.

In direct export, the company gets a larger income yield capacity, because there is no need to pay retribution to any intermediary located in the market of origin to facilitate the operation. This approach allows a greater control of the marketing channel, since it is the company, deploying its own resources, the one that gains access to external markets. This factor enhances a learning capability and operative and commercial functioning of external markets feedback. But, in turn, direct export has a higher risk for the organization, especially when it does not have enough experience in world markets commerce and marketing.

Indirect export allows the company to have access to international marketing, totally or partially delegating the following undertakings to a third party: detection of business opportunities, international offer and negotiation, operative and documentary procedures, management of financing instruments. This intermediary possesses know-how on those aspects and qualified experience in global markets, virtues that are not generally typical of the companies that require its services. In indirect export, the company outsources the process totally or partially, leaving the activities mentioned in the hands of intermediation, thus reducing the risk and uncertainty implied by internationalization.

When indirect export structures are frequently used, the organization may obtain a null or poor learning about international market operation, because that information is concentrated on the structures of the assisting companies. There are some exceptions to this, like is the case with export consortia in which, although there exists an indirect export channel, consortia members participate in export strategy decisions. Generally, indirect export is frequently used by companies in the occasional or experimental export stage, not consolidated in the external market.

## 4. DIFFERENT BASIC INTERNATIONAL MARKETING CHANNELS USEFUL FOR THE SMALL AND MEDIUM-SIZED ENTREPRENEUR

### 4.1. The Export Department

#### *4.1.1. Convenience of its Structuration*

Depending on the company structure, it may be necessary to assign staff for administrative, financial, commercial and operative areas related to international market access. The creation of an internal structure department in the organization, in charge of supervising the development of international operations, shows the difference existing between domestic sales and export activities, and points out the need to design a specialized division or administrative area. The size and structure of this department will be subject to these factors:

— Number and diversity of international operations made by the company. It may be a single department that only performs basic administrative functions, such as the preparation of export documents; or wider activities, like formal or informal market investigations and promotional actions, like trade shows and international trade events attendance. It should be made clear that the operations not carried out by this department will be assigned to some specialized external structure.

— Number of present and potential external markets to operate.

— Exports sales amount in those markets and their relationship in percentage to company total sales.

— Cultural differences, commercial and economic policies, and existing legislations between the national market and the external penetrated markets. When there is a great difference as regards these aspects between the markets of origin and destination, this is known as psychographic distance.

### *4.1.2. Some Relevant Aspects of the Export Department*

Once considered the convenience of the existence of an export department, the company has to evaluate its own different resources (financial, administrative, human, technological, etc.), which are going to be assigned to the different functions of that area. This department may be in direct contact with the marketing area or division. It is also possible that, in a first stage, the company could have a commercial area subdivision for the internal market and other devoted to international business.

However, this department will also be associated to the other areas of the company. For example, it is going to analyze the legal aspects: contractual conditions and clauses (terms, exclusivity, prices, discounts, etc.) of international operations together with the legal section. On the other hand, it is going to analyze the possibility of an export deferred collection, the fixing of deferred financing, the interest rate to be agreed, the use of financial instruments (letter of exchange, letter of credit, etc.) as well as the granting of discounts, among others together with the financial department. It is going to obtain information about costs and sales, and balance sheet detailed information, company results, trends and projections in the different items that may serve as a base for decision taking in international operation, together with the accounting department. Product adaptations to legal issues and consumers' preferences in the destination market in packaging, labelling, components, packing, design and quality will be agreed with the production area people in charge.

As regards minimum technological requirements that the international marketing department must have, there are: personal computers, telephones and fax machines, high speed Internet connection. In some cases, there may exist an internal net that links the different areas of the company (intranet), radio control communication and a system of electronic data interchange (EDI).

The existence of this department within the organization is not incompatible with the development of alternative channels (trading companies, brokers, export consortia, etc.) for certain markets of difficult access or with very peculiar features. Besides, one of the functions of this administrative structure is to develop linkage activities and supervise the different intermediaries based in the destination market (agents, distributors, concession holders, etc.).

### *4.1.3. International Marketing Department Structure*

The department organization has to be adequate to the volume and importance of the world operations that the company makes. At the beginning, it may consist of a department director—who is going to perform the international marketing strategy—in charge of a reduced structure, an auxiliary—who is going to perform support activities like freight hiring, financial institutions procedures and goods insurance—and an administrative secretary—who will be in charge of preparing documents, answering calls and sending messages. If the company only has a few resources, this area may be yet smaller, and all the functions will be concentrated on one person, who will be in charge of all the international marketing operations. As the company consolidates in the external markets, new subareas can be started, with responsible personnel in charge (in the issues of freight and insurance, financing, and other activities). In this case, it is possible to expand department structure, by creating subdivisions, in order to prioritize the most relevant external markets or the type of product internationally marketed.

Regardless of the structure designed, all the members of the department must have exporting conscience and motivation, and the minimum level of qualifications adequate for the functions they perform (knowledge of languages, training in marketing, etc.). It would be important not to develop structures that generate the concentration of activities in only one person, but look for team work, with decentralized functions, and skills complementation of the different people in charge, so as to generate greater product value.

#### *4.1.4. Activities Developed by the Export Department*

Export department activities may vary according to the structure adopted, however, the most important are:

— Contacting potential external buyers and negotiating current operations conditions.

— Hiring goods insurance and international carriage.

— Contacting different external operators, like sellers, agents and distributors, in order to reach consensus about prices, exclusivity, catalogue or sampling and stipulation of minimum activity levels.

— Development of international sales, international agency, international distribution contracts, among others.

— Communication of quotations and international counteroffers.

— Preparation and issuance of certain international financial and commercial marketing papers.
— Management of shipment authorizations and obligatory revisions, required by the different control bodies.
— Implementation of different international promotion activities: trade shows and commercial missions attendance, sampling and catalogue delivery, etc.
— Coordinating integral delivery (packaging adequation, exports logistic follow up, shipment confirmation, etc.).
— Presentations in banking institutions so as to collect operations performed.

## 4.2. Sellers

### *4.2.1. Seller's Function and Retribution*

The international seller is a company employee assigned to business promotion in the external markets. He moves to those markets and gets a retribution for his work, either in the form of a fixed amount of money or by commission.

In practice, sellers always have a minimum fixed remuneration, which is increased by the commission obtained and estimated upon the deals made through their participation. When this channel is used, the company has to consider substantial expenses, like salespersonnel travel allowances which include: trips, food and lodging, travelling, and other expenses in the destination market. The fixed remuneration as well as the allowances determine a minimum level of fixed maintenance costs for this commercial structure, which the company will have to pay regardless of the closing of deals abroad.

### *4.2.2. Advantages and Other Issues in the Use of Sellers*

It is a useful structure for companies that centralize a market's operations on a few buyers. It is a very efficient channel when external buyers need personalized counselling, in order to make a purchase or to get some product technical information, case in which the company personnel is the most adequate channel to offer that information. Besides, the seller appears as a very important data source about external markets news.

The international sales responsible person will have to perform activities according to the company objectives. This is why this person must possess marketing knowledge, a tenacious and sociable personality and great communication skills to advise with precision about the product attributes and the operating conditions. In order to do this, this person will also have to have, an important knowledge of the product marketed and a great tact to approach potential buyers.

There is a subordination and dependency relationship between the seller and the exporting company because both parties are linked by an employment contract according to respective labour laws. Product commercial promotion is the company seller's primary function, so as to close commercial deals. The seller will also be able to, when the organization allows him, close deals on behalf and by order of the exporting company. If the company considers necessary to extend the seller's functions, the financial convenience of that extension of activities as well as the consistency with the company commercial objectives will have to be assessed.

The use of this channel is framed within a direct export, because the seller is based in the destination market, and it is the company the one that performs by itself all the export operative, documentary and financial activities, in the market of origin.

As regards the instructions that the company communicates to the seller, the most significant are: identification of which line of products the seller will promote, minimum sales volume for a particular period, existence of geographical exclusivity, percentage of commission per operation, etc.

## 4.3. Agents

### *4.3.1. Importance of International Agents*

International agents are, unlike sellers, independent as regards the company in origin and their aim is to promote businesses on behalf and by order of the exporting company. When the company makes use of agents' services to gain access to external markets, this activity is framed within direct export. In some cases they may be representative-agents, lawfully authorized by the company to make commercial deals. Their retribution is generally a commission calculated upon deals concerted.

These channels do not take physical possession of the goods, that is, do not buy the goods or resell them. Neither do they acquire the property of the goods to market them. These intermediaries may have an assigned zone in the country-market where they perform their activities (what is called "geographic exclusivity"). This exclusive zone may be a part of a city or a whole city, a state or province, a region or the whole country-market, depending on the extension of the area, the type of product commercialized, the number of agents assigned to that market, the number of buyers, etc.

Agents may also have commercial or economic exclusivity, which means that they cannot promote sales of any other competitive product. Also, there may exist total exclusivity from the commercial point of view, which means that the agent may not sell products other than the company's (be they competitive or not).

Exclusivity conditions stipulation, other contractual clauses that relate the agent to the exporting company, due dates, accounting, and more commercial rights and obligations, will be fixed by consensus in the international agency contract. Other issues to be agreed in the contract are: minimum volume of sales expected from the agent during a period of time and treatment of sales directly made by the company in the area exclusively assigned to the agent.

### *4.3.2. Agents Optimum Features*

The small and medium-sized enterprise has different sources to obtain information about potential agents that may promote its product: query to commercial attachés upon agents' listings for a particular product, participation in commercial events like trade shows and expositions, among others. Factors that entrepreneurs should evaluate about the potential agent before closing an international agency contract are: commercial history in the market to penetrate, experience in like or related products, knowledge of international marketing, commercial contacts and influence upon governmental bodies that it has in the destination market, commercial references on its performance, etc. Other factors to be considered in the selection of the most appropriate agent are: operator time of residence in the market chosen by the company and competence in the language, legal rules, commercial and economic practices in the destination market, which make it more efficient for marketing activities.

An advantage of this channel, in comparison with sellers, is that the agent is permanently based in the destination market, which saves travelling expenses or allowances. Besides, as generally the only retribution of the agent is the commission by sales produced, when there are no sales, there will not exist any marketing expenses for the company that uses this channel. Being permanently based in the external market, the agent has a greater access to knowledge about the dynamics of its functioning and the changes likely to appear.

## 4.4. Manufacturing Contract

### 4.4.1. Channel Relevance

The manufacturing contract, also called "outsourcing of the productive process", consists in subhiring another company for the production of particular goods. The company that makes the order asks the second company, among other conditions:

— Quality product standards.
— Size, weight, components.
— Packaging design and style.
— Number of units to manufacture.

The company that manufactures the product by order, does it according to the subhiring company instructions. In some cases, this contract may anticipate the total or partial product manufacturing (components, pieces and accessories).

### 4.4.2. Different Manufacturing Alternatives

In the case of product total manufacture, the company makes the order, then buys the lot produced to the manufacturing company, and adds its own brand name to commercialize it in the destination market. In the cases when the subhired company manufactures the whole of the product, including the package, this organization may also carry out the imprint of the brand name, legends and symbols from the contracting company, in the package. There is another possibility, in which a company appoints another one to manufacture the product in bulk, so that it is then packed by the first company with its brand, to introduce it in the market.

Two interesting alternatives that may be considered are: one, that the manufacturing company be located in the market of origin, that is, in the same country where the company that performs the order is located. The other option states that the industrial company be located in the external market that wants to be penetrated. In the first case, the company has to buy the product and then export it to the chosen market. In the second case, the manufactured product is already located in the external market, so, there is no export and the company in origin may, using this channel, evade existing access barriers in the country of destination (tariff and paratariff barriers). Besides, this second way may be used to test an external market of which there is not enough commercial information, or there is not a high degree of assurance about product acceptation in that market. The company that performs the production order may make this test with the use of the manufacturing contract, without great investment or resource (productive, financial, human) involvement.

### *4.4.3. Advantage of its Use*

Besides, through the manufacturing contract, the entrepreneur may regulate production orders, starting by small manufacturing orders, and increasing them, as product acceptation in the country-market is achieved. This channel is very useful in very small country-markets because in a first stage, they are not very profitable to perform export from origin or production in destination. Also, its application in those countries with a long psychographic distance with the market of origin, or of which the consumers' market functioning and evolution in aspects like: consumption habits, commercial uses and practices, product usage and other cultural issues are unknown, may be very convenient.

### 4.5. International Marketing Advisors

Advising in external activities consists in a personalized counselling given by a professional expert external to the company, qualified in different international marketing topics. This person offers wide services related to external markets commerce that go from international market investigation to the precise issuance of export documentation. Among other functions there are: offerings to external markets, negotiation of deferred payment and further conditions in each international operation, and follow up of each concerted operation. Also, sampling, compliance with governmental bodies regulations related to international activities, hiring of different export related services (customs agent, carrier, insurance company, etc.).

Among other services there is: advising about barriers existing in the destination market, supplying information about constitution of customs protective guarantees and counselling on registration aspects of international brands. This expert may also make contacts with potential distributors and agents abroad, attend international promotional events with the entrepreneur and guide him or her in the different banking procedures for the collection of exports made.

This professional person may carry out the tasks interdisciplinarily, with other professional people from related areas (legal, financial, logistic), and the retribution may consist in advanced and/or periodical payments. However, it is possible that a fixed amount and/or a percentage calculated on the sales made be agreed as remuneration for his or her services.

### 4.6. Brokers

Brokers constitute a marketing channel with great performance flexibility in the international markets. Their function is to contact a product offer with its international demand. Unlike agents, brokers are linked neither to the buyer nor to the seller, and so, generally, do not represent any of the parties. They represent neither, because they may close a deal at a certain time for a company, and a deal with another at another time; that is, they try to reach commercial agreements, irrespective of the intervening companies; they are opportunists, in the good sense of the term.

Retribution consists of a commission upon operation concerted that can be charged, according to stipulation, to the seller, the buyer, or both. They do not take physical possession of the goods, that is, they do not buy the product and resell it, and may limit the field of action to a particular sector (machinery, food products, commodities, etc.).

## 4.7. Distributors

### *4.7.1. General Aspects*

Distributors make up company structures geographically located in the country of destination, that buy—that is, import—goods for subsequent reselling. As a result, distributor's retribution will be the difference between the cost of the goods and the sale price. As with the agent, the distributor also called "importer distributor", is independent from the exporter. Distributors may also have economic or geographic exclusivity.

The only connection is through an international distribution contract, in which distributor's—also called "import distributor"—and distributee's rights and obligations are defined. The latter is the exporter and generally the product manufacturer, located in the market of origin.

### *4.7.2. Major Complexity of this Structure*

The distributor buys the goods, that is, there is a transference of ownership from distributee to distributor. This is why this channel needs a more complex commercial structure than the international agent, because the latter, unlike the former, does not take possession of the goods. The distributor's organizational structure has to consider all those aspects that permit to appropriately develop activities related to product international buying and selling: warehouses, points of sale for exposition of goods, means of transport, manipulation of goods, personnel in charge of sales functions, storage, administrative accountancy work, among others.

Generally, the distributor is a wholesaler so, he or she does not sell the imported product to the ultimate consumer or user, but resells it to other intermediaries that are part of the internal distribution channel. Some items that have to be included in the international distribution contract are: minimum stock levels that the distributor has to keep available in his or her platform, reselling price policies to be set in the subsequent channel levels, discount policies among others. All these parameters may be negotiated between both parties, but in some cases, the distributor only sticks to the regulations established by the distributee, due to scarce negotiating capacity.

Distributors configure very efficient marketing channels for product massive penetration like food products, cleaning products, and those of low unitary value, or that require little or null technical assistance during postmarketing.

## 4.8. Concessionaires

### *4.8.1. Significance of International Concession Agreements*

Concessionaires possess product reselling monopoly in the destination market, under certain conditions stipulated by the conceding authority, that is, the company located in origin, in a contract called concession agreement, which relates both parties. It has to be made clear that the conceding authority is the one located in the exporting country-market and the concessionaire is the entrepreneur that imports the product and resells it in the destination market.

A concession agreement differs from that of distribution in that international concessions always have a geographical and economic exclusivity, and besides they have to give the consumer or user of the marketed products a series of postmarketing services: repairs, installation, spare parts replacement, warranty coverage, etc. This is why, apart from the infrastructure (premises, warehouses, sale shops, transportation) that the concessionaire must have, it will have qualified personnel to render the services that constitute the "extended product". This commercial channel must consider stock maintenance, not only of goods, but also of pieces and parts to provide those services.

The consumer or user that buys a product from a concessionaire is protected by this commercial structure a longer time period, after the purchase, as compared to other channels. As a result, a higher containment and satisfaction of the buyer's needs is achieved, which allows the buyer to resort to any of the other concessionaires that make up a net in the destination market, in order to get postmarketing assistance; which makes it possible for these services to be rendered by a concessionaire different from the one that sold the product in the first place.

### *4.8.2. Channel Distinct Features*

There are, for the different concessionaires of the net, various commercial compensation variables among them, as well as minimum attention levels which are homogeneous, that is, which are standardized through uniform concession agreements. Concessionaires, in practice, comply with the regulations of the conceding authority, in every issue relative to marketing like price policies, discounts, stocks, which are identical or similar for every concessionaire of the same market.

According to this, the concessionaire does not possess the negotiating capacity to fix the concession agreement conditions, since both parties are linked by conditions, fixed by the conceding authority and accepted by the concessionaire. Thus, this marketing procedures become very useful for famous trademark products or state of the art technology like instrumentation, agricultural machinery, automobiles and building equipment, for which postmarketing is really important.

In comparison to the distributor, the concessionaire generally constitutes a marketing short channel because sales are directly made to the ultimate user or consumer, and not to other intermediary.

## 4.9. Trading Companies

### *4.9.1. Channel Characteristics*

Also called "marketing companies", these international marketing channels make up the group of international penetration policies associated to indirect export. These structures possess vast resources, as well as their developed and complete international markets information systems, so as to perform international marketing operations. Besides, they have a net of international contacts composed by:

— Specialized agents in different countries for different products.
— Various distributors in close relationship with trading.
— Sale branches in different country-markets.
— Contacts with other trading companies through the signing of strategic partnerships.

Generally, the trading company has important updated databases with an important number of business opportunities detected, as well as studies and market profiles performed in different countries. The information this channel has, is very vast, and the net of contacts which is a part of its structure is widely extended worldwide, which allows it to position any product in the global market with speed and simplicity.

### *4.9.2. Structure and Organization of the Marketing Company*

The trading company possesses an important internal structure, divided into functional departments which are in charge of different specialists in each one of the areas. Some of the main areas are:

— ***Administrative area:*** Comprises everything that has to do with trading commercial, financial, and internal preparation of documents, as well as issues like accounting, taxation, and labour registration. Its main function is the preparation of commercial and financial papers required by the external buyer that are in charge of the exporter.
— ***Customs transactions management area:*** It deals with presentation of all the papers in the different customs in origin, classification and valuation of goods and other procedures related to the import or export mechanisms. It also coordinates the strategies of introduction and departure of goods from free trade areas, and performs temporary admission and export procedures.
— ***Carriage and insurance management area:*** It deals with everything referred to processes of loading, discharge,

settling and consolidation of goods. It coordinates the containerized and palletized management of goods. It requests freight and tariff quotations, makes reservations for ship holds, negotiates international carriage conditions contracts. It performs goods insurance when necessary and evaluates different coverage alternatives according to the product, means of transport and destination market.

— ***Area of deal closing:*** It is the area in charge of the international negotiation with the client in the country of destination. It is composed by specialists with deep knowledge of international law to negotiate international buying and selling agreement clauses and conditions, as well as by personnel with solid knowledge of global marketing. It is the sector that performs the initial offer of the goods and the different counteroffers in the development of the international negotiation.

— ***Area of exportable offer generation:*** It is the internal division in charge of contacting the producers that supply the products required abroad. In some cases, for the same order in the external market, this area has to group the exportable production of two or more producers to satisfy international demand. In other situations the exportable product is obtained via import. Triangulation market operation is performed to do this, and this implies import to then export to other market in the same state or with higher national value.

— ***Market studies and international promotion area***: It is an area that develops international exploration undertakings, through the conduction of formal and informal market studies. To do this, it makes a detailed compilation and analysis of external market primary and secondary information. The objective of these activities is to produce profiles of the most attractive markets at international level. Others of its functions are participating in events, like trade shows and international expositions, making deals, establishing contacts and partnerships with other commercial channels. The priority in this area is to feed trading companies with updated information to perform commercial operations. Upon the information on actual businesss opportunities detected by the people in charge of this division, the exportable offer generation area will provide the potential suppliers of the products ordered from abroad. On some occasions, it is also possible for the trading company to try to get information at a producer's request that hires its services in order to export products through this structure.

— ***International collection and payment area***: It is in charge of all the international financing import as well as export operations. For export operations, its activities are: compliance with letter of credit documentary terms and requirements, preparation of the collecting record instructions and presentation of documents to the financial institution (these functions are performed in coordination with the administrative area) and negotiation of financial documents (i.e., letters of exchange or cheques in currency). From the import point of view, it is in charge of the opening of the letter of credit, or it makes international currency payments. As regards the payment of related services relative to international commerce, like insurance, freight, dispatches, consolidations and loading, those activities remain in charge or the international carriage and insurance management area.

For the producer, the use of the marketing company services represents an indirect export, because it is the trading company the one that makes all the export operations. It is very frequent for the trading company to buy the product to the company and then resell it to the external market, and the trading company margin is the difference between the cost and the reselling price. However, in other cases, the trading company may perform an export operation at the manufacturing company's own expense and risk, and charge a commission for services rendered.

### *4.9.3. Trading Company Isolating Effect*

Generally, when the organization uses a channel like the marketing company to gain access to external markets, it does not learn absolutely anything about global markets operative, documentary, financial and commercial aspects. This knowledge remains concentrated on the trading company power and does not reach the entrepreneur. This information is the main "know-how" for a marketing company that constitutes its business, and this is why it does not share it with the company that requires its services.

As a consequence, an isolating effect as regards export operations performed by the trading company is produced; the producer does not have knowledge about the market to which the product is going to be directed, it ignores who the buyer abroad is, it does not know at what price the product was marketed, or what was the means of transport used. The producer also ignores whether the shipment made includes only its product or goes consolidated with other of the same or different kind, and whether it was commercialized with the same package and trade name, or if these were changed by the marketing company. All this information is in the power of the trading company, that exerts the total control upon the marketing channel.

As a result, a specific division of functions is produced; the entrepreneur only manufactures a quality and price-competitive product, and sometimes he or she may also develop an industrial process, according to the parameters required by the trading company, and externalizes all the issues relative to international marketing, which remain in the hands of the marketing company.

### *4.9.4. Other Relevant Questions*

The trading company must be created in agreement with the legislation of the country where it is based, and has to comply with all the legal and statutory registration, minimum capital and functioning requirements established by the corresponding statutes.

This channel is widely used in the first stages of the company in its insertion in the external markets (occasional or experimental export) when the company ignores international marketing operative and documentary issues and how to detect business in the different country-markets. This structure would have to be progressively abandoned, as the entrepreneur consolidates in the more advanced stages of internationalization, which imply ways of direct export and other marketing channels. However, in those stages the company may have a selective use of the marketing company services for specific markets, which may be very complex for direct access.

## 4.10. Piggybacking

### *4.10.1. Piggybacking Functioning*

The company may use a distribution structure already present in the destination market, to market the product. The company "assembles" its products upon the distribution system existing in the external country-market. It is very likely that the distribution structure which the product joins may not commercialize similar or related products, but that it may be adequate and compatible for the company product sales.

Generally, companies that make up the distribution chain in destination are going to accept the entrance of new products to be distributed so as to widen the offer in the market and make it more attractive, and besides, to get additional earnings. These companies are going to accept the management of non-competitive products as complementary to the ones they distribute.

### *4.10.2. Advantages for the Parties*

The main benefit for these distributors is that they may complete their lines with products that, consistently assembled, will allow them to get more margin in their benefits, as well as distribute more efficiently fixed costs of the distribution structure. Piggybacking, also called kangaroo marketing, allows the company in origin to have access to external markets, by using distribution developed and specialized structures with experience and contacts in the country-market chosen. In this way, the difficulty that implies distribution structure development for a company in destination is avoided.

# 5. INTERNATIONAL MARKETING ADVANCED CHANNELS

## 5.1. Complexity of Certain External Marketing Channels

There are certain channels that require more complex implementation activities for the small and medium-sized enterprise. This complexity may be the result of the following factors, which vary, according to the channel:

— requirement of coordination among two or more companies in internationalization decision taking (for example, consortia, cooperatives, coinvestment), the existence of shared control and external activities earnings distribution among two or more companies;

— need of more company financial, commercial, human and administrative resources in the development of company structures for international marketing (this happens in the marketing and production branches in destination);

— development of certain value assets (tradenames, patents, successful business formats, efficient management, etc.), that could be given to other companies (in the case of franchising, licences, technology transference, administration contracts).

## 5.2. Export Consortia

### *5.2.1. Definition and Features*

Considering numerous authors as a necessary reference in the subject (Acerenza, Ullmann, Maeso Ruiz and Daemon), it is possible to define an export consortium as a permanent company structure that pursues, through the creation of a package of exportable offer, international insertion of products of the member companies. These export consortia are partnerships composed by a group of companies with some difficulties to internationalize.

There is total legal independence between the newly constituted partnership (that is, the export consortium) and the companies that give origin to it. These companies are partners of this new partnership. Generally, the consortium functions as if it were an external exports department, as regards its partners.

#### *5.2.2. Activities and Advantages of this Structure*

The most important and specific consortium function is purchasing the production that its members assign for export (that is, their exportable offer) and assign the total of those exportable offers (called "package of exportable offer") to external markets. This partnership comprises a wide range of activities related to international marketing like: issuance of documentation, management of collection and external financing, carriage hiring, goods insurance, management of customs dispatching, compliance with legal requirements of previous official interventions of each shipment and shipment follow up from destination to arrival.

Organizations that constitute the consortium get the benefits of participating in the decisions of a specialized structure devoted to international marketing. Companies participation as members of the consortium generates a greater negotiating capacity, as a result of greater volumes offered to the international market. This greater negotiating skill is shown as regards:

- external market big clients, with which better commercial deals may be agreed on an equal basis.
- intervening intermediaries in international marketing procedures, like customs agents, carriers, insurance companies, through the obtention of lower costs in the services offered.
- *governmental bodies*, so as to get fiscal benefits or credit incentives, towards which a stronger power and pressure may be exerted (lobby).

#### *5.2.3. Company Concerns and Consortium Performance*

Small and medium-sized enterprises that compose the consortium, generally, have some difficulties to gain access to international markets, because of different reasons:

- Lack of knowledge about information sources on international business opportunities.

— Ignorance about international marketing functioning, documentary and financial issues.
— Non-competitive prices in the world environment.
— Scarce exportable volume which does not satisfy the minimum order required by the international demand.
— Lack of funds to perform international market investigation activities or develop international promotion activities.

Consortia allow to centralize the international marketing operations of each of their members. The offer made by the consortium may cover products that satisfy the same need, that is, the same product or ancillary products; or products of different lines that satisfy various needs.

When a consortium markets homogeneous products that satisfy the same need, they are called "mono-offering" or "specialized". When the exportable offer package is composed by a wide variety of products, they are called "generalist" or "polyoffering" consortia.

A consortium, besides, may have marketing activities, or just make international promotion activities, leaving marketing in the hands of its members. There are some consortia called "of guarantee", which serve as a guarantee in order to get financing lines for their members.

### *5.2.4. Consortium Objectives*

The consortium is generally composed by producers. However, there are cases at international level in which there are service providers (carriers or financial companies) or commercial intermediaries (for example, distributor wholesalers) among its members.

The consortium has an instrumental objective, which means that it is the most adequate means of access for the small and medium-sized enterprises that do not have knowledge about external markets.

This exporting structure is based more on shared expectations and objectives, than on related products. For the members of the association, this structure is an indirect export channel, because they assign exportable production to the consortium, so that then it is the latter the one that commercializes internationally, through its own structure, the products.

Even though it is an indirect way to export, associated entrepreneurs start to acquire knowledge about international marketing operation management, because different decisions about consortium internationalization are generated through the participation of the members in consortium meetings.

One of the advantages that the consortium gives is that, by centralizing the exportable production of a series of important producers, external buyers simplify the acquisition of big shipments by negotiating with only one company; that is, the consortium, which represents a series of productive organizations.

### *5.2.5. Evolution and Development of Consortium Activities*

The consortium has to start by entering the external markets with a limited series of activities, like export operative, documentary and commercial issues. It may progressively incorporate functions which are not traditional, like the setting and supervision of uniform quality parameters, for the production that its members assign to the exportable offer package.

Other non-traditional activity may be the creation of a common trade name for all the products commercialized by the consortium. This allows for a more solid positioning of the products offered internationally. The existence of a consortium tradename simplifies promotional activities in the external markets, with the use of an umbrella brandname that includes all the products offered by the associative structure. This brandname may be accompanied by different individual related sub-brands depending on the product, using, in that case, the brands of the partners in the national market.

A function of the consortium consists in getting a more efficient use of transport structures, with the consolidation of shipments and a better use of the space in the containers, in order to reduce freight costs. Other aspects of great importance are the production of market investigation that may be usufructed by all its members, as well as the participation in international promotion events through consortium specialized personnel that may display the products of their partners.

This commercial structure is very effective to perform all the activities just mentioned, because all the resulting expenses are going to be shared by all its members, which will also allow to gain access to more profitable markets with greater purchasing power. These expenses, like market studies, international expositions, quality control, will be difficult to be afforded by a small and medium enterprise on its own, due to their high cost.

### *5.2.6. Consortium Development*

Improvisations in the development of the consortium should be avoided. So, a series of meetings with the potential members, in a stage previous to its constitution, should be carried out to discuss the following items: exportable offer potentiality of future members, relationship of this offer with the demand detected in particular international markets through preliminary investigations, future monetary flow projected on the consortium operative development, more beneficial partnership structure to be adopted, possible managerial and administrative organization of the consortium, marketing strategy and commercial channels to be developed, system for partners' decision taking, project of social contract, control systems of consortium activities, among other issues.

It is important that the potential candidates for associativity project membership have, at least, some commercial experience in the internal market, as a previous step to gain access to external markets jointly. Rights and obligations of the parties intervening in this associative channel have to be made clear enough in the consortium legal constitution as a result of the meetings, previous to the assumption of formal commitments.

### *5.2.7. Consortium Economic Support*

As regards the economic cost for the entrepreneur, relative to the creation and support of the consortium activities, the use of initial capitals—that is, the ones contributed when the consortium is started—and periodical—those that contribute to the administrative functioning, services, specialized consultants' fees, all through the association's life—has to be considered. However, there may exist contributions of its members of exceptional character for actual expenses, like, for example, participations in commercial missions. It would be ideal that the consortium could self-finance in subsequent stages, as a result of the difference between the purchasing costs of the products that the consortium acquires from its members and the *resale prices* in the export markets. Other retribution channel may be through the commissions that the joint structure collects from the international sales that it does at its members' own expense and risk.

#### *5.2.8. Disadvantages of this Channel*

The main inconvenience observed in the functioning of export consortia is the asymmetry of power among its members, that negatively affects the process of decision taking which is monopolized by a few members with the majority of the votes. This problem may be saved by, contractually, assigning a vote to each member regardless of economic power.

Other likely inconvenient, more specifically in mono-offering consortia, is the assignation among its members of an international order inferior to the exportable offer assigned for them. A possible way out for this concern is to make it clear what the external purchase distribution way among its partners will be, in the incorporation agreement, considering parameters like: total sales or production volume for each company, percentage of capital of each partner, or any other valid parameter. Other variable to consider, in this case, is the assignation of a system of turns in which, a first shipment has priority to send the whole of the exportable offer to member A, the second shipment gives priority to member B, and so on.

It is also possible that tensions between partners' individual actions and activities developed within the joint export project might appear. If these conflicts are not faced in time, an external individualism versus associativism issue may arise, where misunderstandings among members are very sharp and may lead to the dissolution of the consortium.

### 5.2.9. *Wrong Entrepreneurial Approach of Synergy of Forces*

On some occasions, companies do not even reach the stage of formal constitution of the consortium, and everything remains at the level of informative meetings for those interested in the project. It is very usual to observe a clear tendency for the businesspeople to translate the internal market competitive spirit to international operations, that is, consider the other company, that may be its partner, like a rival. Those organizations wrongly judge one another, since, even though it is possible that they may have been historic enemies in the internal market, they believe that they will continue being competitors within the exporting association. Business people do not perceive that all the members of the consortium become partners within the joint structure, and that it is their union that gives them force in the international market.

## 5.3. Export Cooperatives

### 5.3.1. *Channel Attributes*

Within the partnerships, export cooperatives, generally, are positioned for the international marketing products of the primary sector. Consortia, however, are related to industrial origin goods with an important added value. However, in practice, export consortia may develop rural international businesses and export cooperatives may commercialize industrial goods.

Export cooperatives have similar features as export consortia from the point of view of their advantages, functions and performance in external environments. However, they are clearly different from consortia from the point of view of the way they operate. The consortium centralizes and concentrates the exportable offer of the members to produce the offer package for the world market; in the national market its members keep autonomy in the fixing of the commercial policy, that is, applying their own strategy of price, discounts, brandname, etc. On the other hand, the exporting cooperative achieves an economic and commercial exclusivity of its members' production, whose marketing activity, for the internal as well as for the external market, is performed only through this structure. This commercial channel has to be developed according to cooperatives' legal regulations and have a social goal, unlike consortia, which are governed by commercial and societary legislation.

### *5.3.2. Other Functions of Cooperatives in the Primary Sector*

Farm export cooperatives may perform joint purchases of raw material and production and primary activity exploitation input (fertilizers, balanced food, herbicides, seeds) for their partners, and besides they may possess productive facilities where all the activities that form part of the primary sector chain of value of their partners are made (for example, product processing and packaging centre, storing silos for stock, and platforms for fractioning). This commercial channel may negotiate the associative acquisition of capital goods at lower costs for their members (wrapping machines, pulverizers, harvesters, filter machines, milkers).

## 5.4. Licences and Technology Transference

### *5.4.1. Importance of Licences*

Licences allow a company to generate an intangible like a brand, a patent of invention, or a design (elements which are considered copyright) to transfer the usufruct of that element for a certain time and according to some conditions. This internationalization channel may be classified within the so-called mixed forms or other forms, which are considered neither export nor production in destination.

The company holder of the copyright element penetrates particular markets through the granting of the licence to be usufructed by a company in the destination market. There is no export, because the product is produced in destination by the entrepreneur who is going to make use, for production and/or marketing, of that intangible. The organization that generates this asset of value remains linked to the company abroad by a contract of international licence in which the rights and obligations of each party are established, its duration, and the retribution of the holder of the asset conceded (it is a periodical payment or royalty made by the company located in destination).

### 5.4.2. Advantages and Disadvantages for the Parties

Trademark licence allows a company that obtains its usufruct to sell the production with a brandname already developed and promoted, which makes commercial activities easier. In the case of the patent licence, the company that obtains it, gets access, for a short time, to information about productive methods, scientific advances and innovations relative to a particular product, which allows to improve its production or manufacture new goods. These methods are a consequence of great monetary investment and long periods of testing. The company that possesses the temporary usufruct of these intangibles lacks resources for the development of new methods; this is the main reason why it chooses this channel.

The inconvenience this marketing way may produce appears especially in the case of trademark licence. It is very likely that the products manufactured by the company that gets the trademark usufruct do not meet the minimum requisites and quality standards required by the company that owns the intangible, which causes damage to the positioning of the brand in a particular market. As a result, a product mispositioning may be produced because there is not an homogeneous quality in the different country-markets where it is identified by the same brandname. To avoid these inconveniences, requisites, minimum quality parameters, and penalties in the case of non-compliance have to be stipulated in the licence contract.

### 5.4.3. Other Issues Relative to Licensing

Internationalization through the granting of licences allows the owner of the assets licensed to develop international business without any investment, because it will be the entrepreneur that gets the licence the one to use his or her resources in destination. The only costs assumed by the holder of the intangible are those relative to the development of that transferable element. Besides, certain benefits are obtained as a result of licensing through the perception of royalties. Likewise, this international marketing channel permits to elude tariff or paratariff barriers in the country of destination, because the export operation is not performed.

### *5.4.4. Technology Transfer Significant Character*

Technology transfer contracts are those celebrated between two or more parties, through which a party transfers only once, or periodically, different elements which are the result of intensive activities of Research and Development (R + D). This knowledge may be about improvement found in the productive processes, development of new material, substitution of functions and components in a particular product, new sources of generation of energy, among others.

In this type of channel there is a company in a particular country that develops that information, which comes from an investigation in strict scientific and productive conditions. Besides, there is another organization located in the country of destination market, to which this knowledge that makes production and marketing of goods easier is transferred.

### *5.4.5. Functioning of Technological Know-how Transference*

The company that develops this expertise gets a retribution from the company that receives this information. The organization that later adopts that informative technology may develop a relationship of dependency with the company that generated the technological assets. The company that receives the intangible may blindly trust the informative provision it gets, and it is likely that no effort be made to generate its own development of innovations.

On the other hand, this channel does not produce internationalization expenses for the company that generated the technology, but those concerning an innovative know-how. A risk for this organization is that the licensee, over time, may become its competitor, due to improvements of the knowledge transferred.

## 5.5. Coinvestment

### *5.5.1. Reasons for the Development of Coinvestment*

Also known as joint venture. This channel is composed by two or more companies from different countries which develop a joint project for internationalization. This joint project may consist in the constitution of a new company (partnership joint venture) or in a contract that links the companies internationally (contractual joint venture).

This access channel to external markets is used when there is complementarity of the companies that develop coinvestment. In this complementation, a company gives another what the other lacks, and *vice versa*; the coinvesting companies are in a system that generates synergies in their performance. Through this commercial channel, more efficiency in the external performance, which consists of the actions developed individually by each company, is achieved.

The reasons for the constitution of a joint venture, following COLAIÁCOVO, may be varied: need, convenience, government demand issues, and company strategy. There is need when a company depends on the existence of other company's resources, which is why there is not another valid alternative to gain access to a particular market but through the joint project. In this case, company complementation is vital. The origin of the joint venture may also be the convenience of this undertaking, when there are different options to gain access to external markets, but the most appropriate is coinvestment. The legal aspects that require the use of this channel, when some legal regulations in the country of destination establish that a company will only have access to that market through its branches (marketing or production) located in that country, if a local company participates, are very important. The last situation clearly describes a requisite of the political and legal environment of the country in destination, that may be considered as a paratariff barrier.

### *5.5.2. Coinvestment Concerns and Advantages*

In the case of a partnership joint venture between two companies from two different countries, the partnership may be located in any of the two countries, or in a third. Some critical inconveniences that present in a joint venture development are: problems of control of the joint project between the companies that constitute it and differences in idiosyncrasy and coinvesting company executives styles, based on the different international cultural environments.

Taking as an example partnership coinvestment between two companies, one from country A and the other from country B, which make up a partnership for joint participation located in country B, the company in country A will be called foreign, and the one in B, local. The foreign company may apply some resources to the joint venture, like capital (necessary to finance the project), qualified human resources for executive and managerial positions in the new partnership, and technology (industrial know-how, patents, designs, etc.). In turn, the local company will provide, especially, commercial contacts in the destination market and connections with official bodies in order to obtain fiscal and credit incentives. As regards the operative issue, the product may be totally manufactured by the company in country A and then exported to the country of destination to be marketed by the coinvestment, what we call "marketing coinvestment" or "coinvestment sales branch". Other alternative may be to export the product unfinished, and complete the productive process in destination (for example, by adding value with activities like assemblage, painting, fractioning). Other option is for the product to be totally manufactured in destination. In the last two cases the project is called "productive coinvestment".

### *5.5.3. Other Aspects to be Considered*

Other advantage that the foreign partner may get could be the access in the country of destination, through this channel, to sources of raw material and materials, or cheaper labour force. The objective is to use these lower cost factors, which may be present in that market, in the productive process so as to get a product more competitive final price.

This marketing channel reduces the risk of access to external markets, since it is shared by the companies that compose the coinvestment. There is also a joint control in the management of the project, which is why it is important for each partner not to concentrate more power than the rest for decision taking. Other factor to be considered is that in the joint venture there are benefits that are not concentrated in only one company, but they are distributed among the partners of the project.

### 5.6. Administration Contract

Through the administration contract, a company that has a great management strategy assigns highly qualified human resources to assist in the direction or management to other company. Through this contract, there is an organization that offers human resources with a high level of managerial formation that replaces, in certain vital positions, the personnel of the company assisted temporarily. In some cases, there may be a codirection composed by the qualified assisting personnel and the senior level of the assisted company. The company that incorporates the personnel with technology knowledge is, in a way, training through these highly qualified human resources. This organization learns from the management developed by the supporting resources form, style and flexibility.

An organizational conduction know-how is transferred in these contracts (from one company to the other one) that is, knowledge about how to run a business. In this penetration policy there is not an export of goods, but of ideas, knowledge and services. This channel is widely used especially in big mining and petrol industry exploitations, tourism and hotelry, among other sectors.

### 5.7. Export Franchise

#### *5.7.1. Format Business Franchise*

As regards this marketing channel, some specialists think it is within the licence group, as a very particular and complex type. However, some opinions define it as a differentiated channel in the universe of commercial channels, including licences.

In export franchising, it is widely used the so-called format business franchise, in which a company—"franchisor"—transfers a form of business management to another company —"franchisee". The franchisor grants the franchisee the usufruct of some elements successfully developed and tested, like: brands, patents (registered by the franchisor as Intellectual Property Rights, IPR), productive and commercial management know-how (non-registrable as IPR). This licence is performed under certain contractual conditions agreed by both parties.

### *5.7.2. International Unlimited Expansion*

There are some important issues for consideration in the international franchising system. The franchisor wants to duplicate or multiply a successful business in different countries in order to get a progressive internationalization of the business. To do it, in the beginning it has invested important amounts to position the brand, to promote the company, its product and client service. This initial development has been carried out through certain pilot tests developed with its own capital in the market of origin. It may have created, in the national market, outlets of its own, carrying operative as well as commercial activity homogeneously and testing knowledge and operation transference from one shop to another, previous step that is necessary for the franchisor to gain access to business.

### *5.7.3. Manuals of Procedures and Training as System Cornerstones*

The information that constitutes the core business—that is, know-how management—and the image that the franchisor positions for consumers have to be easily transferable to the companies franchisee. This information has to be subject to systematization and compilation in the so-called "manuals of procedures" or "operation manuals", which are long reports that contain a vast and precise degree of details about the execution of the different aspects that distinguishes the business subject to franchise from the ones developed by the competition, and that will serve as a guide for the franchisee in its actions. Among the information that these manuals may have there are technical and aesthetic features of the point of sale, employees uniforms, customer care center, outlet operative and commercial organization performed by the franchisee, etc.

Manuals of procedures, together with training activities and direct updating developed by the franchisor training department, include training information for the franchisee and constitute the fundamentals of information transference that looks for business format duplication.

### 5.7.4. Benefits for the Parties

This marketing channel advantage for the franchisor is that no disbursement is needed to internationalize the business. The only amounts paid are those related to development, positioning and testing of the franchiseable business. The invesment implied by the setting of new sales platforms in destination (premises renting, personnel hiring, operative costs, etc.) are in charge of the franchisee, the one who takes responsibility for economic and financial risks.

The franchisor, besides, may avoid tariff and paratariff barriers in destination, since internationalization is not produced via export, but through other ways. This system allows the franchisee to gain access to a business already developed and tested, popular and successful. According to this, the franchisee assigns neither efforts nor resources to position or develop a business, because that way has already been done by the franchisor.

### 5.7.5. Franchisor-Franchisee Relationship

The franchisor and the franchisee enjoy legal independence; they will only be linked by a contract that establishes the rights and obligations of the parties. The franchisor has the duty of assisting not only at the beginning and development of the franchisee commercial centre, but also all through the period stipulated in the contract (pre- and postinaguration of the franchisee's premises support).

The franchisor collects, for the transference of a successful business format, a fee, or initial right to incorporation, which is a fixed amount paid by the franchisee in order to enter the franchise business. It will also collect royalties, which are periodical payments generally calculated like a percentage of gross sales.

Besides, the franchisor may collect additional income paid by the franchisee for the sale of goods or raw material that, due to contractual obligations and with operative goals, the franchisee should buy from the franchisor. It may also receive money sums provided by the franchisee on the item of participation in promotion and advertising activities (done by the franchisor for the franchisee chain).

The franchisee must, apart from the above-mentioned payments, respect all the conditions for the commercial management, following the contractual regulations and the manuals of procedures. Thus, its performance will not produce distortions in the commercial positioning and global image pursued by the franchisor.

In the cases when the franchisee does not honour some issues that affect the development and the position of the business in the market, it will be subject to penalties—and in more serious cases, the contract might be rescinded—, being the franchisee co-responsible of the care and maintenance of the image built by the franchising chain in society.

### *5.7.6. Other Aspects of International Franchising*

International penetration through the franchising system demands the franchisor a detailed and vast study of the legal, societary, contractual, real-estate, commercial and cultural aspects in each country-market where the franchise system is desired to be implemented. The granting of an export franchise generally is not performed through a direct relationship between franchisor and franchisee, but it develops through a system called "masterfranchise", in which there is an intermediary authorized for each country-market, or for particular regions in a country-external market. This intermediary is exclusively assigned to a particular market so as to centralize the granting of the franchise, and has the authorization to evaluate potential franchisees and assign them for participation in the franchising system.

In this international marketing channel there is a risk for the franchisor, that the franchisee learn the management of the business and later, adopting a policy of benchmarking (creative copy approach), generate its own business, with a brandname, becoming a franchisor business competitor.

Other aspect to remark is that although all the businesses different franchisees have in charge have the form of positioning management and image, and homogeneous services, those franchise units get far from total standardization, since regional or local adaptations are produced in most markets, according to economic, cultural, or legal differences.

## 5.8. Marketing Affiliate

### *5.8.1. Sales Affiliate Location*

Better known as "marketing affiliate", it may be of two kinds: branch and affiliate.

The sales branch is only an extension of the company (a division of it) abroad. It is the geographical extension of a part of the company—located in the country-market of destination—commercial department. There is not, in this case, the constitution of an enterprise legally independent from the exporting company, but the branch is part of the same company and it is a division that forms part of its organizational chart.

Generally, international legislation in most countries requires that, in order to trade in its own territory, a company has to constitute a new enterprise in the destination country; in this case it would be a sales filial. In the case cited, these norms may prevent the performance of the commercial operations made in that country from being carried out by a simple extension of the commercial department of the company in origin.

### *5.8.2. Affiliate Commercial Relevance*

The sales affiliate is a new company that generally has to be developed according to the commercial legislation in the country of destination. This company (filial) is totally independent from the legal point of view from the enterprise in origin, known as "parent company". However, there is a clear economic connection between both companies; in fact, the parent company frequently has participation in the capital of the affiliate.

Thus, the parent company directly influences affiliate decision taking, which is going to act with more or lesser autonomy within the regulations of destination. Through this sales channel, the company in origin extends its marketing structure towards the destination market and achieves, in this way, greater contact with it.

### 5.8.3. *Functions of this Channel*

This commercial channel has to have a certain infrastructure that can make logistic and external marketing easier, and its specific functions will be:

- Product import for resale in the market local of destination or in other markets.
- Logistic management of the goods in destination (storage, fractioning, internal dispatch, internal carriage, etc.).
- Exhibition and explanation of the different product qualities, and the other activities of marketing in destination.
- Contacts and commercial contractual relationship with different channels at contractual internal level in the external market (agents, distributors, etc.).
- Contractual rendering of different services connected to the sale of the product (warranty replacement pieces, maintenance, reparation, etc.).

### 5.8.4. *Feasibility of this Channel for a Small-sized Enterprise*

The creation of a sales affiliate implies a higher financial and monetary disbursement by the company that uses this channel. This commercial platform implies a series of initial expenses (constitution of the partnership abroad) and maintenance costs (personal, administrative expenses, hiring of facilities, etc.).

Besides, this channel requires a minimum infrastructure, like building, warehouses, venue for sales and product exhibition, and means of transport. As a result, due to its operative complexity and its economic cost, it does not result in an accessible channel for small and medium-sized enterprises, at least in the first internationalization stages. It is possible that this way of access may be used by these entrepreneurs after a prolonged period of adaptation and consolidation in external markets.

The sales branch may have a greater control over the international distribution total channel, and may orient certain commercial policies in destination in a more vast way than other external access channels, like: fixing retailer price in destination, and promotion at this level of sales. It is important to consider that this sales filial may be created by the company individually or by coinvestment, that is, a joint venture in which a company of the country in destination or of other country participates.

## 5.9. Direct Investment

### *5.9.1. From a Marketing to a Production Approach*

This channel, known as production affiliate or one hundred per cent investment in destination, develops total or partial production in the external market, that remains in charge of a branch. External market manufacturing is partial when, for example, a company exports product parts or unfinished goods that are later assembled or to which an industrial finish process is applied in the branch; however, other possibility is that the product be totally manufactured in the foreign country. In the cases when the product is also manufactured in origin there is a duplication of the productive process.

It is called one hundred per cent investment, since the company in the country of origin has the whole of the participation in the branch, and so, there is no coinvestment.

### *5.9.2. Feasibility of this Channel for a Small-sized Enterprise: Advantages of this Channel*

This international market penetration policy demands a greater investment than the one performed in the marketing channels mentioned through this chapter, because of the need of specialized technical personnel, factory labour work, productive premises and machinery. For this reason, it is out of reach for a small and medium-sized enterprise, especially during its first stages of international market access.

This channel is considered as if it were a transfer or export of the whole (or a part of it) of the productive system towards a particular market. This channel of access implies a relocation of the chain of value from the geographical point of view that may have the following items as reasons: use of more economical resource sources in destination or the obtention of government incentives that favour the location of productive investments in a particular country-market (tax deduction, advantageous credit lines, subsidies, etc.). Other promoting aspect that stimulates the use of this channel is that, through this, tariff and paratariff barriers in destination are avoided, because there is no export.

Generally, from the governmental point of view of the external country, this channel is positively considered, when compared to the export coming from other countries, because the installation of productive structures by the external companies generates a greater level of economic activity, labour work employment from that country, more consumption, greater development and well being in the market assigned for that investment.

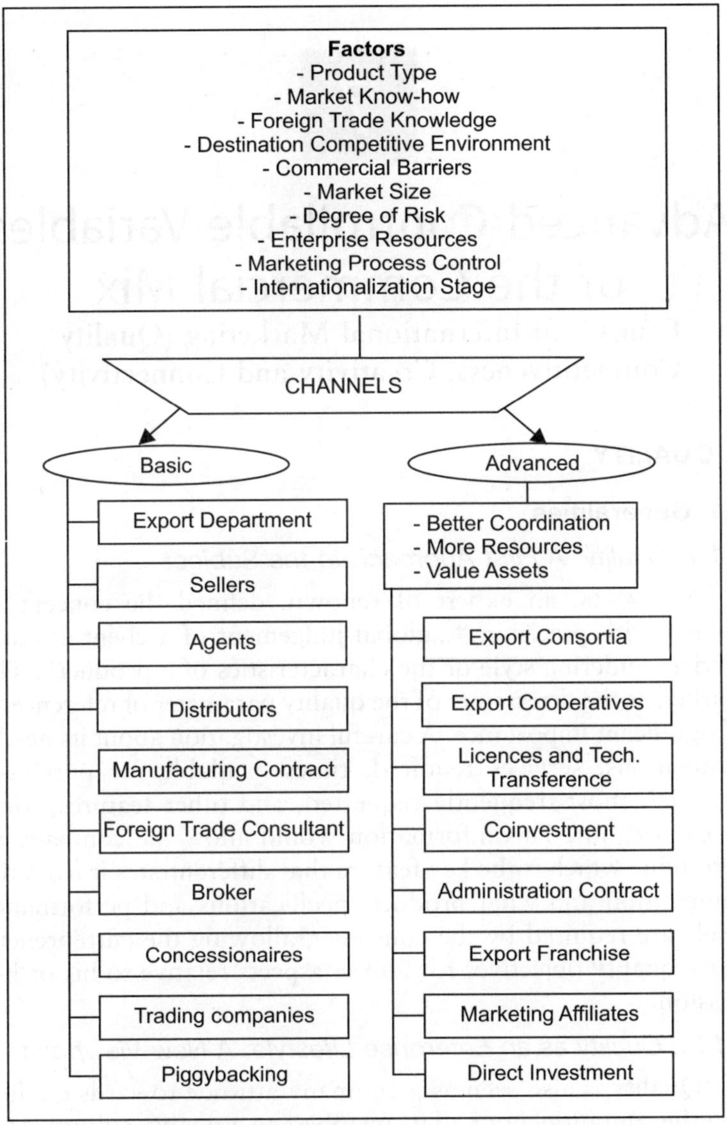


**Figure 6.1.** International Marketing Channels

# 7

# Advanced Controllable Variables of the Commercial Mix

## Four Cs of International Marketing (Quality[1], Competitiveness, Creativity and Connectivity)

## 1. QUALITY

### 1.1. Generalities

#### *1.1.1. Quality: A First Approach to the Subject*

MESTANZA, an expert of renown, defined the concept of quality with precision "...global judgement of a client about a service rendering style or the characteristics of a product". The market, as the determiner of the quality parameter of reference, is of significant importance. A careful investigation about its needs, motivations, services required, times available for purchase, materials most frequently requested, and other features, must be carried out. This information would allow the company to determine which is the key feature that differentiates it from the competition and what product specifications and performance levels are required by the consumer, allowing the entrepreneur to fix quality objectives for all the aspects relative to his or her mission.

#### *1.1.2. Quality as an Enterprise Lifestyle: A New Viewpoint*

Quality is also seen as a company attitude towards quality, and the commitment of all its members to a quality culture. This is a strategic attitude, because it raises the question of quality as a company vision through which every one of its activities will be performed. It is the entrepreneurs' duty to create a propitious

1. This word starts with a C in Spanish: "calidad".

field for the development of quality systems that adequately position the company in the international market, and to pursue results that raise a higher response to clients' expectations in their activities. When, in a global quality approach, clients are mentioned, this term refers not only to consumers, but also, in a more general sense, to the different employees of the company, who are internal clients. The company also looks for a connection with its input processes, that is, the suppliers, and with an indirect client such as the social system, in which the company acts. Quality means coherence at every stage of the entrepreneurial internal and external activity. The company is a net of multiple internal and external interconnections with continuous links with its clients, in a general sense, and those links have to be permeable to quality objectives.

Quality, through responsibility and commitment, has to reduce:

- — design inadequacy of the product for the complete satisfaction of users' needs;
- — multiple production defects;
- — lack of schedule coordination;
- — performance discontinuity of the same product over time;
- — few process inspections;
- — inadequate communication between the members of an internal or external company channel, which produces time and money drawbacks;
- — high levels of waste in the productive process.
- — underuse of resources and duplication of internal activities;
- — lack of understanding of directives imparted by people in charge assigned to different tasks;
- — inappropriate raw material supply.

### 1.1.3. *Quality Awareness within the Enterprise and its Environment*

Quality process is a continuous process that gets feedback from the information provided by the market, and perfects itself at every stage. Quality has to be adopted as a corporative philosophy that interpenetrates every link in the chain of value (research and development, design, production, premarketing, delivery, postmarketing), so that an image of reliability and security, which would in turn promote consumers' repeated consumption, could be positioned in the market.

Such quality relationship allows for a close communicational bond between the company and its suppliers, in which the former asks the latter for specific requirements on materials, physico-chemical features and tolerance degree, and commodity standards as regards the raw material needed for production. Thus, the provision that one of the parties makes to the other will be unequivocally made, according to the company standards. The objective of a quality system is the revision and careful consideration of the contractual conditions that link the parties and the correct testing of the goods supplied.

Every effort in this quality relationship will be aimed mainly at consumers and users, and the entrepreneur will try to fill the needs of their motivations, improving design performance level and product use. It is essential for the consumer to perceive a coherent image of the product-company relationship, different from that of the competition, and in which quality is the main attribute that promotes a new purchase. In order to do that, the company has to develop bonds of trust that link the product to the consumer, trying to build society public acknowledgement. In this way, client loyalty is built through specific activities like: improvement in the perception of the product benefits as regards price, efficient adaptation of the marketed product to consumers' needs, reduction in product replacement and reimbursement rate, shorter delivery times and extra service, in order to please the consumer permanently.

A quality very substantial objective is the reduction of discrepancies between clients' expectations of the product and its real performance as to their satisfaction. The existence of imbalances between the required quality and the quality introduced in the market produces costs which are in direct proportion to the quality system such as: product replacement due to warranty fulfilment, productive process or design modification for adequation to users' expectations, improvement of inspection activities of the different internal stages, etc.; apart from the indirectly system related costs such as: loss of potential sales due to a negative promotion word of mouth and product positioning displacement in a particular segment compared with the competitors, among others.

Some entrepreneurs prefer to implement quality policies on a preventive as well as on a corrective level. However, it is important to consider quality management as a continuous action process that enhances a constant appreciation of the company products.

### *1.1.4. The Importance of a Quality Plan Viable in the Long Term*

Quality relationships stretch into the inside of the company, fostering a cooperative structure among executive, administrative and operative personnel, and an atmosphere of flexibility and motivation, in which each company member is regarded as a fundamental piece for the quality plan development. The members of the organization must avoid hiding defects in internal processes, and incentive the elimination of the various errors that could exist at the centre of the entrepreneurial activity through a participative attitude and following clear efficacious and efficient instructions and rules. The development of a generalized awareness of quality is a priority at the internal level, and at every company level, through steady entrepreneurial activity improvement and coherence. The quality system has to accomplish a greater commitment of all the company members, in the search for internal process uniformity and homogenisation, and in the reduction of organizational operations. The constant development of human resources to develop aptitude and promote protagonism in all the steps of the quality plan, within a frame of excellency is of total relevance to meet those goals.

It is possible for the company objectives and actions towards a quality ideal to have external sources as a reference. Benchmarking refers to the strategic and critic observations that an entrepreneur makes of other companies' outstanding processes and attributes, be it in the same line or in a different one, in order to incorporate them in his or her company. Benchmarking is a process that imitates what is external, and the company can implement the incorporation of outstanding and successful features in two ways: in a direct or literal way, or with the subsequent adaptations necessary to the specifications of the organizational structure. Benchmarking can also be internal, when the company evaluates the favourable and successful aspects of particular processes or internal areas of the company, and extends and adapts them to other departments of the organization. In internal as well as external benchmarking, a permeability towards outstanding quality features is produced.

## 1.2. Quality Management in World Markets

### *1.2.1. Quality in International Operations*

A quality system can be developed according to written or verbal specifications that generally come from the leadership and cover all the functions and operations of the company. But this plan can also be carried out within a system of quality reassurance, in agreement with quality regulations. These norms are not obligatory, but they are nationally or internationally recognized, and their objective is to determine what the entrepreneur has to do to get a quality certification. The company will develop the quality plan, the general and specific procedures and the operative practices, with these norms of standards as a guide. The standardization or adequacy to recognized quality standards improves company's internal control systems and constitutes a guarantee that particular parameters and requirements necessary for excellency standards in the internal organization process have been fulfilled. In certain cases, the requirement of quality norms compliance builds real commercial barriers, matter of factly imposed, to penetrate particular developed external markets. This certification can improve access conditions to those markets and, on the other hand, get a standardization validation from the countries members of a regional agreement. With an adequate quality management, the company generates a more competitive image in the penetrated countries. Besides, the implementation of international quality standards allows the small and medium-sized entrepreneur access to the external markets to get cost improvement and optimization of his or her actions for a greater client satisfaction. In some international markets, standard observance is obligatory in order to penetrate that market, and that standardization is called homologation.

### *1.2.2. International Recognition of Particular Standards*

#### 1.2.2.1. ISO Standards 9000 Version 2000

There are standards with international level recognition. These make up the series ISO 9000 version 2000, issued by the International Organization for Standardization (ISO). These rules point at (unlike others that refer to product related specifications) quality management, and quality and permanent improvement system implementation within a company. However, optimization of the process management within the organization will always affect directly the product or the marketed service. These new standards have a wider scope than the 1994 version, are less oriented to the production sector and are more generic, which makes them available to all the companies, irrespective of product or service type, size and category. These new norms have also reduced significantly the documentary requirements for quality management. Some specialists think this is about an entrepreneurial philosophy more than a group of rules. The ISO 9000 (version 2000) includes fundamental areas such as: quality administration system, leadership responsibility in quality management, resource administration, product or service manufacture, entrepreneurial performance measurement, analysis and improvement guidelines.

These standards are compatible with some international quality norms that are in force for specific sectors like the ones in force for the automobile, telecommunication, software and medical device sectors among others, and most of these specific standards have been adapted and updated to mirror the guidelines of the series ISO 9000 version 2000.

These rules are expressed in a clear and simple language, which makes it more accessible to small and medium-sized organizations. The process based approach presented in the new standards, according to the International Trade Centre newsletter (ITC), "will tend to make sure the systems are documented and implemented in such a way so as to adapt to the particular fashion in which SMEs (small and medium-sized enterprises) do their business" and besides "will make it easier for the SMEs managed by their owners to show strong commitment to the quality management system".

This ISO 9000 family is made up by:

— **ISO 9000:2000**, which specifies and explains the fundamentals and the terms used in the series ISO 9000 (version 2000), as well as the quality management principles. It constitutes a starting point to understand the quality rules of the series.

— **ISO 9001:2000**, which stipulates the requirements for a quality management system through which entrepreneurial capacity to provide products as required by the clients can be demonstrable. They are used for contractual certifications or agreements between suppliers and buyers. It explains what a company has to do, but not how it has to be done, giving great flexibility in the direction and management of the entrepreneurial business.

— **ISO 9004:2000**, which stipulates orientation standards about quality management system permanent improvement issues, in order to fill the needs and expectations of all the interested parties. These norms cannot be used for certification, because they do not set requirements; their main objective is to give orientation about permanent improvement in the performance of an organization. It is based on efficacy issues such as efficiency (this last term means to do the right thing in the right way).

The ISO 9004:2000 together with the ISO 9001:2000 constitute a coherent pair that looks for modern quality management in entrepreneurial processes and activities, and make a special emphasis both, in the promotion of permanent improvement and in the fundamental objective of satisfying clients' requirements.

There are, as a part of the series ISO 9000 version 2000, the ISO/DIS 19001 (guidelines about audits of quality and/or environment management systems). These developing norms, give orientation to perform audits to internal or external quality and/or environment management systems with the purpose of measuring the capacity of those systems in the observance of the stipulated objectives.

The series ISO 9000 version 2000 is based on the following ruling principles:

— client approach (greater client satisfaction through the provision of products according to his or her requirements);
— leadership (it is important to highlight the function and great commitment of the top board to the development and administration of a quality management system);
— participation of company personnel;
— approach based on efficiency-oriented processes;
— management-oriented system, through the identification, understanding and management of the interrelated processes, in a frame of efficiency and effectivity;
— stipulation of permanent improvement as an organization objective;
— approach based on facts for decision taking, which emphasizes data and information analysis to that end;
— understanding of entrepreneurial interdependency with suppliers, and searching for mutually beneficial relationships.

Some other requirements that differentiate these new standards are: stipulation of measurable quality objectives in the different levels and functions, establishment of communication processes inside the company that allow the effective transmission of the quality management system objectives, information relative to client satisfaction follow up in order to quantify the efficacy of the system, among others.

1.2.2.2. ISO 14000 Standards

As with the series 9000, the ISO 14000 standards constitute a system of quality management generic standards that could be applied to any organization (commerce, industry or service organization; public or private). These well-known standards consider specifications and guidelines for environmental management, environmental labelling and ecolabelling, and entrepreneurial evaluation systems and their environmental impact, among their main ecological concerns. These norms allow any industrial or service company of any sector or economic activity to take control over its actions impact on the environment. Some of the direct consequences of the implementation of this environmental quality management system are: drop in industrial waste handling costs, reduction in energy and materials consumption, less distribution costs, improvement of the company image for different economic agents it operates with, continuous improvement in the interaction company-environment.

These norms are voluntary, that is, their implementation does not have legal force. They establish an adequate environmental management frame that demands the company a commitment oriented towards a developmental policy, the establishment of objectives to improve environmental management, the development of a culture of environmental performance, and management development progress or deficiencies objective evaluations.

These standards are based on the following basic principles: development of an entrepreneurial environmental policy, planning of the activities to that end, development of the planned activities and a management evaluation. The ISO 14000 include simple instruments for the protection of the world environmental conditions, promoting an adequate and rational management of the entrepreneurial activities designed to those ends. The reassurance of the companies through these environmental management criteria can become an important competitiveness factor to penetrate the international markets, by showing entrepreneurial actions with a strong commitment in ecological issues. On the other hand, the company image is improved, getting an active co-starring social position in the reduction of global ecological risks.

### 1.2.2.3. Other Important Certifications

A complete anlysis of all the other international certifications of importance is not going to be developed. The objective of this section is to give orientations about the main aspects about which the small and medium-sized enterprise can get international validation through the intervention of authorized bodies. The common factor in the obtention of the different certifications is that they contribute, directly or indirectly, to generate a greater commercial flow in the world markets.

#### *1.2.2.3.1. Organic Product Certification*

These are food products whose certification by an organization or authorized body demands them to comply with a series of accepted standards as to which is recognized as "organic" for various products. The main characteristics of an organic product are: non-use of pesticides nor synthetic herbicides, non-existence of dangerous bacteria in the products, non-use of artificial ingredients or preservatives and non-use of synthetic fertilizers. As regards the production equipment used in the manufacture of organic products, the company has to employ industrial equipment according to environmental care standards, environmental sustainable techniques that protect water resources.

The *Codex Alimentarius Commission* (a body established by the World Health Organization (WHO) and the Food and Agriculture Organization of the United Nations (FAO), has produced guidelines for the production, manufacture, labelling, and marketing of organic products. There are also organic production international standards, such as the ones created by the International Federation of Organic Agriculture Movement (IFOAM), that concentrates about 700 world organizations, many of them producers, of more than 100 countries.

The products certified as organic generally have a higher sale price than the others in the same category due to the care and complexity required by their industrial process and they have a typical labelling and/or packaging.

*1.2.2.3.2. Certification of Non-Transgenic Products*

Particular products could be produced from genetically modified bodies (GMB). A GMB, also known by the name "transgenic", is a plant or an animal that has received the genes of a different species to give it some characteristics of the latter and with specific objectives (product longer commercial life, resistance to adverse environmental conditions and to diseases, improvement in the nutritional features, etc.). These biotechnological experiences are produced in laboratories and are discretionary applied for product transformation; that is, not produced by natural multiplication or recombination.

There are no studies that certify that these products with alterations do not cause damage to consumers' health and the environment, but there are investigations about the side effects (allergies, antibiotic resistance, toxic effects) products with GMB can produce in consumers' bodies. The non-transgenic condition of a product can be determined through tests that evaluate the non-existence of genetically modified bodies.

There are international agreements that require the transgenic products to be identified in order to protect consumers' information rights. There is a consensus in the international regulatory body known as the *Codex Alimentarius Commission* (FAO) about the need to label transgenic food to protect consumers' security rights. However, companies resist GMB product labelling. As regards transgenic product international trade, international agreements about the subject have agreed that those companies willing to market genetically manipulated products should indisputably notify the government of the importer country, which will be able to restrict the entrance of the product if it is considered that either the environment or the health of the population could be affected.

#### *1.2.2.3.3. HACCP Certification*

HACCP certification is the certification relative to Hazards and Critical Control Point Analysis. Based on the Codex Alimentarius guidelines, this system has applied scientific and technical principles, according to STEVENSON, "to every phase in food production, including basic agriculture, preparation and handling of foods, food service, distribution and handling systems, and consumer use". This internationally recognized system guarantees the harmlessness of food through the implementation of specific actions. It is based more on prevention than on inspection principles, and this programme controls the factors that affect the ingredients, the process and the product.

The company that obtains this certification is able to show its ability to administer tools for the prevention of dangerous situations (physical, chemical and biological) in the manipulation of food (as a result of a natural process or by errors in the manufacturing process) before the international community. Certification in these issues allows the company to increase product international marketing opportunities towards markets where the system HACCP is recognized and regulated. Besides, possibilities to integrate this system to other quality management systems such as the ISO 9000 become available.

#### *1.2.2.3.4. Certification of Good Manufacturing Practices (GMP)*

These rules are based on the *Codex Alimentarius* hygiene practices and their objective is to develop good practices for the manufacture of the product and the observation of hygienic and sanitary optimum conditions (so as to avoid contamination problems) in the food manufacturing industrializing premises.

Among the most important subjects these rules deal with: requirements about the establishment (as regards location, product transition and manipulation areas, industrial wastewater disposal, etc.); hygiene requirements (which include equipment and tool maintenance, tidiness and disinfection, subproduct and dangerous substances storage, waste disposal, etc.), personal hygiene related issues of people who manipulate the products (handwash, health state, use of gloves, etc.), as well as manufacture hygienic requirements (as regards raw material use, cross contamination, and employment of water, product packaging, among other issues). Storage and raw material and finished product transportation as well as food control are also included in the orientations.

The GMPs constitute a basic tool for the obtention of products suitable and harmless for human consumption, and they emphasize on questions of process and product hygiene and manipulation related to food.

*1.2.2.3.5. Occupational Health and Security*

At present, organizations are concerned with other areas, such as workers' health and security. To that end, there is international level recognition of certifications on the base of the OHSMS (Occupational Health and Safety Management System) 18001 standards in which an occupational health and safety management system is evaluated inside the company. That is, these standards establish occupational health and security management system requirements which allow the company to control the risks in the system and improve its performance. Obtention of this certification allows the recognition of the existence of an adequate management system of the working aspects within the company by the interested parties, clients, insurance agents, and the community in general. Those norms emphasize the proactive preventive practices by identifying potential dangers and controlling risks at the workplace. Some advantages of this certification are the reduction of work accidents, improductive time and occupational medical expenses, and the improvement in job stability and employers' satisfaction. Other benefits include the obtention of new international business opportunities as a consequence of a demonstrable occupational health commitment, better negotiation with insurance companies, better entrepreneurial position before labour control governmental bodies. This management system is compatible with other systems, such as the ones established by the series ISO 9000 and 14000.

*1.2.2.3.6. Social Responsibility System Certification*

The system known as SA 8000 (or Social Responsibility 8000) has the same ISO management audit techniques and its objective is to certify decent working conditions. The SA 8000 uses a system of corrective and preventive actions and is based on human rights principles (such as the Universal Declaration of Human Rights, the UN Convention on the Right of the Child and the International Labour Organization Conventions). The main areas this system covers are: forced work, children's work, health and security, free association and the right to collective negotiation, disciplinary practices, discrimination, working schedules, compensation and management systems.

This certification allows companies to position internationally as responsible and committed employers from the social and labour point of view.

*1.2.2.3.7. Other International Certifications*

Apart from 14000 ISO Standards and others previously mentioned, some international certifications can validate entrepreneurial activity very specific thematic fields as, for example:

— ***Use of clean sources of energy:*** In general terms, energy (especially the energy that comes from traditional sources) in industrial processes has harmful effects on the development system. However, there are some energy sources which are more efficient or less pollutant and so, their use diminishes development impact. Natural gas and renewable sources of energy, such as solar energy and wind power, which form part of an ecoindustrial management system are also included in these sources.

— ***Development of less contaminating industrial processes:*** These issues are of vital importance to those companies that identify the impact that their activity has upon the environment and try to reduce them. These certifications demand variations in its production process or product design variations in order to use less raw material and natural resources or to minimize the use of contaminating or toxic material. Related to this, there are certain international certifications based on environmental risk analysis and evaluation.

— *Adequate exploitation of waste material:* Recycling companies make sure that some used materials could be reused. These actions are important because there is a decreased use of raw material taken from nature and besides recycling diminishes the amount of waste that impacts negatively on the environment. These certifications could include validations on the non-use of recycled synthetic materials, use of recycled natural materials, as well as requisites and minimum contents required for containers and packaging in order to be recycled.

Other issues are certifications referred to an adequate treatment of dangerous waste (among which there are special, industrial radiation, and pathology wastes) and to the effective observance of laws and international agreements on the subject.

Small and medium-sized enterprises that manage developmentally sustainable industrial systems, and get certifications that ratify them, enjoy a double strategic benefit:

— They contribute to environmental care and population health protection.

— They offer an important differentiation in the market, compared to their competitors and buyers perceive them as friendly and committed to the environment, which allows them to get and keep more clients.

## 2. FOREIGN TRADE COMPETITIVENESS

### 2.1. Competition in the World Market

#### *2.1.1. Small and Medium-sized Enterprise Competitive Strategy*

The small and medium-sized enterprise has a flat structure, with a few hierarchical levels that offer great operative flexibility to adapt to the environmental changes; besides, it has a great ability for structure reconversion, and a movement capacity of improductive activity resources towards more productive businesses. The organization strategy of a small-sized business has to be concerned about the detection of different opportunities that appear in the international market. The perception of potential world opportunities has to be done within a wider scope which could include the analysis of competition in external markets, to position the relative differential advantages that the company has in relation to the others that operate in a particular country.

Entrepreneurs have to assess the entrepreneurial competitive position as regards the consumer, that is, determine what differential of value contributes the company in its product attributes and in the service related to it. It is vital to discover which are the excellence processes or attributes offered to the market, through an analysis of the competing company, as well as of non-competitive companies, so that the very company could adopt and adapt them through a benchmarking strategy.

### *2.1.2. Enterprise Competitiveness: Various Differential Aspects*

Within this strategic study, the company will look through its internal resources (human, image, financial, economic, technological, innovating and marketing resources) assigned to the markets. In relation to the marketing resources, the company should find out which are the competitive advantages that differentiate it from the different existing offers in the international environment. Among the main resources of competitive marketing, there are:

- Performance degree of the international sellers, agents, or distributors that the company uses to gain entrance in the external markets.
- Adequacy capacity with regard to specific and differential environments (cultural, economic, legal, political), in each market-country. The company has to adopt a balanced position between standardization and adaptation of the different variables of the commercial mix, considering barriers and advantages in each individual market.
- Satisfaction ability of consumers' needs and creation of loyalty conditions towards the company brand,

which implies market-oriented external activities. The company may be specialized in particular areas: service, technology, materials used, packaging, that differentiate it from the competition.

- Company staff motivation towards international operations that consider foreign trade a fundamental activity within the entrepreneurial vision.
- Optimum product price conditions. In a wider sense, value has to be considered as perceived by the consumer (that relates the price paid for the product to the benefits obtained by its use or consumption).
- Company capacity of response in the presentation of different services related to the internationally marketed product (claim procedures, premarketing advice on models, technical assistance, punctuality in delivery, effectiveness of the different international distribution functions, etc.).
- Quality levels reached (level and service level, internal process level, suppliers interconnection levels, clients, and entities).
- High levels of flexibility and timing that generate an adjustment capacity to abrupt changes produced in the company environment (local currency devaluations or revaluations, imposition of paratariff barriers on particular markets). This quality embraces a great intuitive capacity of company human resources to diagnose potential commercial scenarios and is centred in an anticipation and prediction strategic spirit to face the different changes in the entrepreneurial environment.
- Team innovation and creativity skill within the company. There has to be a constant generation of alternatives for courses of action, marketing and channel variables available to be used by the organization. One of the main company resources is style and talent of the human capital that produces multiple ideas constantly. An atmosphere of open reflective thinking has to be fostered, for the creation of new visions about the

different concerns that affect the organization in its international operation access and diversification.

- Company communication strategy and information systems that link the company internal and external designing and functioning aspects.
- Predisposition for the constitution of strategic alliances and export or production joint ventures.
- Selection of the most adequate internationally oriented external markets, taking into account rhythm and form of access, product line and resources assigned.
- External market economy of scale generation capacity, that is, a better distribution of fixed costs produced by a price rise in the marketed goods, with more competitive prices as a result.
- Ability to generate economies of scope in the external markets. This concept refers to cost saving in order to widen a product line in a particular market, which allows to share experience and information among the different products offered by the company to that market.
- Efficiency in the positioning developed and in the obtention of more participation (market share) in the external markets.
- Progressive and sustained internationalization experience that the company gets through the development of its international operations.
- Possibility to generate a brand capital as an important asset in the company generation of value.
- Capacity to generate marketing economies and investigation and development economies, in order to increase the number of penetrated markets, which allows for the global use of the marketing and innovation activities.
- Efficient use of the benefits gained by the company due to its positioning in a regional market, which implies the expansion of its commercial activities towards the

different members of the block as well as to the extrazone countries.

— Company balanced attitude when adopting extreme strategies, as market concentration and expansion and the analysis and evaluation of some factors like: level of company commercial development in each market, existence of adaptation requirements of product attributes to each market, sales stability, product lifecycle, etc.
— Persistence to reach the goals devised for the world markets.
— Sustained continuity and earnestness in the undertaken commitments.
— Commercial honesty in the activities developed by the company. The organization has to have ethical behaviour and stipulate clear external operations game rules, getting away from unfair practices such as dumping, commercial fraud, etc.
— Other issues like: patent development, obtention of quality international certifications, which form part of the value resources of the company.

## 2.2. Value Generation and the Entrepreneurial Mission

A company value generation within an international competitive strategy has external beneficiaries such as the external consumer or user, but it also has multiple internal beneficiaries such as partners, management and employees. From a macroeconomic point of view, the State where the company is located can also be considered as another added value addressee by the internationalizing organization, by different factors such as: taxation payment, new employment generation, foreign exchange inflow and productivity rise.

The company has to create new markets in the international environment. In order to fulfil this objective, the organization must not only penetrate the existing segment in a particular country, but also explore the potential penetration in specific market niches which have not been exploited by the competition.

Accordingly, all the strategic approaches that generate value towards the client and that allow a more intimate contact with him or her, in order to satisfy his or her needs will have to be carefully identified. All these activities will have to be developed coherently with the mission of the company, that is, the final goal pursued, and in agreement with its financial, economic and commercial objectives.

The external market entrepreneurial strategies will consist of a series of different alternatives in order to comply with the internationalization objectives, which consider the existing resources. Within the frame of these strategies, the entrepreneur must establish realistic goals to reach certain objectives.

There are factors external to the company that condition the levels of competitiveness to reach, among which could be mentioned:

— entrepreneurial financing cost;
— governmental policies that affect the industrial sector;
— energy inputs cost;
— tax and labour regulations;
— foreign trade infrastructure systems;
— other factors: exchange policy, degree of economic liberalization, state interventionism degree in international marketing activity.

## 2.3. Competitive Advantage of a Sector and of a Country

### *2.3.1. Conditions that Create Competitiveness in a Sector of the National Economy*

In this section, the introductory aspects of company and nation competitiveness are going to be defined, advising the reader to more specific literature so as to study these isuues in depth. According to Dr. PORTER—one of the most relevant specialists in the subject of strategy competitive advantage—, in two of his main books *Competitive Strategy* and *The Competitive Advantage of Nations*, it is possible to determine five forces that interact and influence to develop a company level of competitiveness, within a specific sector of a country's economy.

The first of the aforementioned aspects is the potential entry of new competitors in the market. The intervention of these new operators brings about a price, margin and productivity level reduction within the sector. All the organizations that consider the possibility of getting access to a particular competitive environment will have to carry out a detailed evaluation of the existing obstacles for the company at the time of introduction in the market, such as: economies of scale demands to be competitive, the existence of differentiating elements in their products, requirements of fixed and operative assets to get access to the sector, costs that imply consumers' change from one supplier to another, easy access to an adequate distribution structure, existence of state policies that discourage the entry of new companies and cost advantages not related to economies of scale (for example: governmental subventions granted to certain companies, insufficient supply of raw material).

The second factor is the real or potential existence of substitute products. The existence of these products allows the consumer, when there is a product price rise, to displace his or her purchase to a more economical product, which may equally satisfy his or her needs.

The third factor is buyers' negotiating ability, determined by their influencing power to reduce the company's margins or earnings, and which is related to consumers' volumes of purchase and negotiating advantages that each party in a commercial agreement gets. This aspect is also closely related to the level of differentiation of the product which the company commercializes, and with the relative importance of the product purchase-buyer's total expenses ratio.

Suppliers' negotiating capacity is the fourth important factor; it is related to the existing amount of suppliers in the sector, differentiation degree of the product offered by each one of them, existence of brands and attributes of their own, and the cost that changing suppliers implies for the buyer.

The fifth encouraging factor is the intensity of competitors' actions that can generate positive effects on the commercial or industrial sector such as: rational cost readjustment, higher responsibility in the sector, differentiation degree of the goods offered by the companies, strategic efforts made by the competition to keep its position in the market.

### 2.3.2. Enterprise Competitive Approaches

MICHAEL PORTER declares that competitive advantage can have a cost-oriented or a differentiation-oriented approach within a limited frame; this approach is segmentation oriented, that is, entrepreneurial actions are oriented towards well defined goal markets. From a wider marketing approach, that is, for a great amount of markets and/or a wide line of products, the company can achieve leadership in costs. In order to obtain more reduced costs in an international level sector, it is vital to design efficiency seeking strategies as regards productive scale, with a concern about industrial process innovation. The cost leader strategy implies the improvement of productive processes, an efficient restructuration of the distribution channels, and increasing capital investments in a reengineering process.

Besides, the company can also develop a competitive differentiation strategy through brand, quality, design, reliability, service or any other attribute, which allow it to quickly increase its share in the market and defend its confronting position towards the competitor. The development of this strategy requires certain specific actions like: investment in investigation, production of creative ideas, technological updating, betterment of commercial abilities and building of cooperative bonds among market operators.

### 2.3.3. Competitive Conditions of a Nation

In order to develop a competitive national advantage in some sectors, Dr. PORTER defines a structure of competitiveness diamond which is made up by several interrelated phases: human, intellectual, capital and natural factor availability and infrastructure, its existence in a country and its relations with the productive sector structure; existence of a wide and increasing domestic demand that makes up an important national consumption market, development of companies that help other sector organizations, configuration of an important national dynamic competitive scenario and ability for new entrepreneurial activities.

Two complementary factors of the diamond are the existence of eventual facts, like wars and exchange fluctuations, and the influence of state intervention in the economic and commercial activity of the country, as well as in education. This model, which has been shortly developed, has been reinforced by the strong influence of state activities in some countries, which have sensibly affected the parameters of relative competitiveness among the nations through the production of barriers, regulations, direct investment requirement. The development shown does not either consider in depth the links between the diamonds of two or more countries which, in some cases, could generate and increasing and synergic competitiveness for operations that the companies belonging to those countries make between them. A recognized specialist, Dr. D'Aveni, holds an extreme position in which not one advantage can be sustained for a long time, because those advantages get built and destroyed in a continuous process that opens a frame of hypercompetition, and thus, marketing has a privileged position in market creation and development.

## 3. CREATIVITY IN INTERNATIONAL MARKETING

### 3.1. Creativity and Entrepreneurial Disciplines

#### *3.1.1. Importance of Creativity*

It is common to associate the concept of creativity with exotic or extravagant ideas, and there is a generalized belief that everything that is creative only has a natural bond with the arts. This approach to creativity is very limited and does not admit that creative issues could be extended to other areas not related to the arts. It is important to recognize that creativity can be applied to the entrepreneurial sciences and, more specifically, to the international marketing activities. A creative spirit has to be developed in the different entrepreneurial processes and actions with access to the external markets. A creative vision proposes new ways to perform activities, to get results in agreement with the preset objectives. The original ideas do not make sense by themselves, if they are not put into practice, and have to be the way from a modifiable present situation to a desired future scenario.

### *3.1.2. Attitude of Innovative Options Generation Relative to Internationalization*

For the company which has never exported, taking the decision to internationalize and starting to perform the activities of the external business plan is already a creative process. External market penetration implies an attitude of alternative diversification as regard markets, earnings, risks and assignation of resources and so, the entrepreneurial actions are not limited only to the internal market. The company that performs international activities can explore non-traditional solutions for the challenges that appear in its commercial activity. In an international approach, there are multiple potential strategies that the company can adopt to reach its objectives, some of them obvious ones, and others less traditional.

The first important concept about this subject is that as regards international markets, it is vital for the company to evaluate the greatest number of alternatives about the following features:

- — Solutions to different company problems as regards external markets.
- — Ways to have access to information about the international markets and different approaches to analyze the data obtained.
- — Ways of segmentation to be used in the external market.
- — Presentations (design, colour, shape, size and other features) that a product will have so as to adapt to the selected markets.
- — Ways to position the product and communicate its attributes.
- — Potentially beneficial markets to commercialize the product.

— Ways to avoid or soothe the tariff or paratariff barriers effect existing in the destination markets.
— Penetration channels to be used for international access.
— Existing or potential distribution channels in the destination market.
— Stipulations about the various components of a price policy.
— Ways to react to competitors' attitudes.
— Service variety which will satisfy consumers' needs.
— Marketing general strategy design and analysis of the different potential variables in each of its stages.

### *3.1.3. Lateral Thinking and the Generation of Multiple Options*

The application of a creative approach in the international marketing aims at giving more freedom to the emergence of potentially useful options for the company business, going from beyond the most ordinary and recognizable ones to multiple alternatives, even taking into account, in a first instance, channels of exceptional or non-traditional character. In this way, the entrepreneur can analyze new possibilities, that give rise to a continuous improvement of the company competitiveness in external markets. This approach aims at, in one of its most important aspects, more than one alternative to solve problems and meet internationalization objectives, to subsequently choose the most convenient. This multiplicity of options has to be generated in a frame of spontaneity and suppression of critical judgement. Creativity applied to entrepreneurial activity is characterized by a strong attitude of curiosity and generation of ideas than can be made specific in the development of a project, through innovative actions. The creative approach of international trade implies, in certain cases, a higher risk, which routine and repetitive activities do not possess.

Within what is known as lateral thinking, originally developed by Dr. De Bono, the greatest amount of options to approach a specific topic has to be produced, with the aim of restructuring the mental models of logical reasoning. In a first stage, the adequacy of the multiple generated alternatives is not to be criticized. The important thing is the number of options that are provisionally generated, to subsequently, in a second instance, filtrate it within a rational analytical process. This way of focusing tries to overcome the barriers of conventional and mediocre conservatism that may characterize the company activities and allows to re-imagine new original scenarios for the fulfilment of its goals.

## 3.2. Different Creative Activities Related to External Operations

### *3.2.1. Creativity in the Approach to Internationalization Problems*

As regards the concerns that can affect the company in its process of incursion in the external markets, the problem would have to be divided in different parts, so that each component can be analyzed in detail. For example, the problem of lack of funds in the company as regards the international markets, can be subdivided into:

- Lack of budget for the study of international markets.
- Lack of funds for the purchase of raw material to manufacture exportation products.
- Lack of funds to cover the operative cycle that goes from shipment to encashment.

Each one of these parts can be subsequently subdivided (that subdivision does not necessarily have to be done in natural units), and the main objective of this approach is to obtain multiple alternatives for the effective solution of the problem.

Any concern can be creatively reformulated, through new conceptions of the problem. In relation to the example of the previously mentioned problem, the company lack of funds as regards the international markets can be put like this: the company on an individual basis does not possess financing for the external activities. This new approach that adds the word individual, allows the consideration of other alternatives such as outsourcing, strategic alliances, among others. To reformulate a problem, these things can be done: rewriting, subdividing, adding or deleting some details, making it more general or more specific, changing the centre of attention, or radically transforming the presentation of the concerns.

### 3.2.2. Brainstorming the Internationalization Problem

Brainstorming is a useful method that can also be used to analyze an internationalization problem. This technique implies a programmed meeting that involves members of different areas of the company, and where, within a short time limit (not more than 15 minutes per encounter), the participants express their ideas about a subject interactively, and each idea commented by one person triggers the generation of other ideas in the rest of the attendants. Somebody has to register the event by hand and there has to be a moderator. It is important that neither intrapersonal nor interpersonal criticism exist so that more views about the greatest amount of possibilities for the subject under analysis could appear. Once the expositions have been written down, the most viable alternatives will be filtered in a subsequent stage.

### 3.2.3. Change of Approach for the Internationalization Problem

In some cases, the company does not know which are the crucial obstacles that impede its international access. This is why acute and precise questions should be made, taking into account different contexts and probable approaches, in order to have clear concepts and forceful ideas that include the solutions to the problems. Some encouraging words (for example: why, how, what would happen if...) would be very helpful to start discussion. Whenever possible, internationalization problems should have to be debated in groups, with the participation and complementation of the various sectors of the company that are more relevant (financial, commercial, accounting, legal, etc.) to analyze the problems.

### 3.2.4. Adaptation of Analogies for Problem-solving

It can be found in the resolution of the internationalization problem through creative adaptation of other companies' ways of resolution of similar problems; it is also important to look for the problem connection with analogous situations (that is, those in which there is some point in common, even though they may belong to fields different from the problem to be solved) that might have arisen in other internal areas of the company and which might be useful to face the conflict.

A creative analysis of international marketing concerns implies, not only a vision of the problem in itself, but also a detailed look into the obstacles that may appear, together with the impulses that generate inside the company to penetrate the international markets, as well as the resources that an entrepreneur has for those ends. This implies the questioning of the situation, not only emphasizing the existing obstacles, but also highlighting the opportunity for action provided by it. After a global analysis of the problems, it necessarily follows their resolution, by choosing a creative alternative that could efficiently overcome them.

### *3.2.5. Different Observation, Combination and International Data Application Approaches*

As regards international market information, different forms of analysis should be looked for, with various data combinations administered by different sources. During data evaluation, the company has to take several starting points or referential frames, for example, from the segmentation point of view, the existing commercial barriers or competitive environment, etc. Numerous alternatives of creative reorganizing of the information should be forecast in this analysis, as well as its grouping and partition, to look for new perspectives and implicit elements.

Market-country specific data should be applied to the actions to be developed, but it is also important to evaluate the use these offer to other markets or other company activities, even for internal market operations. That is, the creative interpretation of the international information must not have a unique sense in connection with its interpretation and treatment; it has to be multidirectional, with multiple contributions among the different markets and areas of the company.

This approach implies an interactive and global evaluation of different data, in order to discover the different connections and collaborations provided by the compiled information. The entrepreneur has to make this analysis with an exploratory and open mind so as to find links and associations that offer new scenarios that challenge the conventional ways to do external business. An ample range of related data source has to be consulted to get a broader vision of external market information treatment; similarities have to be found, differences contrasted, and reports importance weighed.

### *3.2.6. Creative Redesign of Market Segments*

The company will also be able to creatively redefine its strategy as regards the segmentation ways to be used in the external market, the product presentations to adapt to the selected markets and the way to position the product and communicate its attributes. As regards market segmentation, the company can look for other segmentation ways beyond the traditional segments, and combine variables in a different way or create new ways so as to make a creative partition of the market possible. It is important to consider that the company can divide already existing segments in subsegments that can be better taken care of, or group segments that can be more efficiently explored in a joint way.

### *3.2.7. Generation of Product New Attributes*

The presentation of the product (way, colour, design, size) is closely related to the redefinition of the segments and the creative approach to this subject may include new containers, materials, design, aesthetics and images, container label, colours, overcover, etc. These new ideas may come out from creative meetings among company employers and advisors in charge of different areas: design, production, commerce, finance, accountancy and legal, in which multifunctional and interdisciplinary evaluations are made.

Nevertheless, creative strategies in the presentation of the product attributes can also originate as a result of Research and Development (R + D) programmed activities that look for creative findings and have a budget assigned to that end. This R + D area is less common in small-sized companies, which is the reason why it would be important in its development there, within the budget limitations that these organizations have.

It is also important to consider the presentations and differential attributes of the competitors in the foreign market to be able to, upon that base, perform the pertinent modifications, combinations, adaptations, additions and fragmentations, suppressions and improvements, so as to get a better positioning in the international environment.

### *3.2.8. Redefinition of the Product Line Offered to the External Market*

Besides, line product reduction, grouping or widening, or modification of the one offered to the external market is also included in the creative actions to be developed by the company. As regards positioning, it is convenient for the organization to develop new product categories beyond the market known standards. As regards communication strategy, various options have to be considered when creating the international promotion mix to foster other ways of communicational impact like: communication alliances among several companies, undercover advertising, virtual advertising, ads discounts, etc.

### *3.2.9. Global Conception and Creative Analysis of External Markets*

As regards the selection of beneficial markets to commercialize the product, the definition of the ways to avoid existing commercial barriers in the destination market, and the choice of the penetration channels and the most adequate distribution ways for the destination market, the company may, from a traditional approach, present hindrances in the search for optimum solutions, and this is why those areas have to be creatively approached in order to build successful alternatives.

Market specific features (current and potential) like existing population, industry structure, purchasing power and consumers' education, competition level, governmental regulations, among others, have to be assessed in order to find the most adequate external markets for the company product. However, from an open and creative thinking, other factors that indirectly affect those markets, like: product adaptation need due to legal or cultural differential issues, the geographic and psychographic distance between the markets of origin and destination, company experience in similar markets and the existing funds to enter the new markets (the latter implies, in turn, creative decisions about the application of those resources) have also to be included in this analysis. So, as regards the selection of potentially beneficial markets for the product, not only the obvious factors operatively attractive for the company, but also other indirect factors or factors weakly associated to them, have to be considered.

Further, it is important for the entrepreneur to assess the capacity to share specific commercial experiences in a market-country with other markets likely to be penetrated. On the other hand, the company also has to consider the possibility of expanding the information and know-how acquired through marketing a certain product in a market to other line products of the company in that market (notion known as "economies of scope").

As regards the existing barriers that affect the company exports in a specific market, some alternatives to avoid or diminish its impact in the marketing, like distributing the chain of value between the origin and destination markets in order to pay less tariffs, the granting of franchising or licences, and the location of the productive structure in the destination market, have to be preconsidered.

### *3.2.10. Creative Transformation in the Distribution Systems*

There are numerous alternatives to distribute the product, and each one of them has different combinations in the service/ cost relationship. From a creative point of view, the organization has to consider the use of non-traditional but compatible with the company product distribution channels. In the distribution system analysis, it is important to subdivide the channel into its levels, looking for the optimum combination among the different existing alternatives for each level assessed. If it is possible, it is necessary to consider the following as valid options:

— suppression or distribution levels leap so as to concentrate functions in a smaller number of intermediaries;

— lengthening of the channel, that is, the addition of intermediaries;

— acquisition of ampler width or narrowing at some channel level.

The entrepreneur has to conduct the study about which the options are for an internalization or externalization process as regards the multiple aspects of international access and distribution. The company can, in some cases, copy creatively structures used in the destination market by other local or foreign companies which commercialize similar or complementary products to the company product.

Other aspects to be examined are: the different location and volume that company product stocks may have and the different existing international transport strategies that generate value for the product.

As regards the election of the marketing channels to be used, it is important to look deeply into the different risk, earnings and control aspects of each one; as well as to verify the channel coherence with the product adequate positioning and with the segment towards which the company is oriented. To those ends, the constitution of creative alliances and coalitions among the different members of the channel to get an effective distribution of functions and retributions can be valid. It can also be important the search for one or more commercial partners for the international adventure, in order to achieve strategic complementation and diminish the degree of vulnerability of external operations.

### *3.2.11. Other Aspects of Change and Creativity in the International Product*

Different factors are taken into account by the company in the configuration of the international price policy, among others: competitors' attitudes, costs of service offered and required by the consumer, variable price alignment with the general marketing strategy. From a creative approach, there has to be an evaluation of the different potential combinations of:

— financing;

— payment instruments to be used (letter of credit, collection);
— collection due dates;
— delivery due dates;
— quoted incoterms and service included in that price;
— minimum or maximum volumes.

In this analysis the tangible as well as the intangible qualities of the product, and other variables which could influence over the price quotation (promotion, distribution, product) such as the marketing mix, have to be considered. It is important to examine the price on the global level and how can the mix affect the quoted price when a component is modified. It is priority to develop multiple alternatives that can both improve the benefit/ price relationship for the consumer, and consider the company economic objectives, promoting a differentiation as regards the competition.

As regard consumer service, as a product plus service, the entrepreneur has to constantly and creatively question the general assumptions about the products and have an emphatic attitude, which would make it possible for him or her to understand the consumer. It is very useful to perform a survey about the market in order to be in tune with it and generate new pleasing consumer service, which considers issues like comfort, security, economicity, practicity, entertainment and adaptability to uses and customs, depending on personal preference. This is about giving the company product, which could be susceptible to analogous adaptation, some attributes which belong to completely different products.

As regards strategy and the company's international stage, the various alternative intermediate approaches between standardization and adaptation for each of the variables and subvariables of the commercial mix have to be analyzed. It is important to consider the market strategy expansion and concentration combinations with the ethnocentric, polycentric, and geocentric approaches.

## 4. CONNECTIVITY IN INTERNATIONAL MARKETING

### 4.1. Rising of a World Digital Economic Scenario

#### *4.1.1. Digital Economic Era Consequences*

In the last decades, within the globalization scenario, a new economic scenario which, according to DON TAPSCOTT is called "digital economy" has started to be developed. It is characterized by the progressive telecommunication (radio, television, broadcasting, etc.) and information technology convergence (hardware, software, service, repairs, etc.) and with the contents (that is, different information systems such as newspapers, books, publications, libraries, etc.). This economic scenario is in a transitional stage and in constant evolution. Its main protagonists are information and intellectual capital, the most relevant resources of the company.

The rising of this new operative space is the result of the technological hustling that has been unstoppingly developing (the constant improvement in new microprocessor abilities is an example of this) and pulling down individual as well as entrepreneurial and national communicational barriers. This process is the result of seriously undertaken activities of Research and Development (R + D) which accelerate changes and reinventions.

#### *4.1.2. Channel Digitalization and Informative Messages*

Information transmission has stopped to be synchronic to be asynchronic and multidirectional; it is digitalized information (essentially made of bits) that interconnects the different operators, generating net structures characterized by a cooperative strong value generation and which somehow affects all the entrepreneurial processes. At the same time innovative infrastructures that allow this digital information immediate conduction, reception and storage start to configure.

## 4.2. E-commerce Development

### *4.2.1. Virtual Marketing Importance*

#### 4.2.1.1. The Worldnet and Electronic Marketing

The development of new digital or virtual channels gives rise to new business models called "virtual businesses". One of main qualities of the Internet is the hypertext. It allows to move from one datum to another in non-synchronic jumps, simultaneously and multimedially, generating a great variety of text, image, and sound links in a server-client relationship.

Virtual marketing is based on the structure developed by Internet an information highway. Internet is part of the www (World Wide Web), which expands as a worldnet, linking every sector of the planet through information highways.

Electronic trade, in the strict sense, can be assimilated to the business and information exchange developed through the net, but, in a wider sense, it includes other ways of electronic marketing (automatic teller machines, electronic machines, etc.) so, it originated before Internet trade. The European Union includes those transactions and businesses in which information or communication technologies are used in electronic trade. The following words, related to the Internet commercial channels, are going to be considered as synonyms in order to simplify criteria for the development of this topic: electronic trade, e-commerce, virtual marketing, and digital marketing.

#### 4.2.1.2. Main Features of Electronic Marketing

Electronic trade is based on the development of websites and webpages that can be visited by any potential consumer of the global market, and on the management of electronic trade or e-mail (in the last case, a more limited electronic trade). Even though there are subtle conceptual differences between site and page, both are going to be considered as synonyms in this book.

Electronic trade implies, among other issues:

— The existence of adequate hardware (PC, modems, etc.), that is, the physical infrastructure to develop the virtual platform.

— Software adequate to develop the different virtual processes efficiently (treatment of graphs, data filing, etc.).

— Virtual space where the page will be located. This means hiring the services of an Internet provider (ISP or Internet Service Provider). Those services may be varied and include: page design, surfing service, technical support and maintenance, site content updating. This may vary according to the space granted to the page, number of mail boxes in use, maximum amount of monthly data to update the site, hours of surfing, speed connection, among other variables.

— Virtual commercial approach complementation with real complementing service such as distribution and personal handing of the acquired products.

#### 4.2.1.3. Virtual Marketing Attributes

International environment electronic trade has the following attributes:

1. **Globalism**

   There are neither limits nor barriers for this commercial way, which accomplishes a wide scope for millions of consumers at a world level using global resources. It makes it possible to reach geographically remote markets with little effort, being the global market the potential audience for the electronic international trade.

2. **Velocity and simplicity**

   This channel develops a dynamic and simple link that connects the different parts involved in the process in an on-line approach.

3. **Multimedia communication**

   Consumers' buying process is enhanced by sound, image, icons and visual effects.

4. **Low cost**

   Marketing costs per contact ratio improves, due to the commercial system global aspect.

5. **Personalization**

Even though global communication structures are used, this channel is efficient in directioning commercial actions, because consumers' insights are considered. This issue may be widely considered when the company has certain website systems, which make it possible to collect useful information about different aspects of the potential buyer. Besides, the virtual organization can adopt a sales extreme personalized approach, through hypersegmentation (that is, partition of the market in segments made up by an only client) which produces visitors' greater loyalty.

6. **Interconnection and interactivity**

The commercial process is developed through interactive connections that link the company (through its websites or pages) with the potential client. Thus, market places, that is, virtual business spaces that put the company into contact with clients, suppliers, commercial partners, middle entities and governmental entities, are generated. To this respect, as regards suppliers and commercial partners, the adoption of certain systems and state of the art equipment allow the organization to establish EDI (electronic data interchange) communication vias and just-in-time data loading. These systems are safer in the transmission and collection of information, and allow virtual storage of documents and commercial reports transferred (price lists, quotations, leaflets, purchase orders, catalogues, etc.). This electronic exchange of information reduces costs of data delivery, making intercompany communication more efficient. Besides, the company, through intranet channels (that is, development of company internal nets) achieves an intraorganization connection, to link the different company sectors and reduce failure in the treatment of the information sent.

7. **Low entry barriers**

   Internet marketing allows to compare SMEs with big enterprises, because the basic investment requirements in technological equipment and system design required by e-commerce are only a few.

8. **Virtual rise of brands**

   The company, through its Internet domain (that is, the virtual name for access site registered by the organization) or electronic brandname, generates value for the products offered and defines a policy of differentiation among consumers. A correct international positioning of the brand has to be accomplished, by associating it to different attributes of the virtual company, like functionality, page access speed and timing in responses to the consumer, in order to get a positive image of the company, and the present and potential markets objectives. The virtual brand has to be supported by promotional activities off-line, which ratify the excellency and good reputation of the company in its virtual activities and which encourage recurrent and regular visits to the site. It is important for the organization to lawfully register all the global brands to be able to use them according to the law. If the company is commercial, the brand can consist in nameofthecompany.com (.com stands for commercial) and, besides, it can have the abbreviation assigned for each country, as for example: Argentina: .ar, Brasil: .br, Chile: .cl. In some cases, an only domain within a global strategy could be more convenient; in others, the registration of several domains can be previously considered with differential specific markets in mind because of cultural, economic, and political issues, for a more effective positioning.

9. **Comfort**

   The consumer can visit and explore the company offers 24-hour a day, every day of the year, for as much time as he or she considers convenient.

10. **Synchronicity**

    In a virtual marketing entrepreneurial structure: activity coordination of premarketing, marketing, distribution and postmarketing, has to be a fundamental objective.

11. **Reformulation of intermediaries roles**

    In some cases, electronic trade brings about a marketing channel shortening and the suppression of many international intermediaries (wholesalers, retailers, agents, through a disintermediation accelerated process. Virtual marketing channels are more direct than the traditional ones and encourage the appearance of new intermediaries, called virtual or cyber intermediaries (e-intermediaries) that provide new service (an example are virtual directories that concentrate offers from different companies through a searching category group).

12. **Multiobjective**

    Electronic trade can be used for product marketing and/or place, ideas or service promotion. It can be used by companies as well as by individuals, and by public and private organizations.

13. **Alliances**

    Electronic trade is a fertile field for the generation of alliances between different virtual operators. An example is the consensus of agreements between the virtual company and an outsourced distribution structure. Or the development of membership programmes, in which the virtual company commercializes goods from other virtual company in its page, charging a fixed commission for the operations closed. Other similar case is the one in which a real or virtual company pays a site to advertise their products through virtual banners. Apart from this, there are agreements as regards exchange of virtual advertising, in which a virtual company advertises another in its own page, with reciprocity conditions. A new alternative of coalition can be the association or fusion of several sites into one.

14. **Complementary activities**

    Virtual commercial activities are always accompanied by real activities such as: physical transportation of goods, redesign and updating of page contents, telephonic question answering to visitors and buyers, implementation of promotional actions off-line like graphic advertising, television, etc.

#### *4.2.2. International Marketing "E-strategy" Design*

The company can design a strategy with electronic trade as the only international market access channel or can implement a business plan composed of real trade and e-commerce. The organization may use webpages as another way of communication of its attributes in the market world, without making use of that structure to close commercial agreements, or may globally commercialize products through that system (that is, conduct virtual sales). In this option, the organization will evaluate whether the product is apt for virtual marketing. There is a large variety of products susceptible of being sold by the Internet (electrical appliances, videos, perfume articles, books, disks, pharmaceutical and food products, etc.) that will constantly expand. Besides, the company will analyze which strategy competitors to adopt, visit their sites, and study what activities and service they perform in order to assist the client and the novelties presented in their virtual contents, as well as their pages aesthetic design.

#### *4.2.3. Types of Electronic Marketing*

Webpages show different approaches to electronic trade:

##### 4.2.3.1. According to the Intervening Parties

- — G2G (government to government): It deals with the relationhip between governments of different nations, as well as between different country governmental departments, through the net.
- — G2B (government to business): It refers to public administration data transfer to different private organizations.

— G2C (government to consumer): It consists in the public administration information transmission to the consumers.

— B2C (business to consumer): It includes the virtual commercial relationships developed by the company for consumers.

— B2B (business to business): It is about interentrepreneurial virtual commercial relationships. It is possible that new bonds among the companies generate and extend beyond the short term, generating cooperative attitudes.

— B2G (business to government): It includes public market management activities through the net.

— C2C (consumer to consumer): Its objective is the development of transactions between consumers. Example: virtual auction sites.

— C2B (consumer to business): It consists of groups of consumers, who perform joint buying of products from companies, with a greater negotiation capacity than at individual level.

— C2G (consumer to government): It has to do with private individual payment of taxes through the net.

#### 4.2.3.2. Page Functions and Provisions According to the Contents

There is a wide variety of webpages with a general and varied content. Others, on the other hand, have a high degree of specificity and detail in the information declared. At present, there is a proliferation of pages with different subjects and approaches (informative, commercial, scientific, social, etc.).

Among the main site categories there are:

— Pages of different agents linked to international trade (binational chambers, trade chambers, entrepreneurial centres, embassies and consulates, trade centres or trade points, etc.).

— Search engines: They allow to look for information about other pages, with the indication of key words associated to the search. Some of these pages, also group the information by sector, which makes searching easier. These can be generic or specialized engines, and they have companies and organizations listings.

— Personal entrepreneurial pages that give information about a particular organization: industrial, commercial, advisory, and other financial, transport, and tourism services.

— Virtual shopping centres: These pages commercialize a great variety of articles of different companies.

— Publications or specialized virtual bulletins which may have economic, statistical, commercial or financial reports and articles, companies listings and commercial opportunities advertisements.

— Virtual directories: Like electronic phone directories that allow to look for detailed information about a city, region or country people and companies.

— Virtual platforms with information about international business opportunities: Information is orderly and codified by subject. They include commercial requirements additional information about the companies involved. The advantage of these pages is that data in the page is classified and filtered. In some cases, these pages allow the company to advertise for free.

— Virtual sites with international marketing information. For example, information issued by the United Nations, the World Bank and the International Trade Chamber.

— Pages that announce trade shows, expositions and other commercial events to be held in a particular market.

— Sites with legal information about foreign trade, statistics, bibliographic publications, tariffs and paratariff barriers, entry requirements, etc.

— Consultancy pages in international and marketing foreign trade agents (carriers, customs agents, brokers, etc.).

- Different regional market sites with official information (ALADI, Mercosur, European Union).
- Pages with foreign trade promotion information about each country state bodies.
- Virtual publications about commercial partners requirements to perform international businesses (strategic alliances, coinvestment, etc.).
- Virtual publications about offers and contracts with different country governments.
- Discussion forums: they are virtual sites in which a specific issue is debated among the participants.
- Chat rooms or virtual conversation rooms, in which people or companies communicate on line. There are rooms of different types: social, entrepreneurial, academic, etc.
- Multi-subject portals that include several of the items previously mentioned.
- Institutional pages: Universities and education centres, state departments, non-governmental organizations, libraries, international bodies, professional associations, etc.

### *4.2.4. Electronic Mail Efficient Use for International Activities*

#### 4.2.4.1. E-mail Possible Uses

The electronic mail or e-mail allows international communication of different character at a low cost and it is used, among other things for:

- Production of offers or quotations to the external market. In these cases, the message has to be clear and precise, unnecessary explanations and writing ambiguities in the electronic text have to be left aside. Besides, the webpage company name as well as its links or hyperlinks towards other interesting webpages that can interest the addressee, may additionally be added.
- Company loading notification (with indication of departure date, ship and flag, and estimated arrival

date) and consignment or presentation of commercial and financial documentation at the bank.

— Alterations request about some buyers' requirements like: documentation, packaging, product model, etc.
— Delivery of enclosed files with product price lists or reports about the company or the marketed product line.
— Delivery of enclosed files with scanned brochure or catalogue with a description of the products offered by the company.
— Shipment or sampling demurrage notification.
— Sending of the pro forma invoice so that the importer can start the different customs, insurance and banking formalities.
— International freight, port expenses, international insurance quotation request.
— Company operations promotion towards potentially interested clients in different markets. This kind of message must contain a reference to the origin or resource from where the company obtained the electronic addresses of the addressees (for example: commercial attachés, chambers, etc.), so that the message can enjoy more reliability.
— Communication with intermediaries based in destination country related to the company (agents, distributor, etc.).
— Information request about external markets (importers listings, events, statistics, barriers, prices in force, etc.) to the different foreign trade agents (chambers, commercial attachés, governmental institutions, etc.).

#### 4.2.4.2. Virtual Mail and Electronic Message Features

The electronic mail is an excellent means to initiate a primary bond of trust with the external operator quickly and at a low cost. This instrument, however, has to be complemented and strenghtened with non-virtual means such as the telephone, the fax machine, commercial samples, or personal trips, so that transactions are made in a atmosphere of transparency. The message has to be personalized and a unique massive standardized message, or bulk e-mail, must be avoided, irrespective of whether it is with a visible copy or an ocult copy, because this makes the message less serious. Message contents have to be written in the destination place language or a language usual in international trade, such as English. It is very important to be kind and polite in every virtual communication produced by the company.

The organization has to be very careful about SPAM practices. These are massive messages with special offers, unasked by the addressees. To avoid confusion, it is important to make it clear that the message sent is not SPAM, and indicate clearly the information source of the addressed company data, with the condition, at the end of the text, that the receiver may optionally require not to be contacted again.

## 4.3. Communication through Websites

### *4.3.1. Website Media Features: Icons, Links and Virtual Symbols*

Website communication has multiple dimensions that include icons, tridimensional graphics, sound, animation effects, image transformation and juxtaposition and symbols that have to be harmoniously combined. Site design should avoid too much necessary visual ornamentation which may saturate visitors' concentration capacity. Graphics used in page structuring should be small and light or with magnifying clicking options, so that the page could be quickly loaded and opened, in optimum surfing conditions.

Company site different links have to be accessed in a fluid and creative way. The visitor searching information in the Internet must experiment a strong desire to continue exploring the place in-depth. Besides, the page must have elements that make it original and different from the others in the market, and must have an appealing sensory aesthetics. It is important to consider whether the company site design undertaking will be internally approached or outsourced.

Virtual environment has to look for the surfer complete receptivity of the site contents, the page design has to be aligned with the international marketing strategy of the company. Page loading speed and links access speed is a very important factor to preconsider.

### 4.3.2. Site Contents

The page is a part of the company communication global strategy, and must be appropriately updated all through its contents range. The information spread by the page has to be useful, available in several languages and may include, among other data:

- — Company information, path, main operations and markets.
- — Products line, models, varieties, specific characteristics, presentations, etc.
- — Company contacts in each of these areas.
- — Map of the site visual design.
- — Company product and premises digital photographs.
- — Price lists with financing conditions and delivery costs.
- — Fixed or rotary banners or billboards.
- — Site modes menu.
- — Shopping cart, a devise for virtual purchase.
- — Others interesting sites (links) preferred by the company and recommended to visit.
- — Visitors' frequently asked questions (FAQ).
- — E-mails, chats and a telephone number in order to get contacts, advice, searches and suggestions.
- — Seasonal offers of some products.
- — Site visitors' measuring mode, which adds up every page visitor.
- — Other possible elements may be: product users' comments, or client-companies references, etc.

### 4.3.3. Other Webpage Related Issues

The company has to position its page in the main virtual market search engines. This process can be done manually or by using specific software. Various alternative ways to collect information about visitors through the page should be looked after. Surfers can be offered to fill in a registration form with their most important personal data, encouraging them to ask for further information about new products and services offered by the company. In this way, the company can assess potential consumers' needs precisely to subsequently send personalized messages with information interesting to the profile shown in the records, and carry out an adequate client follow-up.

Every piece of information issued in a webpage has to be true to the description of the product, design, model, price, etc.; and the company has to offer warranty of the marketed product quality. Achieving a highly interactive degree of communication that could allow customization for the visitor must be the goal of electronic trade.

If the visitor wants to buy one of the products, he will have to use the website application called "shopping cart", that allows the visitor to buy on-line while there is an accumulative registration of the items bought and the subtotals to be paid. The total price of each virtual commercial operation should include in detail destination postage and packing. It is important for the company webpage to have an information and stock system interconnectivity, so that an adequate control of the inventory levels, in relation to the sales done could be carried out.

When a virtual buying and selling operation is done, it can be paid by credit or debit card, and on delivery, among other ways. As regards the distribution and product delivery service, the virtual company can externalize those activities, diverting them to international transport or postal companies specialized in logistics and international documentary operative formalities. It is possible that distribution channels could take some time in the electronically marketed product delivery process; this is why the virtual company has to communicate the addressee an approximate delivery date. It is essential for the organization to consider the complementation of every information or service provided by the company, by real supporting lines such as the fax machine or the telephone.

Some companies offer digital validation authenticity service of a particular page, to offer the client the assurance that he or she is really doing virtual operations with the company in the site; that is, this is the way to certify the truthfulness about the existence of the e-commerce company. Some consumers feel reticent to give information about websites registration forms, because they are not sure about the virtual company confidentiality, for which it is vital that the electronic organization assures them the protection of the informed data. Other remarkable issue is that most countries have great legal voids about electronic trade which affect issues like: what the applicable legislation in an e-commerce transaction is, protection issues against virtual fraud, hackers' actions, among other topics.

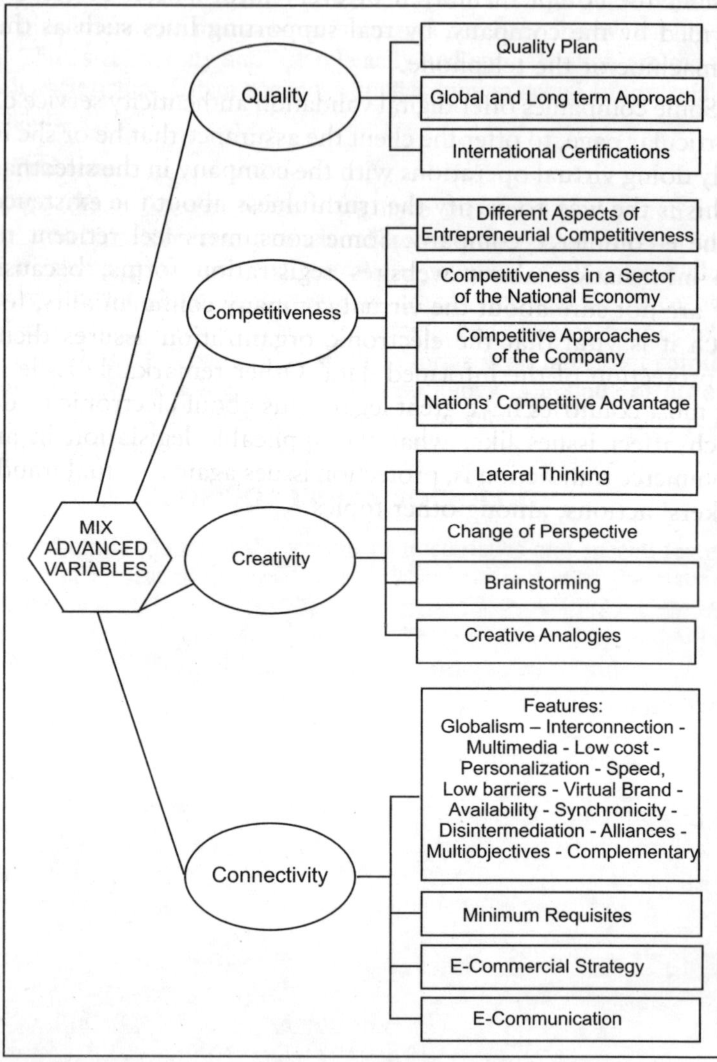


**Figure 7.1.** The Four Cs Commercial Mix Advanced Variables

# Conclusion

Within the global tendency, there is a sustained telecommunication technology development that increases substantially the volume as well as the speed of the worldwide circulating information. This background of continuous progress and innovation encourages companies to the introduction of new substitute products in the international market.

In the last decades, there has been a progressive decrease of tariff barriers negotiated within the GATT and the WTO frame, and a constant proliferation of paratariff obstacles has developed, all within a regional frame, with the constitution of commercial agreements that create discrimination areas between intrazone and extrazone trade. Furthermore, commercial negotiations as regards goods, services, intellectual property rights and primary products have been developed within the WTO frame.

In the international context, also, interconnection among the various national economies has increased significantly, due not only to the increase in commercial volume of goods and services but also to the globalization of financial markets. On a world scale, there exists a very unstable aggressively competitive field, in which transnational trading channels and global strategic agreements, which distribute their chain of value in different countries and do not compete on the local level, develop, but with the market as a unique whole. Besides, there are some market-countries called NIC or *Newly Industrialized Countries* (the Asian Tigers), whose companies compete on the international level and have high levels of productivity and low prices, pushing other external competitors.

Within this continually changing reality, the small and medium-sized enterprise has to efficiently solve the problem of access to external markets. Some of their concerns are related to: access to business opportunities information, lack of funds for exportation, and consolidation of an adequate volume (in terms of quality, quantity, and price) to get access to world markets. To do this, companies have to look for creative solutions to internationalization and high quality standards in product conception, production process, and organization, in order to satisfy international consumers.

It is essential for a company to adopt a flexible strategy so as to adapt product attributes, with external markets requirements as well as regional and worldwide changes in mind. This entrepreneurial flexibility allows the company to create alliances and cooperative projects to improve volumes and offer more competitive prices in more profitable markets.

Internationalization requires the company to develop an adequate and updated information system capable of finding, collecting and analyzing international business information. Furthermore, it is substantial for the company to gain progressive access to knowledge on the dynamics of foreign trade through a double channel: by means of gradual and sustained export activities and by company training at every level as regards international marketing (events, courses, workshops and seminars attendance).

Small and medium-sized enterprises must try to improve every stage in their chain of value, through creative alternatives and a sustainable strategic plan, and it is relevant to get an adequate balance between product standardization and adaptation, keeping cultural, economic and legal market requirements in mind. A very important alternative is to explore and detect transnational segments that exceed a country-market border, and whose consumers share similar needs. This kind of segment allows the entrepreneur to reduce the incurred costs of each variable in the commercial mix, and communicates the product image globally. Another option, in its international operations subsequent stages, is an efficient localization of its productive or commercial process in different countries, through production and sales branches or coinvestment, distributing the chain of value at an international level.

All the actions of the company should be aimed at achieving a sustained development, that could meet the needs of the present time without putting future generations into risk, by trading products that are environmentally safe (organic products, without artificial preservatives, biodegradable, recyclable and non-pollutant).

This creative approach must accompany not only product design, sales and communication, but also the resolution of exporting problems, market selection, change of approach of the services offered in the satisfaction of consumers' needs. The company will be strategy oriented to market niches that position it competitively and differentially due to quality or other attributes offered, and to its creative attitude.

As regards the use of technological information, enterprises have to consider their connection to the international net by using e-mail and websites to look for information, make offers, communicate deliveries, transmit files with catalogues and close e-commerce operations. As regards logistics, the entrepreneur has to develop a close interconnection with the different total distribution channel levels in order to increase efficacy from origin to destination (with the use of containerized and palletized loads, among other aspects), as well as the management of transactional and communicational aspects inside the channel.

However, if an entrepreneur takes external compromises with occasional remainders unsold in the internal market instead of using stable volumes for its international operations, it will be going along the wrong way. It is necessary to have a wider vision for external activities, so that the small and medium-sized entrepreneur could project the possible scenarios for his or her international operations in order to implement his or her strategies, and to evaluate the diversions produced to make the most convenient adjustments for internationalization practice. At a long term, a strategic vision is needed; one of stable commitment assumptions, and of accumulative resources assignation towards international actions, very far from a vision of exportable surpluses.

The small entrepreneur has to get convinced that only perseverance and gradualism, as exporting conscience qualities, make the companies operatively efficient at the international scale. In the first stages, companies only perceive the difficulties and uncertainties of markets they know, but shortly after, the company will have to think of international activity as something vital and fundamental with the adequate help of the different foreign traders (consultors, brokers, agencies, chambers, etc.), with a patient and committed attitude. And so, it can consider internationalization activities as its entrepreneurial mission.

# Supplements

## SUPPLEMENT I: EXPORT DOCUMENTS

### Most Usual Documents

*Commercial*

Commercial documents are those referred to any aspect of the export operative sequence (invoicing, carriage, insurance, etc.), with the exception of those related to the collection of the international operation.

Issued by the Exporter:

— **Offer or quotation:** It is a document that informs the potential buyer of the exporter's conditions in a commercial transaction. Its contents include a technical, commercial and customs-related issues: description of the merchandise, the transaction unit (kilos, cubic metres) and the amount offered (fixed, maximum or minimum), price (unitary, total, including incoterm and quotation currency), shipment date/s and means used, forms of payment and financing terms. After this document is issued, there may exist another one called "pro forma invoice", which contains an operation specific conditions under process of approval, that is, like a rough copy of an operation budget subject to confirmation.

— **Export invoice:** This monetary document is ruled by the laws of the country of origin, and certifies the international deal. Apart from the elements contained in an invoice for the domestic market, the following items are added: place of load and discharge, classification code, bank and means of payment used and total price (incoterm, currency and monetary numbers). Prices quoted in CIF conditions, will have international insurance and freight discrimination.

— **Consular invoice:** It is the commercial invoice in which the country of origin consulate takes part.

— **Packing list, weight list and contents list:** They are documents that give more detailed descriptions of non-monetary aspects which are not considered in the exports invoice. The packing list gives weights, measures and bulk marks; the weight list makes more emphasis in weights (gross, net, total, unitary), and the contents list gives a more detailed description of bulk contents. They are used by Customs and insurance to control the goods.

— **Certificate of manufacturing:** It certifies specific aspects of the production process (manufacturing place and date, lot number, etc.).

Issued by the Customs Agent:

— **Customs document** (also called "shipping permit"): It gives a description of the merchandise, its cost and classification, taxes and benefits that affect it, as well as information about the intervening parties: customs agent, exporter, carrier, etc.).

Issued by Specialized Public or Private Bodies:

(with either obligatory or voluntary presentation, depending on the case)

— **Certificates of origin**: Their function is the identification of the origin of goods (as regards a country or regional market), and are ruled by the regulations in origin. In regional markets they may be requested by the importer in order to get tariff advantages. They are issued by foreign trade chambers or lawful enterprises.

— **Other certificates:** Phytosanitary, quality, disinfection, radioactivity, etc.

Issued by Insurance Companies:

— **International insurance policy:** It states the amount insured, type of insurance, policy holder, beneficiary of compensations, types of risks insured.

Issued by the Carrier (through its representative):

— **Airway bill (Air transport)—Bill of lading (Waterway) —Freight bill (Ground):** These documents must include: carrier name, shipment date and place, description of goods, carriage costs and, if it has already been paid, goods imported. In the case of the bill of lading, it may be endorsed, if issued to order.

Financial:

— **Cheque in foreign currency:** It is similar to an internal market cheque. It is issued by the importer against its account in foreign currency, and it is generally paid to the exporter through bank collection.

— **Bill of exchange:** Issued by the exporter against the importer, so that the latter pays the former an amount, against document acceptance. If this document is accepted but not honoured, it may be protested. It includes the names of the parties, amount, date of issuance and expiration date.

— **Promissory note:** It is a promise of payment from the importer to the exporter payable at a due term. It is little used.

## SUPPLEMENT II: INTERNATIONAL CARRIAGE, CONTAINERIZATION AND UNITIZATION

### Rail Transport

It is a very economical means of transport which permits massive loads, and possesses different types of train cars adequate to the type of commodity, and a wide range of services. In some cases, however, it is slow, and the railway line system is not sufficient. Besides, the load is subject to two transfers, which may result in product damage in the case of train car coupling.

Freight costs are less than ground costs for long distances (parabolic tariff).

### Ground Transport

It is fast and adaptable; it is very useful to reach inaccessible regions to get to by other means, although load volume is more limited than railway load. It allows to perform trips house to house and it has a significant rate of accidents, mainly road accidents. It is more expensive than rail transport for long distances.

### Waterway Transport

It is very efficient (very low cost and large load capacity) for big volumes, there is an important variety of vessels (liquid or solid bulk container ships) for different kinds of products. It is the slowest means of transport, which implies an important financial stoppage and non insurance, which demands for better insurance conditions and a reinforcement in shipped goods packaging. Ocean transport is the most widely used in international trade, whereas river transport is used in regional international trade.

In sea transport, there are vessels that belong to conferences (grouping of carriers) that fix uniform itineraries and freights among their members. There are also outsiders that have neither prefixed itineraries or prices, what makes negotiation of transport conditions the result of the interaction between supply and demand. The person in charge of information about freight, dates and other shipment conditions is the marine and cargo surveyor, who represents the carrier. The bill of lading, which is the transport document, may be issued to the order (transference of goods ownership by endorsement), nominative (transfer of goods ownership by cession of rights) and bearer form (free cession).

### Transport by Air

It is the fastest (very high speed) and safest (lowest accident rate) means, but it has the most expensive rate of all the means of transport, and is used for goods of large volume as compared to weight. It is ideal to deliver samples and certain valuable, fragile or state of the art products, among others. The rate is determined by considering the volumetric weight (volume-weight ratio). There are general as well as specific rates per type of product. The transport document functions as a contract, receipt, invoice and sometimes as certificate of load insurance. Advise on tariff and other regulations are provided by the air cargo weight and balance agent who represents the company carrier. There are some goods that are considered dangerous for this kind of transportation.

### Segmented Transport

Only one means of transport is used.

### Combined Transport

More than one means of transport is used (water, ground, air) and each carrier is responsible for its stretch.

### Multimodal Transport

There is only one main document (multimodal transport document) and only one person in charge (multimodal transport operator) for the whole of the international itinerary, which includes several modes (also called "multimodalism").

### Containerization

It is the use of a container as a standardized link in the international transport chain. It is a load equipment unit that allows for repetitive use and improves load and discharge times; it protects the goods transported against potential risks and avoids load breakage, which makes it ideal for multimodal transport, since it improves load follow-up conditions. There are different types of containers (refrigerated, ventilated, open, for liquids, folding, etc.). Standard size includes: 20 feet (6 × 2.44 × 2.60 m—measures that vary, according to the type—and with a maximum weight capacity between 17.6 and 21.80 tonnes). Other standard size is 40 feet (12 × 2.44 × 2.60 m—measures that vary, according to the type—and with a maximum load between 26 and 26.50 tonnes). The acronym TEU (twenty equivalent units) refers to a unit of measurement equivalent to a 20 ft container. Containers can go full (FCL) or incomplete (LCL—less than container load), and the same container can carry loads from different companies (that is, it can consolidate loads to maximize use).

### Palletization

It refers to the use of pallets, which are structures composed by platforms made up of two decks (double-face). They can transport goods, secured by hoops and thermocontractile material, which makes them an efficient unit for load (easy to manipulate, transport and store, by using forklifts). Standard sizes include: de 600 × 400 mm, 1,200 × 800 mm, 1,200 × 1,000 mm and 1,200 × 600 mm.

## SUPPLEMENT III: INTERNATIONAL COLLECTION MEANS

### Letter of Credit

It is a collection instrument widely used in the international environment and the safest for all parties. The applicant of a letter of credit (the importer) fixes the conditions (that is, terms and documents) that the exporter will have to comply with, in order to collect the operation. The bank which acts on behalf of the importer (the issuer of the letter of credit), issues and notifies the external party the text of the letter according to the form completed by the applicant, and the exporter's (confirming bank) notifies the exporter the text of the letter. The exporter (or beneficiary) has to provide documentation to the corresponding bank (the issuing bank or the confirming bank), within the terms provided to collect the operation. The bank is going to examine the documents presented to insure they are correctly presented and if the letter of credit is callable (that is, payable once it is presented along with the necessary documents) it pays for the operation; if it is a deferred payment letter of credit it accepts the credit securities provided (bills of exchange). *It is the exporter's responsibility to comply with the presentation of documents to the bank, in the conditions required and within the terms stipulated by the importer.* It is the function of the bank to review the documentation provided and verify that it coincides with what has been stipulated in the letter of credit. If all the requirements are met, there is no discrepancy, and the corresponding bank guarantees payment or pays the exporter the amount of the transaction. There are different types of letters of credit:

— *revocable*, it is the one that may be revoked by any party until before the exporter's presentation of documents;
— *irrevocable*, it is the one which may only be revoked by agreement of all the parties;
— *confirmed*, when there exists a co-guarantee (advising bank) of payment between the issuing and the confirming banks;
— *unconfirmed*, when the document bears the guarantee of only the issuing bank.

The letter of credit is the most secure financial instrument for the parties.

## Collection

It may be simple (collection of financial documents), or documented (collection of commercial, or commercial and financial documents). The exporter starts the procedures by presenting the documents to the bank, so that it can start incoming collection procedures. The bank is going to act according to a minute of instructions prepared by the exporter. The bank will send the minute and the documents to the importer market bank, so that the papers could be introduced for collection in the case of sight collection, or the financial documents accepted in the case of deferred payment. In the last case, papers accepted for collection will be presented at expiration date. Financial documents that can be presented for collection are: cheques in foreign currency, promissory notes and bills of exchange.

## Bank Draft or Transfer

It is when debits in the importer account are produced. Funds are credited in the exporter account in order to pay for an operation; payment may be prior to merchandise delivery (in advance) or after shipment (deferred). This procedure presupposes a bond of trust between importer and exporter.

## SUPPLEMENT IV: INTERNATIONAL NEGOTIATION FUNDAMENTALS

According to experts in the subject (COLAIÁCOVO, MARTÍN, WEISINGER), international negotiation is composed by elements intuitive as well as rational; it is both, an art and a science. It consists in the interaction of two or more people who will exert influence upon one another so as to satisfy their mutual needs. In international trade, negotiation seeks a profitable commercial exchange among the participants in the process. In any negotiating environment each party has to be aware not only of its own needs, but also of the other party's wishes. Time management is very important to introduce proposals, to maintain a rhythm in the process, to make the terms stipulated flexible, to generate anticipation about the other party's reactions and to respond effectively to the counterpart's requirements.

There are two very definite negotiating styles: collaborative and competitive. Collaborative style seeks to create value for both parties and promotes the joint compliance with participants' expectations. There is a balance of power; negotiated issues are dealt with in polite and friendly interactions. In competitive negotiation, a party wins at the expense of another; there is a strong emphasis on bargaining, each party is indifferent to the other party's needs, and lobbies for getting advantages from the other party in order to win. Style used will depend on many factors: people involved, their degree of power, regularity of commercial relationships, negotiating terms, interests at stake, among others. In general, consensus reached during the negotiating process is satisfactory only when it produces results that make up for the needs of both parties.

In negotiation, each participant has to gather precise, truthful and reliable information with the following objectives: supporting its arguments, generating negotiating power, making adequate decisions, and clarifying and simplifying the discussion process. A correct use of time, which compensates between delaying and accelerating procedures is important; each party must know the other's terms and forecast reactions at the arrival of deadlines. Quick response times must be procured, as a clear evidence of interest for the party's expectations. In negotiation, each party has to analyze which the objectives pursued in the process are, and be consistent as to its arguments, proposals, as well as performance, within a frame of objective equity and discretion.

Negotiation has to be planned through a prenegotiating or metanegotiating stage in aspects like: different objectives and proposals, both parties' strengths and weaknesses, information adequate for the process, main conflicts and their different alternatives for solution, terms for the agreement, among others. A clear and precise communication of proposals and an active and empathic listening attitude (being an attentive listener), which would allow to understand very important features of the negotiator. The fact that strengthening economic transactions beneficial for both parties is an objective, must not be overlooked since, in some cases, communication may be affected by existing differences in the cultural environments of each country.

A first impression of reliability, responsibility and commitment may develop strong credibility and bonds of trust. Suppositions about the message produced or received have to be avoided; when in doubt, it is advisable to paraphrase the question (or paraphrase), in order to leave aside ambiguity in the communication process. Counterproposals should consider more than one possibility to offer, with negotiator's requirements in mind. Questions asked by interlocutors will be aimed at getting crucial information to reach a commercial agreement. When creating proposals and counteroffers, open and conditional questions may be asked (for example: What is your opinion about...?, Who is your current supplier?, If we send X volume and/or quality, would you accept...?).

As regards the closing of a deal, there are different options like: simple verbal or written confirmation, by fax or e-mail, reception of purchase request, reception letter of credit text opened by the issuing bank, signing of a purchase-sale international contract.

Criticism by any of the parties during a negotiation process has to be constructive, timely, and precise. Each party has to make sure that the other understands the reason for criticism, and prolonged criticim as well as insistence have to be avoided. In general, criticism have to be made in the first person, and offer incentive to the other party so that the changes proposed could be accepted.

It is important to know that, in generalized disputes and conflicts between buyer and seller on a particular commercial operation, international arbitration, an institution to solve controversies that requires the participation of a third party (or arbitrator) to whom the conflict is presented so that he could find a way out, may be used and the participants will have to respect the resolution issued by the arbitrator.

## SUPPLEMENT V: BASIS FOR COMMODITY CLASSIFICATION

The classification of commodities consists in the assignation of a code number for univocal individualization. Such code, called the harmonized tariff schedule, is assigned through logical principles and following certain rules that look for the classification of every commodity that may be commercialized at international level.

Further, commodity codes are expressed in an order together with their description, in a summary called "tariff nomenclature". This shows commodities grouped in categories: sections, chapters, subchapters, tariff items and subitems. Goods are expressed in a sequence that includes products with little added value in the first chapter, which will turn into more industrialized goods as classification progresses.

The objectives of the system is a simple and precise classification, without ambiguity in a product tariff item in order to specify:

— what control requirements are necessary in the market of origin so as to be imported or exported and custom cleared;

— what duties and rights have to be paid for nationalization;

— what exports rights and repayments reach international operations;

— what economic and non-economic prohibitions affect the trading of those goods.

It also allows for comparative statistics on international marketing information of certain products. Entrepreneurs can make an objective and unequivocal reference, when identifying the merchandise so as to request and offer quotations and ask for information about business opportunities to the different foreign brokers.

The HS (International Harmonized Commodity Description and Coding System) comprises a series of general rules of classification of goods that briefly express:

— Titles of sections and chapters, heading or sub-headings do not have legal force as regards classification; they are just referential. Classification has to take into account: item text, section notes, chapter notes and sub-item notes (these notes are references or explanations that group products or exclude them, referring them to other parts in the nomenclature). To simplify the classification, incomplete and dismantled products are considered as complete or assembled, as long as they represent the product profile.

— Any reference to an item composed by material, refers to it as pure material or mixed with another. When two or more items can describe the commodity, it is classified according to the most specific description, which will prevail over the more generic. In the case of mixed or assorted products, the product will be classified as if it consisted of the essential component referential item, and, if even in this case it were not possible to be classified, it will then be assigned the last item in a numerical order among all the items susceptible for classification, or the one with which it shows more analogy.

— As regards packages, cases and containers presented with the product, they will be classified together with the article, provided they are regularly used from the commercial point of view, with the exception of those used repetitively.

### Example of Tariff Item

0106.11.19 Rabbits. Other. OTHER LIVE ANIMALS

01 commodity belongs to chapter I in the nomenclature.

06 it refers to item 6 in chapter I.

11 are the HS sub-item headings and sub-headings at the level of the first and second digit.

19 it is the description at the level of regional suffix number 19 within chapter I. In the case of regional markets like the Mercosur, the tariff item may have additional sub-divisions and control digits.

# Bibliography


Aaker, D. y Day, G. (1989), *Investigación de mercados*, McGraw-Hill/Interamericana, Mexico.

Acerenza M.A. (1997), *Marketing internacional. Un enfoque metodológico hacia la exportación.* Editorial Trillas, Mexico.

Amor, D. (2000), *La revolución e-business. Claves para vivir y trabajar en un mundo interconectado*, Prentice Hall, San Pablo.

Arese, H.F. (1999) *Comercio y marketing internacional. Modelo para el diseño estratégico*, Grupo Editorial Norma, Buenos Aires.

Arnaud, W.G. (1996), *Mercosur, Unión Europea, Nafta y los procesos de integración regional*, Abeledo-Perrot, Buenos Aires.

Avery, D. (1998), Salvando el planeta de plaguicidas y plásticos. Hudson Institute, Buenos Aires.

Badia Jiménez, A. (2000), Calidad: Modelo ISO 9001, Gestión 2000, España.

Balassa, B. (1961), *The Theory of Economic Integration,* RD Irwin Homewood, Londres.

Ball, D. y McCulloch, W.H. (1997). *Negocios internacionales, Introducción y aspectos esenciales,* Irwin, Madrid.

Beck, U. (1998), *¿Que, es globalización? Falacias del globalismo, repuestas a la globalización*, Barcelona, Paidós.

Bekerman, M. y Benjamín, H. (1998), "La globalización economica y sus dilemas para los paises perifericos", Universidad de Buenos Aires, Facultad de Cinecias Economicas, Instituto de Investigaciones Economicas, CENES, Centro de Estudios de la Estructura Economica.

Bery, T.H. (1992), *Cómo gerenciar la transformación hacia la calidad total,* McGraw-Hill, Santate de Bogota, Colombia.

Bertran, J. (1997), *Marketing Internacional avanzado. Departamentos de exportación, redes comerciales, acciones de promoción para pequeñas y medianas empresas,* McGraw-Hill, Madrid.

Bescos Torres, M. (1990), *Factoring y franchising. Nuevas técnicas de dominio de los mercados exteriores,* Ediciones Pirámide, Madrid.

Billorou, O.P. (1992), *Las comunicaciones de marketing,* El Ateneo, Buenos Aires, 1992.

Biasca, R.E. (1991), *Resizing, Reestructurando, replanteando y recreando la empresa para lograr competitividad*, Ediciones Macchi, Buenos Aires.

Biasca, R.E. (2001), *iSomos competitivos? Análisis astratégico para crear valor*, Ediciones Granica.

Bloch, R.D. (1997), *Las economias regionales y el comercio internacional*, Ad Hoc, Buenos Aires.

Bordeje Morencos, F. (1981), *Diccionario militar estratégico y politico*, Editorial San Martin, Madrid.

Brown, L.O. (1972), *Comercialización y análisis de Mercado*, Selcon Editorial, Buenos Aires.

Buzzell, R.D. y Quelch, J. (1992), *Administración de la mercadotecnia internacional. Lecturas y casos,* Addison Wesley Iberoamericana, Estados Unidos.

Calvo Orra, A.; Gutierrez De Villar, J.M. y Merino Cantos, J.A. (1997), *Como hacer negocios en internet*, Paraninfo, Madrid.

Carpenter, P. (2000), *Marcas electrónicás, Como crear un negocios en internet a velocidad vertiginosa,* Grupo Editorial Norma, Colombia.

Carson, D. (1961), *International Marketing: A comparative systems approach,* John Wiley & Sons Inc. Estados Unidos.

Cateora, P.R. (1995). *Marketing Internacional*, McGraw-Hill, Mexico.

Centro de Comercio Internacional (UNCTAD/OMC), Export Quality Boletin No. 70, noviembre de 2001, "Una introduccion a las ISO 9000:2000".

Ciampa, D. (1993), *Calidad total. Guia para su implantación,* Addison-Wesley Iberoamericana, Estados Unidos.

Colaiacovo, L., *Exportación, Comercialización, Administración internacional*, Editorial Alfa, Peru.

Colaiacovo, L. (1992), *Negociación y contratación internacional*, Ediciones Macchi, Buenos Aires.

Czinkota, M.R. y Ronkainen, I. (1997), *Marketing internacional,* McGraw-Hill, Mexico.

Czinkota, M.R.; Ronkainen, I. y. Tarrant, J. (1995), *The Global Marketing Imperative,* NTC Business Books, Estados Unidos.

D'Aveni, R. (1994), *Hypercompetition: Managing the Dynamics of Strategic Maneuvering,* Free Press, Nueva York.

De Bono, E. (1994), *El pensamiento lateral. Manual de creatividad,* Paidos, Buenos Aires.

De Bono, E. (1996), *Seis sombreros para pensar. Una guia de pensamiento para gente de acción,* Ediciones Juan Granica, Barcelona.

De Dios, J.J.E. (1994), *Transporte internacional de mercancias,* ESIC Editorial, Madrid.

Di Gioia, M.A. (1995), *Envases y embalajes como herramienta de la exportación,* Ediciones Macchi, Buenos Aires.

Di Liscia, A.F. y Vanella, R.G. (1997), *Claves para exporter. Manual del exportador argentino*, Nuevo Hacer Grupo Editor Latinoamericano, Fundación Exportar, Buenos Aires.

Drucker, P. (1986), *La innovación y el empresario innovador,* Edhasa, Barcelona.

Fajardo, J. (2000), *Fundamentos de e-commerce*, MP Ediciones, Buenos Aires.

Fitoussi, J.P. y Rosanvallon, P. (1997), *La nueva era de las desigualdades*. Manantial, Buenos Aires.

Folgar, O.F. (1996), *ISO 9000: Aseguramiento de la calidad*, Ediciones Macchi, Buenos Aires.

Revista Forum del Comercio Internacional, CCI, agosto de, 2001.

Fratalocchi, A. (1993), *Marketing y comercio exterior*, Editorial Cangallo, Buenos Aires.

Garcia Cruz, R. (2000), *Marketing internacional*, Editorial ESIC, Madrid.

Garcia Mestanza, J. (1997), *Calidad total*, Imagraf Impresores S.A., Malaga.

Giddens, A. (1994), *Consecuencias de la modernidad*, Alianza Editorial, Madrid.

Giddens, A., *La tercera via. La renovación de la social democracia*, Madrid, Taurus.

Gil-Robles Gil Delgado, E. y. Jerez Riesco, J.L. (1992), *Marketing internacional*, ESIC Editorial, Madrid.

Goleman, D.; Kaufman, P. y Ray, M. (2000), *El espiritu creativo, La revolución de la creatividad y cómo aplicarla a todas las actividades humanas*, Javier Vergara Editor.

Grana, R.; Bonavita, L.; Gatica, L.; Perez, I. y Hernandez, C. (2000), *Ecologia y calidad de vida. Sociedad y naturaleza*, Editorial Erre Eme S.A., Buenos Aires.

Harrington, H.J.; Hoffher, G.D. y Reid, R.P. (2000), *Herramientas para la creatividad. Cómo estimular la creatividad en las personas y en las empresas*, McGraw-Hill Interamericana, Santafe de Bogota.

Hermida, J.A. (1994), *Marketing para gigantes y pigmeos. Un análisis sobre la actual realidad competitivy las dificultades para encontrar y mantener espacios dentro de los mercados globalizados* Ediciones Macchi, Buenos Aires.

Hernandez Fernandez, S. (1995), *Ecologia para ingenieros. El impacto ambiental,* Colegio de ingenieros, de caminos, canales y puertos, España.

Jarillo, J.C. y Martinez Echezarraga, J.I. (1991), *Estrategia internacional. Mas allá de la exportación,* McGraw-Hill, Madrid.

Juran, J.M. (1951), *Manual de control de la calidad,* Editorial Reverte S.A., Barcelona.

Kashani, K. (1992), *Managing Global Marketing: Cases and Text,* PWS Publishing Company, Boston.

Kastika, E. (1999), Los 9 mundos de la creatividad en management, Ediciones Macchi, Buenos Aires.

Keegan, W.J. y Green, M.C. (1997), *Fundamentos de mercadotecnia internacional,* Prentice Hall, Hispanoamericana, Mexico.

Kotler, P. (1996), *Dirección de mercadotecnia, Análisis, planeación, implementación y control,* Prentice Hall, Hispanoamericana, Mexico.

Kotler, P. (1989), *Mercadotecnia,* Prentice Hall, Hispanoamericana, Mexico.

Kramer, R.L. (1964), *Mercadotecnia internacional,* Compañia General de Ediciones, Mexico.

Kuazaqui, E. (1999), *Marketing internacional, Como conquistar negócios em marcados internacionais,* Makron Books, San Pablo.

Ledesma, C.A. y Zapata, C. (1993), *Negócios y comercialización internacional,* Ediciones Macchi, Buenos Aires.

Le Moneer Framis, F. (1994), *Marketing ferial Cómo gestionar y rentabilizar la participación en salones profesionales,* Ediciones Gestión 2000, Barcelona.

Levin, M. y Gealt, M. *Tratamiento de residuos tóxicos y peligrosos. Selección, estimación, modificaión de microorganismos y aplicaciones.*

Levinson, J.C. (1990). *Tácticas de guerrilla aplicadas al mercadeo,* Editorial Norma, Bogota.

Levy, A.R. (1977), *Logistica de comercialización*, Ediciones Macchi, Buenos Aires.

Lobejon Herrero, L.F. (2001), *El comercio internacional*, Ediciones Akal, Madrid.

Maeso Ruiz, A. y Deamon, D. (1997), *Consorcios de exportación en Uruguay, Experiencias internacionales*, Fundación de cultura universitaria, Montevideo.

Makuc, A. y Bun, E. (1997), *Comercio exterior*, Errepar, Buenos Aires.

Martin, M.A. (1994), *Negociación racional introducción a la negociación profesional*, Ediciones Interoceanicas, Buenos Aires.

Moreno, J.M. (1995), *Marketing internacional, Contenido, politicas y estrategias exitosas*, Ediciones Macchi, Buenos Aires.

Moreno, J.M. (1985), *Manual del exportador, Teoria y practica exportadora,* Ediciones Macchi, Buenos Aires.

Nieto Churruca, A.; Llamazares Garcia-Lomas, O. y Cervino Fernandez, J. (1997), *Marketing internacional, Casos y ejercicios practicos,* Ediciones Piramide, Madrid.

Paz, E. (1998), *Como exportar, importar y hacer negocios a traves de Internet.* Gestión, 2000, Barcelona.

Porter, M.E. (1997), *Estrategia competitiva. Tecnicas para el análisis de los sectores industriales y de la competencia*, Compañia Editorial Continental, Mexico.

Porter, M.E. (1991), *La ventaja competitiva de las naciones*, Javier Vergara Editor, Buenos Aires.

Pranteda, N. (1997), *Clasificación de mercancias en el comercio internacional,* Guia Practica del Importador y Exportador, Buenos Aires.

Ries, A. y Trout, J. (1989), *Posicionamiento, El concepto que ha revolucionado la comunicación publicitaria y el marketing.* McGraw-Hill/Interamericana de España. Madrid.

Santambrosio, E.E. (2001), *Tecnologia y medio ambiente*, Colección Cuadernillo UCEL, Rosario.

Secretaria de Agricultura, Ganaderia, Pesca y alimentación, "Análisis de peligros y puntos criticos de control (HACCP)", Boletin de Difusión.

Secretaria de Agricultura, Ganaderia, Pesca y Alimentación, "Buenas practicas de manufactura (MBP)", Boletin de Difusión.

Stanton, W.J.; Etzel, M.J. y Walker, B. (1996), *Fundamentos de marketing*, McGraw-Hill, Mexico.

Stenhardt, R.J.M. (1971), *Geografia en marketing. Problemas de comercialización; criterios para zonificar y evaluación de vendedores,* Ediciones Macchi, Buenos Aires.

Stevenson, K. y. Bernard, D. (1995), *ARPCC-HACCP. Establecimiento de programas de análisis de peligros en puntos criticos de control,* The Food Processors Institute, Washington, D.C.

Tapscott, D. (2000), *La economia digital. Las nuevas oportunidades y peligros en un mundo empresarial y personal interconectado en la red,* McGraw-Hill, Santiago.

Tugores Ques, J. (1994), *Economia internacional e integración económica*, McGraw-Hill/Interamericana de España, Madrid.

Ullman, R.R. (1984), *Estructuras empresarias para el comercio internacional*, Ediciones De Palma, Buenos Aires.

Vidal Villa, J.M. y Martinez Peinado, J. (1995), *Economia mundial*, McGraw-Hill de España, Madrid.

Villegas, C.G. (1993), *Comercio exterior y credito documentario*, Editorial Astrea, Buenos Aires.

Weinstein, A.K. y Fargher, K.H.F. (1970), *Case Studies in International Marketing*, Edward Arnolf Publishers Ltd.

Weisinger, H. y Lobsenz, N. (1983), *Nadie es perfecto. Cómo criticar con exito*, Grijalbo, Barcelona.

Yip, G.S. (1993), *Globalización, Estrategias para obtener una ventaja competitiva internacional,* Grupo Editorial Norma, Bogota.

